perspectives

on Criminal Justice

DATE DUE

MAY 0 8 2001		
DEC 1 3 2001		
DEC 1 0 2005		
NOV 2 7 2007		
DEC 0 1 2010		
GAYLORD		PRINTED IN U.S.A

perspectives

Criminal Justice

Academic Editor
Alejandro del Carmen
University of Texas at Arlington

coursewise
publishing
inc.

Bellevue • Boulder • Dubuque • Madison • St. Paul

Our mission at **coursewise** is to help students make connections—linking theory to practice and the classroom to the outside world. Learners are motivated to synthesize ideas when course materials are placed in a context they recognize. By providing gateways to contemporary and enduring issues, **coursewise** publications will expand students' awareness of and context for the course subject.

For more information on **coursewise,** visit us at our web site: http://www.coursewise.com

To order an examination copy:
Houghton Mifflin Sixth Floor Media 800-565-6247 (voice) / 800-565-6236 (fax)

coursewise publishing editorial staff

Thomas Doran, ceo/publisher: Environmental Science/Geography/Journalism/Marketing/Speech
Edgar Laube, publisher: Political Science/Psychology/Sociology
Linda Meehan Avenarius, publisher: **courselinks**™
Sue Pulvermacher-Alt, publisher: Education/Health/Gender Studies
Victoria Putman, publisher: Anthropology/Philosophy/Religion
Tom Romaniak, publisher: Business/Criminal Justice/Economics
Kathleen Schmitt, publishing assistant

coursewise publishing production staff

Lori A. Blosch, permissions coordinator
Mary Monner, production coordinator
Victoria Putman, production manager

Note: Readings in this book appear exactly as they were published. Thus, inconsistencies in style and usage among the different readings are likely.

Interior design and cover design by Jeff Storm

Library of Congress Catalog Card Number: 99-90097

ISBN 0-395-97319-8

Printed in the United States of America by **coursewise publishing**, Inc.
1559 Randolph Avenue, St. Paul, MN 55105

10 9 8 7 6 5 4 3 2 1

from the
Publisher

Tom Romaniak
coursewise publishing

Every time you open the newspaper, you read about it. Every time you watch the evening news, you hear about it. Every politician wants to take a stand against it. What is it? Crime.

Our society is fascinated by crime. We even watch for it by tuning in for the latest courtroom update on this case or that case. Some of the most popular movies and television programs (including two of my "must-see" programs) are based on crime.

But how many of us have a solid understanding of the systems that deal with crime? How many of us really know enough about the criminal justice systems to intelligently decipher and analyze what we see in the news, on television, and at the theater? Very few of us, I'm willing to bet.

For you, that's about to change. You are taking a course about criminal justice systems. These systems cover what I like to refer to as the three Cs—cops, courts, and corrections. Your instructor and your textbook will provide you with the basic kernels of information, including theory. This reader will complement and apply that instruction with articles depicting recent issues and events.

Perspectives: Criminal Justice was carefully crafted by Alejandro del Carmen. Alex is a young, bright, energetic professor at the University of Texas at Arlington. I met him while he was still a graduate student at Florida State University and have been impressed with him ever since.

Alex is passionate about both criminal justice issues and his work. He is dedicated and efficient and has done a great job of putting together this volume for you. Alex won't let obstacles get in his way. If I told Alex that he needed to run through a brick wall in order for me to publish this reader, he'd carefully survey the wall to find its weakest point and then plow through it.

This reader is accompanied by the **courselinks**™ site for Criminal Justice, a collection of web resources designed to enrich your learning process. At **coursewise,** we are committed to connected learning—helping you to link classroom theory to real-world issues. Our goal is to provide you with useful learning tools that don't cost an arm and a leg. We would love to hear from you. Feel free to drop me a line to let me know how we are doing.

Good luck with your study and understanding of the criminal justice systems!

Tom Romaniak
tomr@coursewise.com

Alejandro del Carmen is an assistant professor of criminology and criminal justice at the University of Texas at Arlington. He received his bachelor's degree from Florida International University, and his master's and doctorate from Florida State University. Dr. del Carmen has taught several courses, including criminal justice, criminology, corrections, law, and victimology. He and his wife Denise have a child, Gabriel. Outside academic work, Dr. del Carmen enjoys listening to classical music.

Dedication

To my son
Gabriel

from the
Academic Editor

Alejandro del Carmen
University of Texas at Arlington

The criminal justice system has recently been the source of a great deal of controversy. This has been largely the result of the media attention given to a few controversial criminal trials at a time when the citizenry seems obsessed with the notion that crime should be controlled at all cost. We all seem to recall where we were at the time the O.J. Simpson verdict was read. At times, it seems as if the opinion we formulate regarding a particular case is directly influenced by the reaction of experts and the media. Many argue that the different opinions regarding the outcomes of some of these controversial cases have led to a great ethnic and cultural separation in America. Despite this, few people engage in the quest to understand the complexities surrounding our system of justice. Thus, you should consider yourself fortunate that you will have the opportunity to examine some of the issues surrounding the criminal justice system in America, which, although often discussed, are seldom understood.

The criminal justice system is comprised mainly of three social control agencies: the police, the courts, and corrections. Although each of these is independent of the others, all three work together toward the common goal of controlling crime while ensuring justice. The academic study of the criminal justice system is concerned with the nature and extent of crime, as well as the reactions of these social control agencies toward the breaking of laws. As the Academic Editor of *Perspectives: Criminal Justice,* I have selected a series of readings dealing with the three social control agencies in the criminal justice system, as well as with other areas of interest, including race and crime, and victimology. Specifically, these readings not only address an array of issues that directly affect the operations of the criminal justice agencies but also examine other topics, such as the impact of race and the rights of victims in the justice system.

The first three sections of this reader deal with the social control agencies in the criminal justice system—the police, the courts, and corrections. You will have the opportunity to read articles examining such areas as police brutality, the jurisdiction of the Supreme Court, and the operations of the new supermax prisons. The last two sections examine areas pertaining to race and crime, and to victimology. I hope that the wide variety of topics discussed within each of the five sections will lead you toward a more comprehensive understanding of some of the complexities surrounding the system of justice in the United States. More important, I sincerely hope that this reader introduces you to new ideas while challenging the basic underlying assumptions we often make about the criminal justice system, which is one of the most important subjects you will have an opportunity to examine throughout your tenure as a college student. In the words of George Washington (see *Letter to Randolph,* 1789), "The administration of justice is the firmest pillar of government."

Editorial Board

We wish to thank the following instructors for their assistance. Their many suggestions contributed to the construction of this volume and to the ongoing development of the Criminal Justice web site.

- **Course Overview** This is a general description of the typical course in this area of study. While your instructor will provide specific course objectives, this overview helps you place the course in a generic context and offers you an additional reference point.

- **www.orksheet** Focus your trip to a R.E.A.L. site with the www.orksheet. Each of the 10 to 15 questions will prompt you to take in the best that site has to offer. Use this tool for self-study, or if required, email it to your instructor.

- **Course Quiz** The questions on this self-scoring quiz are related to articles in the reader, information at R.E.A.L. sites, and other course topics, and will help you pinpoint areas you need to study. Only you will know your score—it's an easy, risk-free way to keep pace!

- **Topic Key** The Topic Key is a listing of the main topics in your course, and it correlates with the Topic Key that appears in this reader. This handy reference tool also links directly to those R.E.A.L. sites that are especially appropriate to each topic, bringing you integrated online resources within seconds!

- **Web Savvy Student Site** If you're new to the Internet or want to brush up, stop by the Web Savvy Student site. This unique supplement is a complete **courselinks** site unto itself. Here, you'll find basic information on using the Internet, creating a web page, communicating on the web, and more. Quizzes and Web Savvy Worksheets test your web knowledge, and the R.E.A.L. sites listed here will further enhance your understanding of the web.

- **Student Lounge** Drop by the Student Lounge to chat with other students taking the same course or to learn more about careers in your major. You'll find links to resources for scholarships, financial aid, internships, professional associations, and jobs. Take a look around the Student Lounge and give us your feedback. We're open to remodeling the Lounge per your suggestions.

Building Better Perspectives!

Please tell us what you think of this *Perspectives* volume so we can improve the next one. Here's how you can help:

1. Visit our **coursewise** site at: http://www.coursewise.com

2. Click on *Perspectives.* Then select the Building Better *Perspectives* Form for your book.

3. Forms and instructions for submission are available online.

Tell us what you think—did the readings and online materials help you make some learning connections? Were some materials more helpful than others? Thanks in advance for helping us build better *Perspectives.*

Student Internships

If you enjoy evaluating these articles or would like to help us evaluate the **courselinks** site for this course, check out the **coursewise** Student Internship Program. For more information, visit:

http://www.coursewise.com/intern.html

Brief Contents

Contents

At **coursewise,** we're publishing *connected learning tools*. That means that the book you are holding is only a part of this publication. You'll also want to harness the integrated resources that **coursewise** has developed at the fun and highly useful **courselinks**™ web site for *Perspectives: Criminal Justice*. If you purchased this book new, use the Passport that was shrink-wrapped to this volume to obtain site access. If you purchased a used copy of this book, then you need to buy a stand-alone Passport. If your bookstore doesn't stock Passports to **courselinks** sites, visit http://www.courselinks.com for ordering information.

section 1

Law Enforcement

section

2

Courts

section
3

Corrections

section
4

Race and Crime

section

5

Victimology

Topic Key

This Topic Key is an important tool for learning. It will help you integrate this reader into your course studies. Listed below, in alphabetical order, are important topics covered in this volume. Below each topic, you'll find the reading numbers and titles, and R.E.A.L. web site addresses, relating to that topic. Note that the Topic Key might not include every topic your instructor chooses to emphasize. If you don't find the topic you're looking for in the Topic Key, check the index or the online topic key at the **courselinks**™ site.

Appellate Courts
10   The Jurisdiction of the Supreme Court
18   The Misperception of Public Opinion toward Capital Punishment: Examining the Spuriousness Explanation of Death Penalty Support
25   One Crime, Two Sentences: Blacks See Bias over Cocaine

Legal Information Institute
http://supct.law.cornell.edu/supct/

Causes of Crime
30   Disintegration of the Family Is the Real Root Cause of Violent Crime

Centre for Research on Violence Against Women and Children
http://www.uwo.ca/violence/

Community Corrections
21   Defining Community Corrections
22   Fewer Sex Offenders on Community Release Programs Than Other Criminals

The Sentencing Project
http://www.sentencingproject.org/

Corruption
3   When the Bad Guys Are Cops: While Professionalism Is Increasing, a Vicious New Breed of Rogue Officer Has Experts Worried
4   Discipline Philosophy
7   Why Not Hire Civilian Commanders?
8   Do Appellate Courts Regularly Cheat?
11   Lack of Conviction

Shielded from Justice
http://www.hrw.org/reports98/police/index.htm

Crime Prevention
5   On the Waterfront: Police Unions Are Arresting the War Against Crime
6   Teaching Youths about the Law

Preventing Crime: What Works, What Doesn't, What's Promising
http://www.ncjrs.org/works/index.htm

Drugs
25   One Crime, Two Sentences: Blacks See Bias over Cocaine
27   Is Justice Color Blind?
31   Hispanics: The New Irish in the American Criminal Justice System?

Web of Addictions
http://www.well.com:80/user/woa/

Due Process vs. Crime Control
12   Courting the Middle Ground
16   Three Strikes and You're Out! The Political Sentencing Game
24   Race and the Criminal Justice System
26   "Stop or I'll Shoot": Racial Differences in Support for Police Use of Deadly Force
28   The Color of the Law
40   Watching "As the Jury Turns"

National Center for Policy Analysis
http://www.ncpa.org/studies/s219.html

Effects of Crime
33   Crime Victims and Psychological Injuries
36   Guilty Victims: How States' Failure to Separate the Innocent from the Guilty Is Costing the Victims Compensation Program Millions
37   Should Doctors Be More Proactive as Advocates for Victims of Violence?
39   Training Enhances Victim Services

National Crime Victims Research and Treatment Center
http://www.musc.edu/cvc/

Inmate Rights
12   Courting the Middle Ground
20   Legal Education for Juveniles

American Civil Liberties Union
http://www.aclu.org/issues/prisons/hmprisons.html

Juveniles
6   Teaching Youths about the Law
9   Juvenile Offenders: Should They Be Tried in Adult Courts?
20   Legal Education for Juveniles

The Monitoring the Future Study
http://www.isr.umich.edu/src/mtf/

Minorities and the System of Justice
24   Race and the Criminal Justice System
25   One Crime, Two Sentences: Blacks See Bias over Cocaine
27   Is Justice Color Blind?
28   The Color of the Law
29   Races Worry about Crime and Values, Disagree on Government
34   Paying More Attention to White Crime Victims
38   Violence: Are the Disabled More Abused?

U.S. Department of Justice, Bureau of Justice Statistics
http://www.ojp.usdoj.gov/bjs/crimoff.htm

Parole
14   History of the Federal Parole System: Part 1 (1910-1972)
15   History of the Federal Parole System: Part 2 (1973-1997)

Parole Watch
http://www.parolewatch.org/welcome.htm

section

1

After studying this section, you will know

- that citizens' support for police pursuits declines when the offense committed by suspects is not serious and when citizens are presented with information regarding the dangers of pursuits.

- that, due to the emotional nature of their jobs, police-beat reporters should receive psychiatric counseling in an effort to help them cope with severe levels of stress.

- that job stress among police officers is blamed for police misconduct.

- that law enforcement agencies must develop a disciplinary system in order to control and prevent the abuse of power among police officers.

- that the effort to prevent crime could be enhanced if it were managed at the local rather than the state or national level.

- that most police agencies can benefit from civilian service at all levels of management.

WiseGuide Intro

One of the most challenging and interesting careers anyone could pursue is that of a law enforcement agent. It is no secret that law enforcement personnel risk their lives daily in order to "protect and serve" the public. This risk, which some law enforcement officers describe as being their constant companion, is often augmented by the complex issues affecting their job. Thus, for this particular section, I have selected several articles that address some of the most important issues affecting law enforcement agents and agencies today. Some of these issues include, but are not limited to, the role of police unions in the war against crime, the development of a disciplinary system to control and prevent abuse of police power, and the temptations surrounding undercover police officers.

Before reading the articles in this section, you should recognize that some of the previously mentioned law enforcement-related issues have been in existence since the early days of policing. The changing factor since has been the degree of attention given to these issues today by the mass media and the public. Recently publicized cases that depict poor police practices have found a receptive audience, as some citizens—especially those who belong to minority groups—are increasingly becoming dissatisfied with the practices of law enforcement agencies.

In the United States, there are three major types of law enforcement jurisdictions: federal, state, and local. Most law enforcement agents in the United States work for either a state or a local agency. Only a handful work for federal law enforcement agencies. However, despite their limited size, some federal law enforcement agencies seem always to be the source of public attention. Among these are the Federal Bureau of Investigation (FBI), the U.S. Secret Service, and the U.S. Marshals. The attention given to these agencies often derives from Hollywood movies that depict federal agents as being superheros who, after being faced with numerous life-threatening situations, usually apprehend the subject in question. Thus, as a result of this erroneous view, the public often ignores the fact that all of the law enforcement agencies in this country, including those at the state, local, and federal levels, equally carry the important responsibility of reducing or eliminating criminal activity in general. Thus, it is only through the analysis of the complexities affecting the state, local, and federal law enforcement agencies and their agents that we can begin to understand their remarkable similarities while appreciating the uniqueness of their individual roles. I hope that the articles selected in this section will allow you to either start or continue this educational process.

Questions

Reading 1. What do studies on attitudes toward police pursuit reveal?

Reading 2. Why should police-beat reporters receive psychiatric counseling?

Reading 3. Do you feel that police misconduct is largely the result of job stress? Explain your response.

Reading 4. What are the possible benefits associated with the implementation of a standard disciplinary system on law enforcement agencies?

Reading 5. Name the key factors in an effective anticrime policy.

Reading 6. What is the main purpose of teaching youths about the law?

Reading 7. What are the critical functions performed by all police managers? Could civilians perform these?

What do studies on attitudes toward police pursuit reveal?

Public Attitudes toward Police Pursuit Driving

John M. MacDonald

*Department of Criminal Justice
and Criminology
University of Maryland*

Geoffrey P. Alpert

*College of Criminal Justice
University of South Carolina*

Introduction

Studies of police vehicle pursuits include information from official agency forms, officers and even suspects (Alpert, 1997; Lucadamo, 1994; Alpert and Fridell, 1992; Falcone, Wells, and Charles, 1992). Although empirical studies have reported the risks and benefits of pursuit driving, as well as the attitudes of law enforcement personnel, little is known about the public's perception of pursuit. The research on pursuit policy development, pursuit outcome, and civil liability has identified four critical factors important to police in reaching a pursue/don't pursue decision (Alpert and Fridell, 1992; Alpert, 1997):

1. known violation,

2. area in which the chase occurred,

3. traffic conditions, and

4. weather conditions.

A fifth consideration should be the public's understanding of and support for pursuit. This study reports information on the public's support for pursuit.

Previous Research on Attitudes Toward Pursuit

It was not until the 1960s that police pursuit was considered a critical issue for either the police or the public. During that decade, two juxtaposed positions became the focus of the pursuit debate: the benefit of pursuit, or need to enforce laws and apprehend violators; and the risk of pursuit, or the importance of public safety. While these two concerns have been the cornerstone of the pursuit argument and the courts have balanced them in their opinions, precious little information has been collected on the views of officers or the public on the issue.

During the late 1960s, an effort was made to determine the public's response to pursuit driving. A small public opinion survey was conducted to measure the support for police pursuit dri-

ving. According to Fennessy et al. (1970:11), a random sample of the driving population of Fairfax County, Virginia was questioned about pursuit driving and penalties for fleeing from the police. Each subject was given a short scenario in which a motorist did not stop when signaled by a police officer's emergency signals. Sixty-four percent of the subjects agreed that the police should chase the fleeing suspect, 33 percent responded that they should not chase the suspect, and 3 percent did not reply. In addition, members of the driving public were asked to indicate whether a fleeing motorist should be sent to prison, lose his license, receive a heavy fine, or receive a light fine. Almost 11 percent responded that the fleeing motorist should be sent to prison and almost 63 percent reported that the motorist should lose his license. Twenty-six percent wanted the law violator fined heavily, and no one reported a light fine as an appropriate punishment. From the data reported in the survey, it certainly appears that the public in the late 1960s was less than unanimous in its support for pursuit driving,

Reprinted from *Journal of Criminal Justice*, Vol. 26, No. 3, John M. MacDonald and Geoffrey P. Alpert, "Public Attitudes Toward Police Pursuit Driving," pp. 185–194. Copyright © 1998, with permission from Elsevier Science.

but regarded fleeing from a police officer as a serious law violation deserving relatively heavy sanctions.

Unfortunately, this early survey provided only one scenario. It did not ask those surveyed about other offenses for which the suspect might have been chased. Similarly, the research did not address risk factors associated with pursuit driving; however, the study was important as a first step in determining the level of the public's support for pursuit as a police tactic.

Although the focus of this study is on the public's perception of pursuit, the lack of research on attitudes toward pursuit permits the review of all attitudinal research, including studies of both public and officers' opinions. Eight studies were found that analyzed attitudes toward pursuit. Each had some methodological imperfection, but, nonetheless, contributed to a knowledge of pursuit. The first study conducted in 1991 by the University of Utah for the Salt Lake City Police Department, measured the public's attitude toward chasing. In a state-wide survey of residents (805 subjects), 28 percent reported that police should routinely pursue suspects. Fifty-six percent said that police should only pursue in cases involving forcible felonies and 8 percent reported that police should not pursue suspects at all. Five percent reported other answers and 3 percent reported "don't know" (Reese, 1991).

The second study was conducted by Falcone, Charles, and Wells (1994). Falcone has been a leader in the design, collection, and analysis of officers' attitudes and beliefs about pursuit. His research included a sample of officers and agencies in Illinois. The data from this research included opinions from almost all of the responding officers that pursuits are "somewhat" or "absolutely essential" for controlling crime and maintaining order (Falcone, Wells, and Charles, 1992:104–5). Further, Falcone and his colleagues reported that the respondents had different opinions about the offense categories that would justify pursuit. The categories ranged from traffic offenses to driving under the influence (DUI), and included misdemeanors, felonies, drug offenses, and forcible felonies (Falcone, Wells, and Charles, 1992:73). The authors acknowledged that there appeared to be an attitudinal split between law enforcement officers in some areas. Some officers admitted the risks of pursuit and avoided pursuing suspects, while others considered that the benefits outweighed the risks. These officers readily pursued suspects (Falcone, Wells, and Charles, 1992:73).

Although differences existed among the respondents in Falcone's research, several consistent themes emerged. As one would expect, the seriousness of the offense was positively and strongly correlated to the need to pursue. Most officers reported (in declining order) that reasons to terminate a pursuit included traffic conditions, certain speed zones, dangerousness of offense and weather conditions. More than 84 percent reported that a pursuit should be permitted for a forcible felony (Falcone, Wells, and Charles, 1992:106). Most officers reported that they did not believe that the majority of citizens would run from them if their agency had a no-pursuit policy. Falcone, Wells, and Charles (1994:150–51) concluded the following:

Actually, officers thought that somewhere between five and 15% of the population would be so encouraged . . . . Most officers also mentioned that many of the would-be offenders would probably attempt to elude them despite the presence of a no-pursuit policy.

Insight into why officers continue pursuits was provided by the research of Falcone, Wells, and Charles (1992:81):

Most officers interviewed agreed that it became difficult to call off a pursuit once they became involved in such an activity. Not only did they report that the chase often became a personal challenge requiring them to win over the violator, but they frequently admitted to a high state of excitement that often shaded their good judgment.

This view has also been presented by other research (Homant and Kennedy, 1994a:116):

All too often, an officer becomes so personally involved in the capture of a suspect that the safety of others is forgotten. The chase then becomes a matter of professional pride in driving skill: the officer concentrates only on winning.

While the officers reported general resentment on any limitation to pursue aggressively, it was acknowledged that "discretionary pursuit behaviors are not institutionally rewarded, are not given clear support by the majority of their peers [and] are not part of their public safety mandate inherent in their departmental mission" (Falcone, Charles, and Wells, 1994:152). Perhaps the most important conclusion drawn from these data reflects on the response to restricting officers' discretionary pursuit actions. In a comparative analysis of police agencies, Falcone, Charles, and Wells (1994:154) reported: "The data suggest that civilian departments which discourage pursuit policies experience no increase in attempts to elude and show that actual pursuits were lower than in departments with more permissive policies."

The third study, conducted by Britz and Payne (1994), was designed to determine if attitudes toward pursuit policies differed between line officers and administrators. The researchers surveyed police officers in a state agency. The officers reported serious deficiencies in the language of their pursuit policy, as well as problems with training (Britz and Payne, 1994:115, 131). Specifically, the results of this study indicated that 38 percent of the officers found the pursuit policy difficult to understand (and implement); 80 percent of the supervisors reported that no training on pursuit was provided to their patrol officers; and 35 percent of the officers had been in pursuits that were not reported. As expected, there were significant differences among the ranks concerning "perceptions of policy, supervisory support, the adequacy of training, liability issues and discretionary issues regarding police pursuit" (Britz and Payne, 1994:131).

In a fourth study, conducted by Picolo (1994), a mall intercept method and a quota sample were used to investigate the public's attitude toward pursuit driving. This innovative study also examined whether exposure to information about risks influenced attitudes toward pursuit. Picolo approached and received permission to interview 200 males and 200 females of age twenty-one years or older (50 percent White and 50 percent Black) and who were randomly assigned to control and experimental groups. Members of the "control" group

were provided with only a standard definition of pursuit. Members of the "experimental" group were provided the same definition, as well as a series of risk statistics from Alpert and Dunham's (1990) study of pursuit driving. Finally, each subject was given a nineteen-item survey concerning attitudes toward pursuit under adverse conditions. Picolo reported that there was, generally, only moderate support for pursuit and quite low support for the most risky scenarios. Further, Picolo concluded:

[W]hite men seem to be exceptionally different from white women, black men and black women in their attitudes toward the use of hot pursuits. Over and over again, white males are overwhelmingly more supportive of pursuits regardless of the seriousness of a criminal offense, the road and weather conditions, and the locations in which they occur (1994:77).

White males were the group most affected by the introduction of risk factors. While the other racial and gender comparisons revealed insignificant attitudinal differences based upon introduction to the risk factors, the white male "experimental" group was the only one that reported significantly less support for a continued pursuit and more support to terminate a chase. Picolo attributes these differences to the crime control orientation of White males and the relative importance of the knowledge about risks.

The fifth study, by Homant and Kennedy (1994a), involved a survey of registered voters in a suburb of approximately 80,000 people near Detroit. The researchers mailed out survey instruments to their sample and received a 40 percent return. The members of the public who responded reported that police offi-

cers use good judgment in deciding whether to engage in a high speed pursuit (76 percent). Interestingly, 60 percent reported that the police should be allowed to engage in a high speed pursuit only to prevent the escape of someone known to be a dangerous criminal. Although it is not clear, this could suggest that 36 percent of the respondents did not support a pursuit for even a dangerous felon. Fifteen percent of the respondents reportedly would be tempted to elude if it was known that the police would not follow in pursuit. The authors report that the 15 percent plus a 6 percent "unsure" response is a low estimate because registered voters may be more prosocial than nonregistered voters.

The sixth study, also by Homant and Kennedy (1994b), was designed to examine pursuit tendencies among patrol officers from departments with different policies. Officers from seven state agencies completed the questionnaires and formed the sample for this study. One part of the study asked officers to respond to scenarios by indicating their willingness to pursue. The researchers reported, "As predicted, states with the most permissive policies had officers who were most inclined to pursue, while the more restrictive states had officers that were less inclined" (Homant and Kennedy, 1994b:103).

A seventh study conducted, by Steele (1995), explored officers' attitudes toward pursuit as a police tactic. More than 200 officers from a suburban county were surveyed to determine their attitudes toward pursuit and to determine if knowledge of risks associated with pursuit affected these attitudes. The methods of this study incorporated the same concepts and measures as Picolo's (1994) research discussed above. Steele's research found that experienced officers were more likely to terminate a pursuit than officers with less experience; exposure to risk had little to do with the formulation of their attitudes.

In the eighth study, Alpert and Madden (1994) reported the attitudes of students majoring in criminal justice, police recruits, and police supervisors. Groups of subjects were provided a set of pursuit scenarios. Each scenario contained four bits of information depicting the environment of a pursuit: the need to immediately apprehend the suspect (known offense), area in which the chase occurred, traffic, and weather conditions (risk factors). The results demonstrated that supervisors were most likely, and the students least likely, to support a general decision to pursue. Police supervisors weighed the need to immediately apprehend a suspect as more important than the risks to the officers and the public. Law enforcement was given a higher priority than public safety. Students ranked the risk factors as more important than the need to immediately apprehend criminal suspects: public safety was ranked higher than the apprehension of offenders. It was anticipated that police recruits would support pursuit driving to a greater degree than the students; however, their responses were in between the other two groups. Thus, the dilemma of pursuit as a police tactic was underscored. Police supervisors, who can terminate a pursuit, viewed the tactic differently from a group of young citizens studying criminal justice and a group of young citizens learning to become police officers.

Summary of Research Findings

The information gleaned from these eight studies provides insight into the attitudes held by officers and the public concerning pursuit driving. Together, this information indicates that pursuit driving is a controversial tactic that is viewed differently by various groups or samples. Previous research showed that officers resented having their discretion reduced or controlled; policies were not understood; training was not received or remembered; and officers got caught up in the heat of the chase. Despite these facts, many of these same officers realized the need for restrictions and placed public safety over the need to immediately apprehend certain suspects. It may be that the officers who most resented the institutional control engaged in pursuit driving, but did not always report it. The little these studies learned about the public's attitudes toward pursuit indicated that citizens view pursuit with a cautious eye and provide only limited support. There is a great deal the public does not know about the benefits or costs of pursuit.

Methodology

The present study examined attitudes toward police pursuit held by citizens in Aiken County, South Carolina; Omaha, Nebraska; and Baltimore, Maryland. The survey instrument presented pursuit scenarios by creating categories that corresponded to the existing empirical information affecting officers' decisions to engage in pursuit driving (Alpert and Fridell, 1992). The benefits of pursuit or the *need to immediately apprehend* included eight levels of potential law viola-

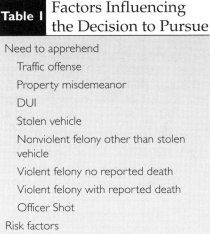

Table 1	Factors Influencing the Decision to Pursue
Need to apprehend	
Traffic offense	
Property misdemeanor	
DUI	
Stolen vehicle	
Nonviolent felony other than stolen vehicle	
Violent felony no reported death	
Violent felony with reported death	
Officer Shot	
Risk factors	
1. Chase area	
Freeway	
Commercial	
Inner-city	
Residential	
2. Weather conditions	
Wet	
Dry	
3. Traffic Conditions	
Congested	
Noncongested	

tions, under high-risk and low-risk conditions. The potential costs or *risks to the public* included three categories: area of pursuit, traffic, and weather conditions. The areas in which the chase occurred had four levels. The traffic and weather conditions each had two levels (see Table 1).

Subjects were asked to imagine that the police had initiated a traffic or felony stop and that the suspect refused to pull over and actively attempted to flee and avoid apprehension. Consistent with prior research and discussions with officers after pretesting the instrument, subjects were asked not to rank the aggressiveness or degree of pursuit, but to respond with a simple "yes" or "no" dichotomy. The factors and levels are presented in Table 1.

Systematic sampling was used in Aiken and Omaha to generate a random probability sample. For a probability sample, each sampling unit must have some known nonzero chance of being selected and, before sampling takes place, every possible sample of a given size must be capable of being specified from the population. The primary advantage of a probability sample is that it allows statistical inferences of the results to the target population.

Interviewers were given the following instructions for sample selection: (1) Select the bottom name in the first column for each page in the telephone listing pages received: and (2) If there is no answer, the line is busy, or it is a business or inoperative number, dial the number directly above.

To ensure that the sample was representative of households with unlisted as well as listed numbers, the plus-one dialing method was used by the interviewers. In this method, the interviewer adds one to the last digit of the phone number selected through the systematic sampling method, and then dials that number. (For example, if the telephone number of the last name in the first column is 777– 6074 the interviewer dialed 777–6075.) In Aiken, a sample of 255 residents was interviewed. According to the most recent census data for Aiken County, the sample interviewed was similar to the population according to age, gender, and geographic area.

In Omaha, 300 telephone surveys with randomly selected Omaha residents were conducted in the same way as those administered in Aiken County. The interview schedule and training guide included the same questions and instructions as the one used in Aiken. As in Aiken County, the sample interviewed was representative of the population in Omaha.

In Baltimore, the survey was conducted from a sample of all residents, eighteen years and older. A random sample of phone numbers was purchased from Survey Sampling, Inc. of Connecticut. Each phone number was called twice to obtain a response. Four hundred and forty-four numbers purchased from Survey Sampling were appropriate for the study. Out of these 444 eligible numbers, 275 refused to answer the survey. As a result of these methods, the final sample of respondents was 169, which represented a 38 percent response rate. Similar to the Aiken County and Omaha samples, the Baltimore sample overall was representative of the city's population.[1]

Two survey instruments were administered in Baltimore. The first instrument was similar to the one used in the other two areas. The second survey instrument provided citizens with some general statistical information about the outcome of pursuits and then asked for responses to specific questions. Specifically, respondents were told that approximately 40 percent of pursuits result in accidents, 20 percent of the pursuits result in injuries, and 1 percent of the pursuits result in a death. Additionally, respondents were told that nationwide, there are between 350 and 400 people killed per year as a result of police pursuit, and the police have no way to stop a fleeing vehicle without setting up a roadblock, ramming the car, or shooting it. The first instrument that did not provide information to the subjects was completed by ninety-two citizens (54 percent). The second instrument that provided the information about pursuits was completed by seventy-seven of the subjects (46 percent).

Findings

The data presented below include results from all three jurisdictions and are presented for comparison, but are limited to the high-risk, low-risk level questions. The first analysis includes responses to questions concerning general support for pursuits under high-risk conditions.[2] Second, responses to questions concerning general support for pursuit under low-risk conditions are presented.[3] Finally, the differences in responses of Baltimore residents to the instrument that provided results of pursuit driving and the one that provided no information is presented under low-risk conditions.

High-Risk Conditions

The data for high-risk conditions are presented in Table 2. Under high-risk conditions involving traffic violations, approval for police pursuits was given by 13 percent of the respondents from Omaha, 30 percent of the respondents from Aiken County, and 27 percent of respondents from Baltimore. Property crime-misdemeanor pursuits were approved by only 21 percent of Omaha respondents, 38 percent of the respondents from Aiken County, and 36 percent of those from Baltimore. Property crime-felony pursuits (other than those involving stolen vehicles) were supported by 48 percent of the respondents from Omaha, 61 percent of those from Aiken County, and 50 percent of those from Baltimore. When a vehicle was stolen, 44 percent of respondents from Omaha, 77 percent of respondents from Aiken County, and 48 percent of those respondents from Baltimore supported the police when pursuing the suspect. Seventy-one percent of

Table 2	High-Risk Conditions: Percent of Respondents Approving Pursuit for Specified Offenses		
	Aiken County (n = 255)	Baltimore (n =169)	Omaha (n = 300)
Traffic violation	30	27	13
Property crime—misdemeanor	38	36	21
Property crime—felony (other than stolen car)	61	50	48
Stolen vehicle	62	48	44
DUI	77	70	71
Violent felony—no reported death	74	68	88
Violent felony—reported death	90[a]	83[a]	96[a]
Police officer shot	91	86	97

[a]All three categories were statistically significant at the $p < .05$ level.

Omaha respondents, 77 percent of Aiken County respondents and 70 percent of Baltimore respondents approved pursuits for DUI. Violent felony–no reported death pursuits were approved by 88 percent of Omaha respondents, 74 percent of Aiken County respondents, and 68 percent of Baltimore respondents. Violent felony–reported death pursuits were approved by 96 percent of those from Omaha, 90 percent of those from Aiken County, and 83 percent of those from Baltimore. The difference between all three samples was statistically significant at the .05 level. Cases in which a police officer was shot were approved by 97 percent of those Omaha, 91 percent of those from Aiken County, and 86 percent of those from Baltimore.

At this high level of risk conditions, the least serious offenses received one of the largest differences among respondents. A pursuit for a traffic offense was supported by 13 percent of the Omaha respondents and 30 percent of those from Aiken County. Incidents involving property crimes–misdemeanors received 38 percent support from Aiken

County respondents and 21 percent support from respondents in Omaha. Sixty-one percent of respondents from Aiken County supported pursuit, while 48 percent of respondents from Omaha supported pursuit for incidents involving property crime felonies. Incidents involving stolen vehicles received 62 percent support from respondents in Aiken County and 44 percent support from respondents in Omaha.

Low-Risk Conditions

The data on low-risk conditions are presented in Table 3. Under low-risk conditions involving traffic violations, approval for a police pursuit was given by 47 percent of the respondents from Omaha, 68 percent of the respondents from Aiken County, and 81 percent of respondents from Baltimore. Property crime–misdemeanors pursuits were approved by only 50 percent of respondents from Omaha, 66 percent of those from Aiken County, and 62 percent of those from Baltimore. In property crime–felony pursuits (other than those involving stolen vehicles), approval for a pursuit was given by 83 percent of respondents from

Omaha, 84 percent of those from Aiken County, and 73 percent of those from Baltimore. In stolen vehicle pursuits, 84 percent of Omaha respondents, 83 percent from Aiken County, and 91 percent from Baltimore approved. In Omaha, 93 percent of respondents approved DUI pursuits, with approval coming from 88 percent of those in Aiken County and 82 percent of those in Baltimore. Violent felonies with no-reported death were approved by 97 percent of the respondents from Omaha, 91 percent of those from Aiken County, and 85 percent of those from Baltimore. One hundred percent of respondents from Omaha, 99 percent of those from Aiken County, and 83 percent of those from Baltimore approved pursuits for violent felonies with a reported death. Ninety-nine percent of respondents from Omaha, 98 percent from Aiken County, and 80 percent for Baltimore approved of a pursuit when a police officer was shot. A striking finding in the Baltimore sample is that approximately the same percentage of respondents approved of pursuits involving traffic violations (81 percent, $n = 137$) as for the

Table 3 Low-Risk Conditions: Percent of Respondents Approving Pursuit for Specified Offenses

	Aiken County (n = 255)	Baltimore (n = 169)	Omaha (n = 300)
Traffic violation	68[a]	81[a]	47[a]
Property crime—misdemeanor	66	62	50
Property crime—felony (other than stolen car)	84	73	83
Stolen vehicle	83	91	84
DUI	88	82	93
Violent felony—no reported death	91	85	97
Violent felony—reported death	99	83	100
Police officer shot	98	80	99

[a]All three categories were statistically significant at the $p < .05$ level.

Table 4 Low-Risk Conditions: Percent of Respondents Approving Pursuit for Specified Offenses

	No information	Information	Difference
Traffic violation	87	73	14
Property crime—misdemeanor	65	58	7
Property crime—felony (other than stolen car)	75	70	5
Stolen vehicle	95	87	8[a]
DUI	83	80	3
Violent felony—no reported death	88	82	6
Violent felony—reported death	88	77	11[a]
Police officer shot	85	74	11[a]

[a]Significant at the $p < .05$ level (1-tailed).

shooting of a police officer (80 percent, $n = 135$).

As under the high-risk conditions, the largest differences were in the least-serious offense categories, including traffic and property crimes. A pursuit for a traffic offense received support ranging from 81 percent of the respondents in Baltimore to 47 percent of the respondents in Omaha. The differences across all three samples were statistically significant at the .05 level. Property crime–misdemeanor received 66 percent support from Aiken County respondents and 50 percent support from Omaha respondents. Pursuits for property crimes involving felonies were supported by 84 percent of Aiken County respondents as compared to 73 percent of the Baltimore respondents.

Educating the Public on Pursuit Risks

The final set of analyses includes the differences of opinions reported by citizens of Baltimore who were provided with some information concerning the outcome of pursuit and those who were not. The citizens were asked to respond to the questions assuming low-risk conditions. The term "information" indicates that the respondents were given information concerning possible outcomes of police pursuits prior to responding to a set of questions. The term "no information" indicates that the respondents received no information about possible outcomes of police pursuits before answering questions.

Respondents gave less support for police pursuits when given information about possible outcomes. The differences are presented in the last column of Table 4. When given no information on pursuit outcomes, respondents approved police pursuits by a higher percentage across all offenses than when given information of pursuit outcomes.

Pursuits for traffic violations received approval from 87 percent of Baltimore respondents who received no information about the hazards of pursuit. In contrast, 73 percent of the Baltimore respondents gave approval when informed about the outcome of pursuit driving. Sixty-five percent of Baltimore respondents gave approval of a police pursuit for incidents involving a property crime–misdemeanor when no information about pursuit was provided compared to 58 percent approval when these dangers were explained. Baltimore respondents gave 75 percent approval to a police pursuit for a property crime–felony when no information of the hazards was provided compared to 70 percent approval when information of pursuit outcome was provided. When a vehicle was stolen, respondents with no explanation of pursuit dangers gave 95 percent approval compared to 87 percent approval of those who were given some information of the likelihood of an accident, injury, or death. Eighty-eight percent of respondents approved of a police pursuit for a violent felony–no reported death when no information was provided, while 82 percent of those approved of a pursuit after information of pursuit outcome was provided. Support for pursuits in a crime involving a violent felony–death reported was given by 88 percent of those who received no information about pursuits and 77 percent of the respondents supported pursuit after information of the possibility of a negative outcome was provided. When a police officer shooting occurred, 85 percent of those respondents approved of pursuit when given no information on pursuit hazards, while 74 percent

approved of pursuit after being told about possible pursuit outcomes.

The largest differences were reported in the least serious offense category. Incidents involving a traffic violation reflected a 14 percent difference among respondents who were provided information about pursuit outcomes and those who were not told about the dangers of pursuit driving. This difference was statistically significant at the .05 level. There were also differences between those who had been told about pursuit outcomes and those who had not been informed when respondents expressed opinions about property crime felonies (5 percent), property crime misdemeanors (7 percent), and a stolen car (8 percent). Additionally, for the most serious offenses (a police officer shot and a violent felony with a reported death), there was an 11 percent difference between groups who had been told about pursuit outcomes and those who had not been informed.

Conclusion

The impact of public perceptions on officers' performance generally has the potential to improve compliance with departmental policy and individual accountability. The analysis of citizens' responses to police pursuit scenarios demonstrates public reaction to this dangerous practice. The results of this research suggest that the public overwhelmingly supports pursuits for serious criminal offenses. This support echoes the results of earlier public opinion research on pursuit driving. The data presented here, however, also show a clear trend in which the public's support for pursuits diminishes with the seriousness of the of-

fense for which the pursuit was initiated. This general trend across sites is supported, although regional and site-specific differences are reported.

This study did not focus on police officers' attitudes, however, it is worth noting the similarities between officers and members of the public. The general trend of support appears to be similar from each group and controlled by the seriousness of the offense. Support for pursuit is strong and criticism is minimal, if it exists at all when a police officer is shot or a felony committed. Support is minimal, especially under high-risk conditions, when a traffic violator is pursued.

The public opinion surveys conducted in Aiken County, Baltimore, and Omaha demonstrated that citizens support the police trying to capture suspects of serious crimes; but, the support diminishes when the nature of the offense is not as serious. In addition, public support for pursuit decreases when information about the dangers of pursuit is presented. The findings suggest that an informed public is less likely to accept the necessity of police use of pursuit for less serious offenses. If the public becomes more knowledgeable of these dangers, police departments may have to develop stricter pursuit policies.

In making those decisions, however, it is also important to recognize two potential benefits of pursuit as well as the costs. First, many suspects who attempt to flee the police will be arrested for crimes unrelated to the underlying violation that caused the pursuit. Suspects are sometimes arrested for outstanding felony warrants, possession of drugs or weapons, as well as offenses related to reckless driving (Alpert and Dunham, 1990). The question remains, how many arrests will be made for serious felonies? Second, the question of deterrence must be considered. That is, if the police do not pursue, how many people will be encouraged to drive recklessly because they know the police will not follow? Similarly, how many drunk drivers will stop if they are not chased by police? The critical question is this: Will more injuries and deaths occur if the police decide not to chase instead of continuing to chase?

Although there is no clear empirical evidence, the police in some areas where pursuits have been restricted to violent felonies report that there has been no change in crime because of the change in pursuit policy. There also has not been a change in the number of suspects who attempt to flee the police.[4] Clearly, future research should address those issues.

Acknowledgements

Support for this research has been provided, in part, by the National Institute of Justice Grant #93-IJ-CX-0061. Opinions stated in this paper are those of the authors and do not necessarily represent the official positions of the National Institute of Justice.

Notes

1. Whites in the Baltimore sample were overrepresented by 9 percent according to census figures.
2. High-risk conditions were defined as a pursuit that takes place on congested inner-city streets at night in wet weather.
3. Low-risk conditions were defined as a pursuit that takes place on a noncongested roadway during the day in clear weather.
4. These comments were made by Tom Arnold, Deputy Director, Metro-Dade Police Department, at the Police Executive Research Forum(PERF) 20th Anniversary Meeting, May 1997. Interestingly, similar comments were made by former Tampa police Chief Eddie Gonzales at the PERF annual meeting in 1994.

References

Alpert, G. P. (1997). Pursuit driving: Planning policies and action from agency, officer, and public information. *Police Forum* 7:1–12.

Alpert, G. P., and Dunham, R. G. (1990). *Police pursuit driving: Controlling responses to emergency situations.* Westport, CT: Greenwood Press.

Alpert, G. P., and Fridell, L. A. (1992). *Police vehicles and firearms: Instruments of deadly force.* Prospect Heights, IL: Waveland Press, Inc.

Alpert, G. P., and Madden, T. (1994) Police pursuit driving: An empirical analysis of critical decisions. *American Journal of Police* 4:23–45.

Britz, M., and Payne, D. (1994). Policy implications for law enforcement pursuit driving. *American Journal of Police* 13:113–42.

Falcone, D., Charles, M., and Wells, E. (1994). A study of pursuits in Illinois. *The Police Chief* 61:59.

Falcone, D., Wells, E., and Charles, M. (1992). *Police pursuit in pursuit of policy: The empirical study.* Vol. 2. Washington, DC: AAA Foundation for Traffic Safety.

Fennessy, E., Hamilton, T., Joscelyn, K., and Merritt, J. (1970). *A study of the problem of hot pursuit by the police.* Washington, DC: U.S. Department of Transportation.

High-speed pursuits: Police officers and municipal liability for accidents involving the pursued and an innocent third party. (1986). *Seton Hall Law Review* 16:101–26.

Homant, R., and Kennedy, D. (1994a). The effect of high-speed pursuit policies on officers' tendencies to pursue. *American Journal of Police* 13:91–111.

Homant, R., and Kennedy, D. (1994b). Citizen preferences concerning police pursuit policies. *Journal of Criminal Justice* 22:415–58.

Homant, R., Kennedy, D., and Howton, J. (1993). Sensation seeking as a factor in police pursuit. *Criminal Justice and Behavior* 20:293–305.

Lucadamo, T. (1994). *Identifying the dimensions of police pursuit.* Master's Thesis, University of Maryland.

Picolo, S. (1994). *Attitudes toward the use of hot pursuits by the police.* Master's Thesis, University of Maryland.

Reese, R. (1991). *Results of hot pursuit poll.* Memorandum to Salt Lake City Police Department, University of Utah, August 14.

Steele, L. T. (1995). *The standard of care: Police attitudes on hot pursuit policy.* Master's Thesis, University of Maryland.

 Article Review Form at end of book.

Why should police-beat reporters receive psychiatric counseling?

The High-Stress Police Beat

A steady diet of violent crime, fatal accidents and human tragedy takes a toll on reporters. Some think newspapers and TV stations should do more to help their staffers cope.

Chris Harvey

Chris Harvey, a former Washington Times *reporter, teaches at the University of Maryland College of Journalism.*

He still remembers minute details from a crash last fall, when a car carrying two sisters to community college classes crossed the center line into an oncoming lumber truck.

The coolness of the morning air. The slickness of the road. The snapshots that had blown out of the car and lay strewn about the road.

Flames had engulfed both vehicles. The truck driver had kicked his window out and escaped. The young women had not.

"It was probably the worst thing I've ever seen," says Matt Nelson, then a reporting intern with Minneapolis' *Star Tribune.* "As they pulled the lumber truck off the car, one of the victim's heads rolled to the side and steam rolled out of her chest.

"We're not trained emergency workers, and that sort of thing sticks with you," says Nelson, 26, now a police reporter for the Duluth *News-Tribune.* "You

go home and hug your family and tell them you love them. And for the next few weeks you wonder when your lumber truck is coming."

Horror and tragedy frequently visit reporters covering the police beat, but they are by no means the only stresses encountered on the job.

Like few other reporters, police reporters must remain ever vigilant, ready to scramble to the scene of a shooting, stabbing, accident or fire. Unlike disaster or war correspondents, they can't leave after a few months if they've had enough.

Many keep their pagers on 24 hours a day, moving them from belt to bedside table. Some surround themselves with the urgent crackle of police scanners at work and in their homes and cars.

"The soundtrack of my life is a police scanner," says St. Paul *Pioneer Press* crime reporter Tim Nelson, Matt's 28-year-old brother. The elder sibling keeps five scanners—tuned to different emergency channels—running in his one-room apartment.

Occasionally, crime reporters find themselves in danger, with a

gun or a knife pointed at them, or a fist in their face. Often, they find themselves trying to pull information from reluctant or distressed sources who, unlike elected officials, have nothing to gain by talking to them.

"My job was to get information from cops who weren't supposed to give me information," and to talk to victims' families "at a time when they really didn't need to be answering personal questions," says former *Washington Times* reporter Margaret Rankin.

A decade of increases in violent crimes has in some cases meant additional work. Between 1984 and 1993, the FBI reports, there was a 31 percent increase nationally in murders. "We just can't keep up with it," says reporter Thomas J. Gibbons Jr., 50, who has been covering crime in Philadelphia for 23 years, the last 14 at the *Inquirer.* "It's to the point now where it's forget about lunch. We can't even go to the bathroom."

Some reporters thrive under the pressure, secure in the knowl-

"The High-Stress Police Beat" by Chris Harvey from *American Journalism Review* July–August, 1995, Vol. 17, No. 6, pp. 28–33. Reprinted by permission of American Journalism Review.

edge that they can produce order from chaos and master difficult situations. "I love the work and I love the rush," says Tim Nelson. "I really get a charge out of it."

Others cope with beat stresses as best they can, picking up unhealthy habits such as smoking or drinking, numbing their emotions to the unfolding tragedies or occasionally finding themselves gripped by nightmares or crying jags.

Some last a few years and then find they need a change. Fear, depression or cynicism overtake them. "I knew I had to get out when I started saying things like, 'Oh, another dead baby story,'" says Rankin, 31, who quit the *Washington Times* in September 1993 to take preparatory classes for medical school. "It's the equivalent of, 'Oh, another nuclear holocaust story,'" she says in disgust.

Dr. Beverly J. Anderson, who runs a counseling program for Washington's police department, worries about crime reporters. "The bottom line is you can't continually expose an individual to high stress or continued stress without it always being a negative factor," she says. "It's the law of diminishing returns. You don't have infinite energy. The hypervigilance uses up defense mechanisms needed to fight illness. . . . Sooner or later you will succumb to illness, emotionally, mentally or physically."

Police and the reporters covering them share many of the same stress factors, she says: work overload; erratic sleep and work hours; exposure to other stress carriers, including bosses and victims; and role conflicts. She says it's tough to be detached and stoic on the street and then come home to a family expecting emotional intimacy.

"People don't ever get used to it," Anderson says. "You tolerate it for a time." But if you don't address the stress, she says, "when it comes back, it's like a stopped-up sewer."

She recommends that police reporters, like police officers and firefighters, be debriefed by a counselor whenever they are exposed to murders, fires, floods, bombings, suicides and barricade situations—incidents "outside the range of usual human experiences that would be markedly distressing to almost anyone."

She says counseling sessions should be mandatory. People need to be told that the feelings and symptoms they are experiencing are normal. "People are much more comfortable with denial," Anderson says. "But you don't ask people if they're going to get immunizations."

When Rankin moved from covering society parties to covering crime in the late 1980's, she thought it would be glamorous and gritty, a ticket to the front page. She also thought it would be instructive. She believed getting up close to the street slaughter in Washington would help her understand why so many young men were killing each other.

"I had delusions of being able to figure this out, but I eventually became disillusioned with it," says Rankin. "Nothing ever made more sense than it did at first."

She remembers being simultaneously fascinated and repelled by her first murder scene, in the driveway of a wealthy family's house. "I was still doing some society stuff. I was in high heels and stockings and a silk blouse" while standing over the body of a teenager leaking rivulets of blood, Rankin recalls.

When officials rolled the teenager over, Rankin could see one eye had been shot out. Still, she moved closer, "until one detective there said, 'You act like you've never seen a dead body before.' And I said I hadn't," Rankin says.

She remembers thinking this was so unlike the deaths she had seen on television. "On TV tragedies, everyone is upset. It seemed [there] no one was."

Body soon followed body. As one of the *Washington Times'* two full time police reporters, Rankin found herself writing about 200 stories a year, most of them "the night's fire, the night's drowning, the night's shooting." In 1993, the year she left the paper, 454 people were murdered in the nation's capital. "I started to think everybody was bad," she says. "You don't feel like you can trust anybody in that world."

She became worried about her safety. When she came home at night to her apartment in Alexandria, Virginia, she would search for potential killers in her closets, "my heart in my throat." She found herself sleeping the weekends away, too lethargic to get out of bed. The job "had a huge depressing effect on my life," she says.

She also found herself crying uncontrollably when interviewing victims' families. One incident particularly distressed her. A mother had left her toddler in her boyfriend's care while she went across the street to make a telephone call. The boyfriend let the child play with a gun and the boy apparently shot himself in the head. "I couldn't imagine," Rankin recalls, "why anyone would give a gun to a child, and that a mother could love someone who could kill her child."

The tragedies that stay with crime reporters are the ones they can imagine striking themselves or their families. For David Simon, 34, a police reporter at Baltimore's *Sun* since 1983, it was a plane crash in western Virginia. A commuter plane headed for Weyers Cave had hit the side of a mountain. Simon says he slipped around the police line and climbed up the back of the mountain to get closer to the wreckage.

"I knew I had to get out when I started saying things like 'Oh, another dead baby story,' " says Margaret Rankin.

Vestiges of the passengers' lives greeted him: Notebooks. A woman's shoe. Luggage burst open. "There's something really humanizing when you walk through the debris," he says. Tired rescue workers punished him for getting so close by making him carry one of the bodies, wrapped in a see-through bag, down the mountain.

He was so shaken, he says, he couldn't bring himself to take a commuter flight back to Baltimore. "I had to drive a rental car all the way back," Simon says. But, he adds, "that was more about me than it was about the bodies." He says he never liked flying.

Car wrecks get to Tom Hallman Jr., a crime beat reporter at the *Oregonian* in Portland. Dead guys in suits remind him too much of himself. "A car accident is something we can all relate to," says Hallman, 39, who in his 13 years on the beat has shifted from covering breaking crime stories to writing crime features. "Most can't relate to a drive-by shooting."

The horror of unexpected tragedy is magnified when the victim is an acquaintance or a friend. David Statter, 40, a general assignment reporter for WUSA-TV in Washington, and Brian Reilly, a crime reporter for the *Washington Times,* say some of the hardest stories they have had to cover followed the November 22, 1994, shooting at police headquarters in the District of Columbia.

Two FBI agents and a police sergeant were killed by a gunman who mistook the sergeant for someone else. Reilly and Statter knew the murdered sergeant and many of the grieving officers.

"I remember somebody was talking to me, upset about what they had seen in the room . . . . I wasn't sure if I was supposed to bring out my note pad or hug them," says Reilly, 27.

For some reporters, the toughest assignments are dealing with the grieving, especially those mourning lost children.

Both reporters had been in a press conference on the same floor of the building when the shooting erupted. Statter had to go live from police headquarters shortly after. "It was very difficult," says Statter, who had known the sergeant for 10 years. "It was all I could do to control my emotions on the air."

During the weeks following the shootings, Reilly says he was certain he was developing ulcers. He had trouble sleeping. His stomach hurt. He was smoking more. "I started buying my own cigarettes. I hadn't done that since the eighth grade," he says. A doctor told him his pains weren't from ulcers, but from stress. He instructed Reilly to drink less and stop smoking.

For some reporters, the toughest assignments are dealing with the grieving, especially those mourning lost children. "If there were things that haunted me, it was the living, grieving people," says Kevin Harrington, a former police reporter for the *Milwaukee Journal.* "Mothers crying at crime scenes. I used to have dreams that included them."

Harrington, 36, left the paper in 1993 to work as a victim-witness specialist for the county district attorney's office. But a crime scene at a Milwaukee public housing project still bothers him.

Two teenagers had been playing with a gun. It went off, leaving one dead. When the victim's mother got to the scene, "she was keening," Harrington says. "It was beyond crying and screaming."

As Harrington walked to his car, he passed a bakery. "And you could smell baking bread. And so for a long time, when I would smell baking bread," he would see that keening mother, Harrington says.

Gibbons agrees that interviewing the grieving can be tough, "particularly if it's a youngster or a teenager." He says he has rarely cried at work, but did this year on Good Friday. He had gone to the home of a "young North Philadelphia lad, a budding athlete who was gunned down the night before while sitting on the front steps of a friend's house."

Gibbons went to the house to get a photo of the 13-year-old boy and to interview the family. "I don't know what it was, whether I let my guard down. But while I was interviewing the dead boy's cousin, I started almost to rack," he says. "I almost had to excuse myself and leave the room. It . . . kind of alarmed me."

Emotions sometimes surface at odd times. Debbi Wilgoren, a *Washington Post* crime reporter from December 1990 to August 1993, says she generally enjoyed the beat. "I really care about people. I like people stories," the 27-year-old reporter says. But while covering crime she would occasionally "get very upset, like it would just come over me."

The most dramatic instance, she says, was one Sunday morning in 1992, when she had spread the morning paper out on the floor to read a story by a colleague that was "supposed to be about people who are shot but don't die." The piece focused on a 16-year-old Marylander who got shot while jogging in Northwest Washington "and was working his way back."

But when Wilgoren turned the page she was confronted with descriptions of the youth's death. Several weeks after the shooting, a fatal blood clot had developed. "I just started to cry," says Wilgoren, who now covers religion for the *Post.* "I was crying for him, but I think I was also crying for all these other people."

Fears for personal safety are not uncommon, or unfounded. Reporters say they feel most threatened when they go canvassing neighborhoods a day or two after a crime, when the police are long gone. But most reject wearing body vests for protection. "If it's very obvious, it's likely to make you a target," says Statter.

"It would hurt me more than help me," says *Washington Post* crime reporter Ruben Castaneda. "What kind of message would that send to people, if I walk up in body armor?"

Castaneda, 34, says if someone wanted to hurt him, they could do it even if he was wearing protective clothes. "Most people in the city are shot at very close range. Body armor doesn't protect the head," he says.

He has had several brushes with danger. Once, he had a long blade pulled on him while trying to interview a group of men hanging out on a Washington street corner. "It was a light feature story about the popularity at the time of bright headbands or skull caps," Castaneda recalls.

The situation turned from playful to menacing when one of the men pulled Castaneda's note book from his hands while another "swooshed the air" with a "small sword, or a really big knife," before stabbing the ground with it. Castaneda managed to regain control of the interview and his notebook.

He says he was also punched by a gang member during the Los Angeles riots and teargassed during disturbances in Washington, D.C.

Gibbons, a former Philadelphia police officer who was shot while on the force in 1970, says he felt threatened two years ago, while reporting "a bizarre story that started with a body found floating in the Delaware River." The investigation took him to a house in South Philadelphia. "A guy, high as a kite, opened the door. He had a gun in his hands."

Gibbons says he told the man to put the gun down, that he was a reporter. The man didn't, but beckoned him inside. They sat talking on the couch. Then the man asked Gibbons to come to the kitchen to look at evidence of a fight. "He's got the gun in his hand and he's behind me. All of my police instincts tell me I shouldn't. I could be horse meat before sunrise."

Gibbons walked into the kitchen, but helped defuse the situation with a joking threat. "I said to him, 'Don't you shoot me, you son of a bitch.' He kind of laughed. . . . We went back in the living room, and I left."

Peter Hermann of Baltimore's *Sun* had to be fished out of the water as an abandoned building burned in the city's Fells Point neighborhood. A firefighter he was walking with and interviewing "took a right and I didn't," says the 28-year-old Hermann, somewhat sheepishly. He lost his shoes, his glasses, his pager and his notes to the murky water of the Inner Harbor.

The harsh realities of the job can also affect a reporter's world—or neighborhood—view. Hermann, who moved from a suburban reporting job to the city crime beat a year ago, casually points out Baltimore landmarks while he drives from an afternoon shooting (no bodies, no story) back to the newsroom.

"This corner here, Homewood and North, is where Nathaniel Hurt lives," says Hermann, as he darts through afternoon traffic in his red Toyota Celica, scanner squawking. "He shot a 13-year-old to death from his second floor fire escape. He was messing with his car," Hermann says of the victim. Hurt was convicted of involuntary manslaughter and is awaiting sentencing.

Driving to the police staging area for an evening drug bust, Hermann passes a park in the southeast corner of the city. The park looks quiet, even serene. It's not. "This is a big prostitution area," Hermann says.

Later that night, driving back to work following the bust that netted police more than a kilo of cocaine, a Hardee's restaurant makes Hermann nostalgic. "They arrested a drug dealer here," he says. "They let him go through the drive-through. But they didn't let him finish his hamburger."

The beat also exposes reporters to facts of life they would rather avoid. "There are certain things you don't need to know," says Melinda Wilson, 37, a police reporter for the *Detroit News.* "One is the sound a woman makes when her child has been shot. The other is how a body looks during various stages of decomposition."

But gruesome scenes and tough neighborhoods aren't the only mine fields crime reporters must negotiate. Newsrooms have their own hazards. Information must often be wheedled, cajoled and manipulated from reluctant sources. Quotes from police officers and prosecutors wishing to remain anonymous must be attributed carefully, so that identification isn't obvious, reporters say.

"Changing a line around can really hurt a beat reporter," says the *Oregonian's* Hallman.

Editors sometimes forget that.

Detectives and prosecutors usually don't.

But editors aren't the only ones who have inserted problems into copy. Wilson says shortly after she came to the crime beat a year ago from the business desk, she wrote a story about a decomposing body that had dripped blood into a woman's apartment below.

She talked to the homicide detective, aware that the city detectives did not like to have their names in the paper. She used his name anyway, assuming he would

The police beat exposes reporters to realities they would rather avoid. "There are . . . things you don't need to know," says Melinda Wilson.

not mind given the unusual nature of the story. "He was crazed," she says. "I sent him flowers. He still hasn't talked to me."

If crime reporters want to stay well, they need to take care of themselves, D.C. police counselor Anderson says. Take vitamins, she advises. Work out. Allow time for relaxation. And learn the "high signs" of stress and seek help when they strike.

Symptoms of problematic stress include irritability, lethargy, attention and concentration problems, and changes in sex patterns. Sometimes traumatic events are re-experienced. "Whether you want to or not, it plays back in your mind," Anderson says.

Other signs include avoidance, "not having any feelings" or not being able to express emotions, Anderson says. They also include feeling isolated and "closed out, even at parties."

Some newspapers are stepping up counseling help for reporters who have covered tragedies. For example, *New York Times* editors are authorized to encourage reporters who seem distressed by a story to seek in-house, confidential counseling, says counselor Patricia Drew.

"It's an opportunity to take care of yourself . . . even if you think you're handling it OK," Drew says. "We like to offer it as a preventative effort, rather than wait until people are so symptomatic that it is obvious to everyone."

Baltimore's *Sun* is considering doing more for its reporters, says City Editor Jim Asher. He says he met with other editors at the paper in May and they agreed counseling "sounds like a good

idea" for reporters who cover tragedies. "But we haven't yet taken the next step" to work out the details, he says.

Wilson of the *Detroit News* says she would like to see more done for reporters industrywide. "Every other profession that deals with this gets some kind of stress counseling. But we're not supposed to be stressed at all. We're not supposed to have feelings."

She says she has been depressed since she came to the beat, and wishes she could find a support group in the Detroit area. A single mother, she says she can't talk to her four- and eight-year-old daughters about work.

"I don't want to share all that sadness with them," she says. "How can you tell a four-year-old kid, 'Mommy is writing about a lady killed in a burnt-out building and they only identified her by her gall bladder scars?'"

Many crime reporters say they are not interested in counseling but have developed other coping strategies.

"Just try and keep your head up and don't be afraid to complain," says the *Inquirer's* Gibbons. "There are other reporters in this room. I get a lot of comfort out of unburdening myself to them."

Some say they resort to humor so dark outsiders would find it repulsive. "People laugh sometimes about tragedy as a way to be tough," says Portland's Hallman.

The *Post's* Wilgoren says she found writing therapeutic. "Look for ways to explore the issues behind the crimes," she says. "It's the way the job ought to be done. And it helps you work through some of the grief."

Many reporters say doing longer projects gives them time to

regroup emotionally. "I just had a break of a month, working on a story on how to survive a fire," says Washington television reporter Statter. "That kept me away from chasing the fires. Now I'm ready to get back at it."

The *Sun's* Simon, who has taken two sabbaticals to research and write books, is a proponent of taking time for more ambitious stories, including those written in the narrative form. He says they're good for both the reader and the writer.

"You can't make a drug murder or arrest story interesting writing it the same way," says Simon, who spent a year with the city's homicide detectives before writing the book, *Homicide.* "You have to go deeper."

He also argues some reporters just aren't cut out for crime reporting and shouldn't be made to do it. "If you have somebody really good on cops, it pays to try to keep him there," Simon says. "But some people temperamentally will be freaked out at the horror show of it." They should be moved to another beat, in Simon's view.

Other reporters say it helps to keep their job—and their role at crime scenes—in perspective.

"We don't see as much as they see," says Hermann of police. "Seeing the body on the ground is a lot different than having to shoot somebody, put them there."

Hallman agrees. "I tell you, I could never be a cop. We dip our foot into this thing. [But] I couldn't do this day in and out.

"It's a dangerous, unforgiving world," he adds. A reporter's mission "is to relay that to our readers."

 Article Review Form at end of book.

Do you feel that police misconduct is largely the result of job stress? Explain your response.

When the Bad Guys Are Cops

While professionalism is increasing, a vicious new breed of rogue officer has experts worried

Gordon Witkin

Americans who thought they had heard everything at the O.J. Simpson trial found out otherwise last week. As the courtroom fell into a shocked hush, the tapes of a screenwriter's interviews with retired Los Angeles Police Detective Mark Fuhrman gave the country something new to think about: descriptions of police brutality and racism so virulent and cavalier that they raised troubling questions about not only the L.A. Police Department but law enforcement across the country.

Fuhrman used the word "nigger" 41 times in his hate-filled discourse about life as a policeman. In explaining his opposition to building a new headquarters in a minority district, Fuhrman said, "Leave that old station. Man, it has the smell of niggers that have been beaten

and killed in there for years." Fuhrman also told of viciously beating suspects after the shooting of two police officers. "We basically tortured them," Fuhrman said matter-of-factly. "We broke 'em. Their faces were just mush. They had pictures of the walls with blood all the way to the ceiling and finger marks from trying to crawl out of the room."

Prosecutors tried to portray Fuhrman's stories as braggadocio, and Judge Lance Ito ruled that the jury could hear just the briefest excerpts. But if only a portion of Fuhrman's discourse is true, what it says about him and L.A.'s police culture is chilling. More important, Fuhrman's comments focused attention on the broader issue of rogue cops in police departments across the country, especially in minority neighborhoods, where friction between law officers and commu-

nity residents often reaches a flash point. With police scandals unfolding in New Orleans, Philadelphia and New York, the question is how much the country's harsh crime-fighting mood is pushing cops into a dangerous, no-holds-barred mentality. "When we tell police officers that they are responsible for crime rates in the inner city, we're putting them into a no-win war," says James Fyfe, a former New York cop and a specialist on police behavior. That leads to frustration, Fyfe explains, "and like some soldiers in a no-win war, they commit atrocities."

Criminal Gangs

Even if police departments are more professional than ever, as many police experts believe, the brazenness and viciousness of today's bad cops troubles even the staunchest defenders of the men and women in blue. In New York, the Mollen Commission investigating police corruption noted last year that the systemic, "look the other way" bribery schemes that plagued the New York Police Department a generation ago had largely disappeared—only to be replaced by a "new and often more invidious" form of malfeasance: police acting as tightknit criminal gangs. Indeed, recent months have produced a host of jaw-dropping tales from around the nation.

Perhaps the most shocking abuses have been in New Orleans, where more than 50 officers have been arrested, indicted or convicted since 1993 on charges including rape, aggravated battery, drug trafficking and murder. The case of officer Len Davis, who faces the death penalty in federal court this January, has shaken this normally laid-back city to its foundations. Davis is charged with ordering the murder last October of Kim Groves, a 32-year-old mother of three who had filed a "confidential" brutality complaint against Davis the day before for allegedly pistol-whipping her friend. The FBI, which was taping Davis as part of a separate corruption investigation, says it heard him make arrangements with a hit man, then yell, "Get that whore!" into his cellular phone minutes before Groves was shot to death in her front yard. In March, another New Orleans officer, Antoinette Frank, 23, allegedly was in the process of robbing a family-run Vietnamese restaurant when she shot and killed fellow cop Ronald Williams, her former partner, who was moonlighting as a security guard. Frank is charged with murder and armed robbery and faces the death

penalty when her trial begins this week.

Philadelphia is being rocked by a police scandal centering on six rogue officers in the 39th Police District. The six have pleaded guilty to charges they framed people, lied to obtain search warrants and stole money. So far, 42 criminal convictions have been overturned. Last week, federal investigators expanded the probe and subpoenaed records that will allow them to search for patterns of abuse among some 100,000 arrests going back a decade.

Blind to Corruption

In New York, nearly 50 officers have been arrested since March 1994 in Harlem and the Bronx on charges of drug trafficking, extortion, brutality and civil rights violations. Those scandals came on the heels of the Mollen Commission report, which said the police department had shown a "willful blindness" to corruption that allowed gangs of cops to deal in drugs and prey on the city's poorer residents. A central figure was officer Michael Dowd, who was sentenced to 14 years in prison after admitting that he organized "crews" of officers to raid the apartments of Brooklyn drug dealers for cash and narcotics. The judge who sentenced him said Dowd's crimes "betray an immorality so deep that it is rarely encountered."

Contributing to such corruption is the fact that only recently has police work been treated as a profession. Traditionally, many departments recruited impressionable kids as young as 20 while requiring no more than a high school education or its equivalent. Several officers in the Harlem precinct implicated in

New York's scandal were high school dropouts or had checkered work histories. Darrel Stephens of St. Petersburg, Fla., is among many police chiefs who have increased the minimum requirement to a two-year associate's degree, and plans eventually to require a four-year bachelor's degree—even though some worry that boosting education requirements may shrink the pool of minority applicants. A related problem has been the lowering of requirements when departments sought to expand their ranks rapidly; in Washington, D.C., dozens of officers employed during a crash hiring binge in 1989 and 1990 have since gotten into trouble with the law.

Communicators Needed

Police recruits have traditionally undergone training regimens that emphasized aggressiveness above all. In Kansas City, says Chief Steven Bishop, a review of procedures that followed a police beating found that 90 percent of the department's training focused on behavior "that got us sued." Only 10 percent of the training dealt with communications and verbal skills, which Bishop feels constitute the bulk of the job. Bishop hiked the communications component to 40 percent.

Stress also drags cops over the ethical line. "Being a police officer is the most stressful job in America, clearly," says Geoffrey Garfield of the Los Angeles Police Protective League. "Imagine being a police officer and having to see the awful, horrible things that people do to each other and, after four or five years, what that does to you." The pounding of their harrowing routine leaves many cops embittered, enraged, paranoid and bigoted. Many cops eventually come to think the ends justify the means.

Progressive departments have brought in psychologists to help, but many cops fear they'll be stigmatized if they see a counselor. One of the main recommendations of the Christopher Commission that investigated the LAPD in 1991 was that officers should be retested regularly for psychological and emotional problems. It hasn't happened yet.

And police departments have done an uneven job of weeding out bad apples. For one thing, civil service and union protections make it difficult to fire cops. Over the last year, for instance, the New Orleans Civil Service Commission has spent almost $200,000 in 25 separate court hearings to finally be rid of Antoine Saacks, a former deputy police chief fired in 1994 for running outside businesses on police department time and consorting with known felons. Saacks claims superiors signed off on his activities.

Flawed System

In addition, a code of silence among officers sometimes makes it difficult to gather evidence, and many departments have disciplinary systems that aren't effective. In New York, the Mollen Commission found a corruption investigation system "that often minimized and even concealed corruption rather than rooted it out." Mayor Rudolph Giuliani and the City Council are now bickering over creation of an independent investigation unit, though similar civilian review efforts elsewhere have proven disappointing. Several departments have had success with "early warning" systems that spot cops with an excessive number of complaints and single them out for counseling and therapy.

Many police executives have come to believe that front-line supervisors may be the most important link in the chain. In New York, the Mollen Commission found that sergeants "were in the best position to know about corruption," but the commission added that supervisors were rarely trained to uncover wrongdoing or held responsible for it and often "failed to serve as a deterrent." To remedy such problems, New Orleans Police Chief Richard Pennington put together a team of officers from the military and the FBI to give 250 sergeants a weeklong course in leadership, discipline and ethics.

Finally, experts say, there must be leadership from the top. In Kansas City, Chief Bishop has expelled more than 100 people from the police department over the past five and a half years, earning him the nickname "Terminator." "You can't set up degrees of integrity," he says. "Even the appearance of wrongdoing is something you can't have." But as the events of the past few months reveal, some cops never get the message.

 Article Review Form at end of book.

What are the possible benefits associated with the implementation of a standard disciplinary system on law enforcement agencies?

Discipline Philosophy

Darrel W. Stephens, M.P.A.

Chief Stephens commands the St. Petersburg, Florida, Police Department.

In *Policing a Free Society*, Herman Goldstein notes that the adversarial nature of policing is a key factor that complicates the control and review of police action and behavior. The public grants the police considerable authority to act on its behalf in an effort to create an environment that is free of crime, drug abuse, violence, and disorder and the fear that accompanies these conditions.

In almost all encounters with the public, police officers and nonsworn employees exercise this authority appropriately. But, there are times when citizens raise legitimate questions about how this authority has been used. And, unfortunately, there are also times when police personnel abuse this authority. Therefore, departments must establish a system of discipline that minimizes abuse of authority and promotes the department's reputation for professionalism.

> "... the police officer expects and indeed needs some insulation from the community being served. But insulation can serve as a shield for the officer who is not so scrupulous—who in fact acts improperly."
>
> **Herman Goldstein**
> **Policing a Free Society**

System of Discipline

The most effective disciplinary system combines the reinforcement of the right set of values in all employees with behavioral standards that are consistently and fairly applied. Each employee must understand and be guided by these standards that have been established in the department's (and city's) general orders, rules, regulations, and procedures.

Employees should be expected to conduct themselves, both in interactions with one another and with the public, in a manner that conveys respect, honesty, integrity, and dedication to public service. In turn, employees should be treated fairly, honestly, and respectfully by everyone in the department, regardless of authority, rank, or position within the organization.

Understandably, employees will make judgment errors from time to time when carrying out their responsibilities. In fact, employees who never make mistakes may be doing very little to try to improve the performance of the department. Each error in judgment, however, offers a learning opportunity for the employee and the department, although some errors will come with greater consequences than others for the public, the department, and the employee.

Even so, the department has an obligation to make its expectations as distinct as possible to employees. At the same time, it has an equal obligation to make clear the consequences for failing to meet those expectations. While meeting both obligations can be difficult, the latter is obviously more complex. Circumstances often contribute to errors in judgment and poor decisions that administrators must consider when determining the appropriate consequences for behavior found to be improper.

Employees often admit that they would like the department to provide a list of prohibited behaviors, along with the penalties

From "Discipline Philosophy" by Darrel W. Stephens, M.P.A., *The FBI Law Enforcement Bulletin*, March 1994, Vol. 63, No. 3, pp. 20–22. Reprinted by permission.

for engaging in those behaviors. Yet, experience shows that employees directly involved in the disciplinary process, either as the subject of the process or in a review capacity, want to consider the results of one's actions in light of the circumstances that might have contributed to the violation. Of course, this is critical to apply discipline fairly and consistently.

Some employees view consistency as the same treatment for the same behavior in every case. If this happens, then the consequences will be fair to everyone.

For the St. Petersburg Police Department, *consistency* is defined as holding everyone equally accountable for unacceptable behavior, and *fairness* means understanding the circumstances that contributed to the behavior, while applying the consequences in a way that reflects this understanding. To ensure fair and consistent treatment of employees, however, discipline for unacceptable behavior must depend on a balance of several factors.

Determining Factors

A number of factors should be considered when applying discipline. Granted, not all factors may be considered in every case, and some may not apply at all in particular situations. There may also be a tendency to isolate one factor and to give it greater importance than another. Yet, these factors should be thought of as being interactive and having equal weight, unless circumstances dictate otherwise. These factors include employee motivation, degree of harm, employee experience, intentional/unintentional errors, and the employee's past record.

Employee Motivation

A police department exists to serve the public. Therefore, one factor to consider when examining an employee's conduct should be whether the employee was acting in the public's best interest.

An employee who violates policy in an effort to accomplish a legitimate police purpose demonstrates an understanding of the broader public interest inherent in the situation. Accordingly, the employee should be given more positive consideration than one who was motivated by personal interest.

Obviously, determining what is in the public's interest will be difficult from time to time. For example, would it be acceptable for an employee to knowingly violate an individual's first amendment right to freedom of speech to rid the public of what some might consider a nuisance? Or, is it in the public's interest for an officer to knowingly violate a fourth amendment right against an unlawful search to arrest a dangerous criminal? Clearly, in either case, improper action by police is not acceptable and should not be condoned; yet, officers address these complex issues daily.

The police have a sworn duty to uphold the Constitution. And, it is in the greater public interest to protect constitutional guarantees, even though it might be argued the public interest was better served otherwise. But, if employees attempt to devise innovative, nontraditional solutions for persistent crimes or service problems and unintentionally run

> ". . . departments must establish a system of discipline that minimizes abuse of authority. . . ."

afoul of minor procedures, the desire to encourage creativity in their public safety efforts should carry significant weight in dealing with any discipline that might result.

Degree of Harm

The degree of harm resulting from employee error is another factor when deciding the consequences for errant behavior. Harm can be measured in terms of monetary costs to the department and community, such as repairs to a damaged vehicle, or in terms of personal injury claims for excessive force.

Another way to measure harm is by the impact of employee error on public confidence. An employee who engages in criminal behavior, e.g., selling drugs, corrodes public trust in the police if discipline does not send a clear, unmistakable message that this behavior will not be tolerated.

Employee Experience

Employee experience also has bearing on the type and the extent of discipline. A relatively new employee, or a more experienced one in a new assignment, should be given greater consideration for judgmental errors. Accordingly, errors by veteran employees may warrant more serious sanctions.

Intentional/ Unintentional Errors

Supervisory personnel need to consider the circumstances surrounding the incident to determine whether the employee's error was intentional or unintentional. Obviously, the type of error will govern the extent and severity of the discipline.

An *unintentional* error occurs when an employee's action or decision turns out to be wrong, even though at the time, the employee believed it to be in compliance with policy and the most appropriate course to take based on information available. For example, a supervisor gives permission to continue a vehicle pursuit on the basis that the vehicle and occupants meet the general description of those involved in an armed robbery. The pursuit ends in a serious accident, and it is subsequently learned that the driver was fleeing because of an expired license. Under these circumstances, the supervisor's decision would be supported because it was within department policy at the time it was made.

Unintentional errors also include those momentary lapses of judgment or acts of carelessness that result in minimal harm (backing a police cruiser into a pole or failing to turn in a report). Employees should be held accountable for these errors, but the consequences should be more

> **". . . department administrators should make every effort to make the disciplinary decision fit each specific incident."**

corrective than punitive, unless the same or similar errors persist.

Employees make *intentional* errors when they take action or make a decision that they know, or should know, to be in conflict with law, policy, procedures, or rules at the time. Generally, intentional errors should carry greater consequences and be treated more seriously.

Within the framework of intentional errors, there are certain behaviors that are entirely unacceptable, to include lying, theft, physical abuse of citizens, and equally serious breaches of trust placed in the police. In such cases, every effort should be made to terminate the individual found to be engaged in such behavior. Granted, determining deliberate errors that result in serious consequences for the department will be difficult. But allowing such behavior to continue will produce even more dire results.

Employee's Past Record

To the extent allowed by law, policy, and contractual obligations, an employee's past record should be taken into consideration when determining disciplinary actions. An employee who continually makes errors should expect the penalties for this behavior to become progressively more punitive. Less stringent consequences should be administered to employees with records that show few or no errors. When determining disciplinary action, every consideration should be given to employees whose past records reflect hard work and dedication to the department and the community.

Conclusion

Serving the community with integrity and in a professional manner should be the goal of every police officer. Employees must accept responsibility for their roles in maintaining this goal.

When employees fail to do so, department administrators should make every effort to make the disciplinary decision fit each specific incident. This needs to be done consistently and fairly. Otherwise, the errors in judgment made by employees pale in comparison to the unfair treatment administered by the department's leaders.

 Article Review Form at end of book.

Name the key factors in an effective anticrime policy.

On the Waterfront

Police unions are arresting the war against crime

Bret Schundler

Bret Schundler is mayor of Jersey City, New Jersey.

President Bill Clinton has made the passage of a federal crime bill a top priority of his agenda this year. Congress is accommodating him with sweeping new legislation that will federalize scores of crimes and use federal funds to put more police officers on America's streets for a five-year period. The bill is complicated and will cost Americans billions more in taxes, but will do virtually nothing to reduce crime.

Why? Because our problem in America is not that we spend too little money on policing, but rather than in return for our money we get too little policing. The solution to this problem is to give local governments more power over police department management. Bill Clinton's legislation does not do this. In fact, if we don't watch out, his increased federal "involvement" in local policing will become increased federal "interference," which together with state government interference is the root of our problem.

Teaching Moral Order

The keys to an effective anticrime policy are not difficult to identify: Teach moral order and enforce it. But as state and federal interference in education and police department management have become greater, teaching moral order and effectively enforcing the law have become more difficult. Sharing state and federal revenues with local governments is appropriate and necessary. But what we in local government really need—rather than more federal money—is more autonomy. What we really need is for state and federal politicians to get out of our way so that we can do our jobs.

Today many talented teachers leave higher-paying public schools for positions in lower-paying private schools simply because they are tired of not being allowed to enforce order in their public-school classrooms. They will readily tell you that federal and state regulatory interference in the public schools destroys teacher autonomy and diminishes student learning. In Jersey City,

we spend $9,000 per child per year in our public system, yet more than half of our public school 9th graders drop out before graduating from high school. Even measuring the less than half of students who do remain in school, fewer than half of these students pass our state-mandated High School Proficiency Test.

But in New Jersey's private schools, there is much less state and federal regulatory interference. Teachers are still allowed to maintain direct control of their classrooms, and student graduation rates and achievement levels are significantly higher. At the Chad School in Newark, spending per child is only one-fourth to one-third of that in New Jersey's public schools. And yet, even though the vast majority of Chad's students come from single-parent, low-income families, 98 percent go on to college. The teachers, free to control their classrooms, maintain a disciplined learning environment and assign over two hours of homework a night. Clearly this workload teaches the students not only basic skills, but also diligence and discipline.

From *Policy Review* Summer 1994, No. 69, pp. 40–43. Reprinted by permission.

If we had less state and federal interference in our public schools, and we funded education through school vouchers, competition would force all of our public schools to become more like the Chad school. With educational power in the hands of parents and teachers instead of politicians, accountability for results would replace accountability by regulation, and our public schools would once again be able to teach moral order effectively. A decrease in crime would be only one of the many positive results.

Broken Windows

Once moral order is properly taught, enforcing it is not conceptually difficult. If we put a well-trained cop—either on foot or scooter patrol—on every other street corner in our city, we would be able to reduce crime dramatically. This approach is just what the Jersey City Police Department did a generation ago. Cops walked a small and very manageable beat, and as a result there was less crime.

The fact is that intensive police presence on the streets deters crime. If an officer walked or scootered past your house every 10 minutes, car and house thieves committing crimes of opportunity—as distinct from crimes of passion or psychosis—would not view your block as a very good place to do business. The incidence of quality of life offenses, such as vandalism, graffiti, and the playing of loud music (three terrible banes of contemporary urban existence) would plummet. Perhaps most importantly, this intensive law enforcement would reinforce the moral teaching that should be taking place at home and in our schools. A child born today into a world of litter, graffiti, open-air drug dealing, violence, and general chaos—where society makes little effort to curb such abuses—does not know that these things are wrong. Even if a child hears that these things are wrong, if that child does not see such things being punished, then as far as that child's experience of life is concerned, such things will be noted as normal and acceptable.

George Kelling and James Q. Wilson have described this mindset as the "broken windows syndrome." Surely all of us, as children, saw an abandoned, deteriorated house with all but one of its windows broken and were tempted to pick up a stone and break that last window. And yet none of us, when we passed a well-maintained home with all of its windows intact, even gave a thought to breaking its windows. Today we are raising children in the inner city amidst the chaos and "broken windows" of unenforced laws. Ours is not a lawless society, but a society of increasingly unenforced laws. The result is that our children see chaos, they internalize chaos, and, not surprisingly, they learn to participate in chaos. Putting a lot more police on the street, and instructing them to rigorously enforce our laws and to re-establish order will be absolutely necessary to bringing up the next generation of children to be law-abiding.

Patronage Paybacks

Of course, putting more police on the street is much harder in practice than in theory. And it is hard precisely because of federal and state political interference in local police management. I know from personal experience.

When I ran for Mayor of Jersey City, New Jersey, in 1992, I promised the voters that my first priority would be to make our streets safe. Despite a very high crime rate, fewer than half of the city's police officers were assigned to street patrol; over 60 percent were assigned to specialist units or were in the precinct station houses shuffling paper. Two officers were actually delivering inter-office mail. This situation was the product of Jersey City's patronage-politics past, where comfortable jobs in all city departments were given as a reward for political service and loyalty.

This corrupt policy has had tremendously negative results. First, the lack of an effective deterrent to crime has encouraged crime. Second, it has weakened the social reinforcement necessary for the moral education of our children. Finally, as far as the police department is concerned, the patronage system has made assignment to street patrol intolerable.

Imagine the circumstances our police officers must confront out on the street. Because there is little deterrence, and because the moral education of our children is ineffective, there is a lot of crime. With too few cops on the street, police response time has grown longer and a response backlog has developed. Those unfortunate officers who are assigned to street patrol, therefore, must spend eight solid hours flying from one crime scene to the next, almost always arriving long after the fact. By the time the police do arrive, the victimized citizens are as angry at the police as they are at the criminals. This situation has made patrolling the streets of Jersey City absolute hell; the first interest of many police officers is to do whatever they can to get off the street and into a desk job as quickly as possible.

Civilian Assignments

I vowed to end this destructive patronage in the police department and to civilianize all jobs in the precinct houses that could reasonably be performed by a civilian. I also promised to put more than three-fourths of our police officers out on street patrol, with half of that number specifically committed to community-based policing. My determination to accomplish these goals helped me win election as Jersey City's first Republican mayor since World War I.

Upon taking office, I immediately moved to carry out my plan. My first goal was to supplement the 300 officers on rapid response—policing in patrol cars—with another 300 police officers performing community-based policing. The city would be divided up into 133 patrol districts, varying in size according to the density of their population and the incidence of crime. Individual police officers would be assigned to patrol specific districts for a period of at least one year without rotation so that a relationship could develop between the police officer and the community.

Once these re-assignments were completed, the next goal would be to properly train the community officers to work cooperatively with distinct residents whom we would form into neighborhood police committees. As a final step, we would institute a professional-standards unit staffed with superior officers and police department civilian managers to meet with the neighborhood police committees on a

Bret Schundler: "Our problem is not that we spend too little on policing, but that in return for our money we get too little policing."

regular basis, in order to ensure that the community officers were performing satisfactorily.

Up against the Union

In those areas of the city where we have been able to carry out this plan, crime is falling and the citizens are happy. But putting this plan in action has been a real challenge. Our efforts to re-assign police officers from desk jobs to street duty ran us smack into the police union. The moment we re-assigned those two police mailmen to street patrol, they initiated a suit against the city charging us with an unfair labor practice. You might ask why it is unfair to ask police officers to do patrol work. The answer, according to the police union, is that a clause in the police contract states, "Police work cannot be diminished except through contract negotiation." What makes delivering inter-office mail police work? The fact that a police officer is doing it, says the union.

According to this reasoning, to have civilians perform duties that prior patronage-oriented administrations have allowed police officers to do diminishes the total number of jobs that police officers perform, and therefore diminishes police work. Reducing the number of police functions must be negotiated in the union contract; it cannot be ordered by executive fiat.

Naturally, I have refused to accept this definition of police work, and fortunately, the city has been successful in the first stage of the officers' legal challenge, winning its case before a

state mediation board. These two officers are now appealing their case to the courts and the case is in litigation. We may ultimately win the suit, and if we do, our community-policing efforts will be significantly bolstered. But it is also possible that we will lose this case, and that is where interference by distant government becomes so evidently and totally destructive.

We now have a score of police suits filed against the city on the same grounds as those cited above. None of these suits would have the slightest chance of success were it not for the offending clause in the union contract which suggests that the supposed diminishing of police work must be negotiated. If I could exorcise this clause from the contract, I could fully implement my community-policing plan.

But that's the rub. Clauses cannot simply be erased from contracts, they must be negotiated away. In New Jersey, we have binding arbitration laws written by the state legislature that govern local government contract negotiations. When we in the city administration want to change a contract clause that impedes effective police department management, the union has the right to just say no, and we are then automatically forced into arbitration.

The arbitrators are not randomly assigned to the case, they must be accepted by the union. Arbitrators are not paid a fixed wage by the state, but earn their pay on a per-diem basis when they are working. The local law firms representing different city administrations before these arbitrators are legion, but the law firms representing the many state police unions are few. Accordingly, the arbitrators know that if they make an award that hurts management they will still be able to find work. But if they give an award that hurts the union, the few law firms that represent New Jersey's police unions can blacklist these arbitrators; if blacklisted, they will never arbitrate in New Jersey again.

Double the Raises

These ludicrous arbitration rules do more than impede effective personnel deployment; they also inflate police department wages, which makes fielding a large enough police force to patrol our streets prohibitively expensive. In Jersey City, the average police officer earns approximately $55,000 in base pay, $15,000 in overtime, a $5,000 longevity bonus, and has a benefits package worth another $15,000. In a low-income city where per-capita income is only $10,000, our average police officer earns a package with a total value of nearly $90,000. Surely if we had the legal means to reduce police department salaries we would still be able to attract many qualified candidates to the force. A wage reduction would allow us to put many more police officers on the street without increasing taxes.

But we don't have the legal right to reduce salaries. In fact, far from declining, or even holding relatively steady, the average police-contract award coming out of recent arbitrations in New Jersey has increased police salaries at twice the rate of inflation.

Inflation is the average rate of the growth in prices in a given economy. If one sector is consistently getting twice the average rate of price growth, then other sectors must be getting less than the average rate. That means an ever-bigger portion of our total

economic pie is going to pay just the police salaries in Jersey City. In fact, even adjusting for productivity gains, one can mathematically demonstrate that if the Jersey City Police Department continues getting salary increases at twice the rate of inflation, and this trend continues indefinitely, there will eventually come a day when it takes all the money in the city just to pay the salaries of the police department.

In Their Faces

It may sound silly to talk about absurd trend extensions, but from where I sit what is really silly is the fact that we mayors cannot more easily re-assign police officers to street patrol, and cannot more easily afford to hire sufficient numbers of police officers to make our streets safe. America is supposed to be a country where government exists to serve the people, not to serve organized government special interests. But in spite of the fact that the New Jersey League of Municipalities has made binding arbitration reform its top legislative priority for the last five years, no reform bill has ever made it to the floor of both houses for a vote.

As I said previously, our crime problem is not the result of our spending too little on policing, but rather of our getting too little policing for our money—and the root cause of this problem is non-local government interference in police department management. In a non-regulated labor negotiation environment that is free of arbitration laws and federal and state interference, I would be free as mayor to do the right thing. If I paid police officers too little, I

would not be able to find quality personnel to do the job well, and the people of Jersey City would blame me for it.

On the other hand, if I paid police officers too much and demanded too little, we would not be able to put enough police officers on the street to effectively enforce the law—as is the case today—and the people would blame me for that too. In either case, because I am the one the people are holding accountable for policing, I would have an incentive to manage the department intelligently, or I would get thrown out of office.

Now let's consider the position of our state legislators. They are removed from the people. If someone gets mugged, I am the one who gets the angry phone call at night, not our state representative. On the other hand, the state legislators have the police union's lobbyists in their faces continually, and the union is dead set against changing the binding arbitration laws in New Jersey. The union is not afraid of telling our legislators that if they disappoint the union, the union will make their lives miserable. Not surprisingly, the state legislators, who are human and self-interested like everyone else, grant the union demands.

A Little Revolution

It doesn't matter if we replace one politician with another; whenever politicians are given power in matters whether they are not directly held accountable by the people, and where their interests are not necessarily commensurate with the people's, it will be the politicians' interests that are served and not the people's. This will always be

The solution to crime will come from reform of federal and state labor laws.

the case, which is why the only solution to our current crime problem is, as Thomas Jefferson might recommend, a little revolution.

Reform is when you change what you are doing. Revolution is when you change who has the power to do things. We need to have a revolution and get the federal and state governments off our backs at the local level so that we mayors, who are held directly accountable by the people, can have the power to manage our police departments in a way that makes sense. Hence it is less regulation and more autonomy that we mayors need right now, far more than additional money, to win the war against crime.

Empower the Mayors

Bill Clinton's crime bill, in the finest Democratic party tradition, does little more than throw additional money at the crime problem while shifting the cost of policing from the local to the national taxpayer. His proposal completely misses the target. If nothing is done to control soaring salaries or permit more intelligent personnel deployment, then more federal aid will do nothing.

Many political leaders in the Republican party are calling for an increase in the building of new jail spaces, and for truth in sentencing laws which would lengthen the minimum time spent in jail by those convicted of serious crimes. These Republican proposals would indeed reduce crime—especially violent crime—since the vast majority of violent crimes are committed by a relatively small number of repeat violent offenders. Still, we could achieve these same ends without the expense of building more jail cells simply by deterring most petty crimes more effectively. And we could easily do this through empowering local governments to manage their police departments more effectively. If we can put enough police back on the streets, we will be able to reestablish general order and deter most crimes of opportunity before they happen. That will leave plenty of spaces available in our jails for the career and psychopathic criminals who we really need to keep locked up.

Most politicians will be reluctant to speak the truth that the solution to crime will come from reform of federal and state labor laws. To do so will antagonize a very organized and powerful governmental interest group—the police union. Indeed, it will always be politically easier to talk about almost any other strategy. But every now and then, when times become bad enough, having the courage to speak about truly revolutionary ideas does equate with good politics, and can lead the way to truly revolutionary, much needed results. Now is just such a time.

 **Article Review Form at end of book.**

What is the main purpose of teaching youths about the law?

Teaching Youths about the Law

Larry Murdo

Chief Murdo commands the Albany, California, Police Department.

With increasing frequency, law enforcement officers around the country are voicing a common refrain: "Today's kids have no respect for the law!" Police administrators often review incident reports involving confrontational field contacts between officers and juveniles. While the tenor of many of these contacts seems to bear out the claim that today's young people do not respect the law, it, in probability, points to a more basic truth— many of today's youths do not *understand* the law.

Americans should be proud of their system of written laws— the oldest in the modern world. These laws usually provide clear parameters that govern acceptable societal behavior and outline the response of the criminal justice system to unacceptable behavior. In essence, the law—as delineated by federal, state, and local courts—provides the practical application of the social contract that citizens and their government enter into to ensure a free and orderly society, in which the rights of the individual are tempered by the rights of society as a whole.

But who can best convey the practical relevance of the nation's laws and legal traditions to today's youths? While traditional government, history, and social studies classes touch upon the major themes that underpin the legal system, they rarely explore the more practical aspects of the law that youths might encounter.

Although junior and high school teachers might not possess the requisite expertise to develop lessons on the practical application of the nation's criminal codes, many law enforcement officers and administrators do. In fact, police work embodies the practical application of constitutional law. Simply discussing the details of police-citizen contacts within the framework of the relevant laws can help students understand what the police do and why.

In recent years, police officers in Albany, California, as in other areas of the country, have experienced a frustrating number of confrontational contacts with young people. Often, the acrimonious nature of these contacts is fueled by the youths' general lack of understanding of their rights *and responsibilities* under the law. In an effort to address this void and the problems it often spawned, the Albany chief of police developed a program to provide area students with practical instruction about the law and the methods law enforcement officers and the criminal justice system use to uphold it. Since it was introduced in spring 1992, the course has proven to be an effective way to communicate important information to this young and impressionable audience, while cultivating an enhanced understanding of the role police play in society.

The Instruction

Constitutional Law/Practical Applications Instruction for Youth is delivered each May to students in the city's public middle and high schools. The chief meets with 8th grade students as they prepare to advance to high school and with high school seniors as they prepare to graduate. By delivering the instruction twice—in slightly modified formats—the program reinforces the principles at pivotal points in the students' lives.

From "Teaching Youths about the Law," by Larry Murdo, *The FBI Law Enforcement Bulletin*, July 1997, Vol. 66, No. 7, pp. 19–21. Reprinted by permission.

Concepts Addressed

The day-long instruction program covers a wide range of topics. These include

- Exigent circumstances allowing warrantless residential searches

- Specific legal points related to the scope of warrantless vehicle searches

- An individual's expectation of privacy

- Searches incident to arrest

- Legality of "pat-down searches"—when and why they may be conducted

- The safeguards—and limitations—of the Fifth Amendment protection against compelled self-incrimination.

The instruction stresses the balance the law seeks to strike between the rights of individuals as protected by the Constitution and the responsibilities of citizens. The curriculum explains, for example, that no constitutional right exists to resist arrest or defy a court-ordered sanction.

During the free-flowing discussions with the students, it quickly becomes evident that, prior to the classroom instruction, they received most of their information regarding the police or the legal system from television, motion pictures, and other products of the entertainment industry. The rampant misinformation featured in such entertainment makes it a poor teacher in an area as complex and vital as the application of constitutional standards.

The students' lack of a balanced and accurate sense of the law becomes most clear early in the discussion when the youths respond to a series of questions designed to gauge their grasp of practical legal matters. The students rarely articulate informed responses to such questions as:

- If police officers stop a car, can they order all of the passengers out and conduct personal searches? Can officers search the interior of the vehicle? Can they search individual bags or cases within the passenger compartment without a warrant?

- If a police officer stops a citizen in a public place and begins to ask questions, must the citizen respond?

- Can police officers lawfully enter a private residence, without a warrant, to arrest the homeowner or someone else in the home?

The concepts of probable cause and related issues are introduced to students so that they can formulate informed and accurate responses to such questions. While students may not always agree with the laws and judicial rulings presented, most gain a new appreciation for the reasoned approach the law must take to balance maintaining order and protecting personal freedoms.

A comprehensive handout given to each student reinforces the lecture component of the program. The written material covers areas of police field operations such as consensual encounters, detentions, and arrests. These issues generally spark lively discussions, which provide an opportunity to explain to the youths how their observable behavior—e.g., threatening posture or abusive language—may impact the tenor of an encounter with police officers. These discussions help the students appreciate that officers must respond to what they *observe* about an individual's behavior at the time of an encounter because they cannot know the person's mind-set.

Adding to the Program

After the *Practical Law* instruction had been delivered to several different classes, Albany school officials and the chief met to evaluate the curriculum. The evaluation panel determined that adding instruction from an attorney's perspective might encourage a broader appreciation for the scope of the law. A constitutional law attorney from the nearby city of Berkeley agreed to volunteer her time to the instruction program and now copresents a revised curriculum with the chief.

Sessions now begin with opening remarks from the attorney and the chief. Students then pose questions to the instructors, both of whom respond to each question. The resulting discussions, often marked by spirited debate among the students, help bring to life the concepts of constitutional law and abstract theories about the proper role of law enforcement in a free society.

As the presentations unfold, students often are surprised to find that the police chief and the constitutional law attorney agree on more points than they disagree. Through this expanded forum, the students learn that both the police and those who represent criminal defendants operate from a position of respect for the Constitution.

Developing a Program

Departments interested in developing a practical-law instruction curriculum should begin by crafting a comprehensive student handout that covers the intended scope of the class. Department administrators should consult their agency legal advisor to aid in the development of the lesson plan. They then should submit the plan to the local school board for approval. Although school administrators may want to monitor development of the instruction, most school systems would fully embrace the concept of a practical law course for students. As with the Albany program, this type of instruction would be delivered most effectively as a supplement to the civics or government components of the regular school curriculum.

"The instruction stresses the balance . . . between the rights of individuals as protected by the Constitution and the responsibilities of citizens."

Instructors do not have to be lawyers to teach the fundamentals of the law and the legal parameters within which the police operate. Nor is it necessary that a department's ranking officer deliver such school-based instruction. Rather, the individual accepting the opportunity to present the material must possess effective and demonstrable communication skills, especially an ability to relate to juveniles. The presenter also must possess a thorough and pragmatic knowledge of the Constitution, most notably the Fourth Amendment. While some formal teaching experience may be helpful, such experience should not be considered an absolute requirement. An appreciation for and understanding of the law combined with enthusiasm for the subject matter and an interest in helping youths in a positive forum represent the most important qualifications.

Conclusion

As the most visible component of the criminal justice system, the police always have represented different things to different people. For too many young people, the police have come to represent an oppressive force that views youths contemptuously and treats them unfairly. Unfortunately, this perception becomes understandable given the steady stream of distorted and often-negative messages youths receive about law enforcement via the media and the entertainment industry. These images not only reinforce a negative view of law enforcement, but they also undermine respect for the law, which is essential to the functioning of a free society.

But law enforcement can take steps to correct the misinformation youths receive. By taking the time to discuss practical aspects of constitutional law, as well as the complex role police play to maintain order and ensure individual rights, agencies can help nurture a deeper appreciation for the law among youths. As youths come to see the positive aspects of the laws they are asked to live by, they gain a more balanced view of law enforcement and the role police play in society.

 Article Review Form at end of book.

What are the critical functions performed by all police managers?
Could civilians perform these?

Why Not Hire Civilian Commanders?

Joseph L. Colletti, M.P.A.

Chief Colletti commands the Emeryville, California, Police Department.

In 1828, Sir Robert Peel, the father of modern law enforcement, said, "The police are the public and the public are the police. . . . " Over time, attempts to remove corrupt influences from American police agencies forced many law enforcement officials to adopt a paramilitary organizational structure and to reject the possibility of any civilian roles in policing. While this stance helped distance police organizations from corrupt political influences, as an unintended consequence, the police became estranged from the very communities they served.

The time has come, however, to revive Peel's notion of the police and the public as one entity, sharing common goals and desires. The community-oriented policing philosophy emphasizes focusing a law enforcement agency's talents and energies on problem solving and changing the social conditions that give rise to crime. It seeks to empower both police personnel and community members to resolve problems.

The community-oriented policing philosophy has opened the door to using civilians in key management positions as a way for departments to tap into the vast reserves of managerial expertise available in the private sector. It also fosters greater confidence and rapport with their communities and dispels the antagonistic relationships that might exist between the citizenry and the police. A civilian in upper management can serve as a bridge between the community and the department.

Job Dimensions

To understand the role civilians can play in law enforcement agencies, one first must examine the critical functions performed by all police managers. Among other requirements, a person in the upper management of today's law enforcement organization is expected to:

- Oversee the operations of uniformed forces or technical support personnel who respond to emergencies, enforce laws, and maintain records

- Take command of personnel in emergencies and direct complex public safety events and special investigations.

- Use discretionary authority in dealing with complaints from the public

- Ensure that reports, memoranda, and correspondence prepared by the staff are complete, accurate, and ready for the executive to sign

- Respond to difficult questions about regulations and policies.

Effective managers have good decision-making skills. They can judge alternatives and realize the ramifications of each decision. They look at long-term consequences and implications, rather than merely handle short-term crises. Their decisions are consistent with the department's mission and goals, even when those decisions might be unpopular.

Analytical skills enable good managers to identify problems and their causes and to break complex problems into components more amenable to examination. These managers recognize gaps in data and can conduct

From *The FBI Law Enforcement Bulletin*, Oct. 1996, Vol. 65, No. 10, pp. 8–11. Reprinted by permission of the United States Federal Bureau of Investigation and the widow of Joseph L. Colletti, M.P.A.

research to obtain necessary information using a variety of sources.

Upper-level managers must be able to set priorities, coordinate and schedule tasks or events logically so as to obtain the most benefit from staff and material resources, and increase efficiency. Today, these qualities exemplify a trait often referred to as "entrepreneurial."

Above all, upper-level managers are leaders. They coordinate, delegate, and follow up on the work of subordinates. They guide and motivate people to achieve tasks and solve problems. They take initiative and do not shy away from action.

The list of managerial duties and characteristics could continue, but what is most noteworthy is a task the list does not include—making arrests. Managers are not technicians. They must have education and experience in the duties of managing a complex organization, not necessarily in the specifics of policing.

Use of Civilian Commanders

Law enforcement agencies assign the title of commander, captain of police, lieutenant, or deputy chief to positions in charge of a division or bureau, with the incumbent reporting directly to the chief of police or agency head. Whether the division conducts administrative, investigative, or field work, the scope of duties and responsibilities for the commander remains essentially the same.

Civilian division commanders have worked in law enforcement for some time. Even though their presence is not new to the profession, many departments still might not realize the unique strengths they can bring to an agency. Unlike police officers who rise through the ranks, civilian employees typically make lateral entries into law enforcement organizations and are selected because of their special qualifications. As a result, they bring a fresh perspective to their positions and to police work. The public also might afford them a certain credibility due to their civilian background and experience.

In addition, simple economics justifies the wide-spread use of civilians. The cost of employing a sworn division commander significantly exceeds the expense of a civilian because of considerable differences in pay and retirement rates.

In many police agencies, civilians command the support services or administrative branches of their organizations. The highly technical aspects of administration—budgeting and accounting for example—can be learned and perfected in the private sector and then applied efficiently to the realm of policing.

Another position in which civilian command could be advantageous is internal affairs. Rather than calling for the creation of an external review board, citizen complainants might view a civilian as being more fair and neutral than a sworn commander.

These represent a few of the many positions civilian commanders can fill. Police executives contemplating the use of civilians should consider the full range of possibilities.

"A civilian in upper management can serve as a bridge between the community and the department."

Challenges

Through decades of vigilance and effort, law enforcement as a whole has sought to banish political corruption and influence from its midst. As law enforcement agencies embrace the valuable concept of hiring civilian commanders, precautions should be taken to ensure that the gains made in years past will not be compromised now. Strict hiring standards should be developed (preferably on a statewide level) and uniformly applied to all civilian applicants to avoid political intervention.

In order to perform effectively, civilian division commanders, as well as any other civilian employees, must be treated equitably and considered equal to their sworn counterparts. They should be inserted into the normal department hierarchy or rank structure. In addition, civilian commanders should be able to rotate to other division assignments, just as captains or deputy chiefs do. As second-level commanders, they should be trusted to act in the absence of the agency head, just as their sworn peers would.

Law enforcement executives who decide to bring in civilian managers will need to take steps to gain the acceptance of civilians in the police culture. It is important to emphasize that hiring civilians in no way devalues the contributions of sworn officers; it simply provides a way for the agency to take advantage of the expertise available within the community.

Officers might worry about how hiring civilian commanders

Potential Civilian Command Assignments

Depending on the size and needs of the agency, the following assignments exemplify some suitable posts for civilian commanders.

- Accounts Payable/Receivable
- Affirmative Action Administrator
- Audit and Inspection Program
- Budget Administration
- Code Enforcement
- Computer Systems Management
- Contract Administration
- Cost Recovery Program
- Crime Analysis
- Cultural Awareness Director
- Custodian of Records/Personnel Files
- Environmental Design Review

- Graffiti Abatement Program
- Internal Ombudsman
- Jail Management
- Neighborhood Watch/Business Watch
- Outreach Program Development
- Payroll Supervisor
- Personnel Recruiting and Selection
- Records and Communications
- Risk Management Program
- Television Programs
- Training Program Development and Administration
- Workers Compensation Administrator

will affect promotional opportunities for sworn personnel. For example, as a cost-saving measure, some police departments in California have placed civilian commanders in management positions traditionally held by sworn personnel. This does, indeed, affect the career ladder for sworn officers within these departments. However, the effects are no greater than those of the increasingly prevalent practice of hiring upper-level sworn commanders from outside an agency. Lateral entries—sworn or civilian—bring benefits and drawbacks; police executives must weigh these carefully when making hiring decisions.

Civilian commanders need not be used solely to replace sworn commanders, however. In the Emeryville, California, Police Department, as in many other agencies, civilians have been hired to enhance the department by providing technical or managerial skills not found within the ranks. Thirty-four percent of Emeryville's employees are civilians. They bring expertise in computers, writing, public affairs, record-keeping, communications, and other areas to support the mission of the department and to allow sworn personnel to focus on their areas of expertise—enforcement and investigation. Sworn and civilian employees at all levels complement one another, integrating their talents to benefit the agency as a whole.

A concern equal to persuading officers to accept civilians is preventing civilian law enforcement professionals from becoming co-opted by traditional police thinking. Executives must encourage civilians to maintain their unique perspectives and not lose the very strengths they bring to the organization.

Conclusion

The traditional law enforcement agency is composed almost entirely of sworn personnel. If civilians work in an agency, they often are relegated to first-line job assignments and rarely used in supervisory or management positions.

Today, however, the paradigm is shifting. Purposeful police executive leadership is a full-time job. The contemporary police agency should include talented civilians at all levels of the organization, especially upper management. Law enforcement managers are effective because they possess certain qualities, traits, and skills, not because they have arrest powers.

Bringing civilian division commanders into a law enforcement organization can infuse the agency with fresh thinking. Carefully chosen, qualified civilian administrators bring new ideas into an oft-closed group. What better way to foster the notions of community-oriented policing than to bring members of the community into the police department?

 **Article Review Form at end of book.**

WiseGuide Wrap-Up

- Public support of police pursuit of serious offenders is high, but it diminishes when the nature of the offense is not serious and when information about the dangers of pursuit are presented.

- Police misconduct scandals are often blamed on job stress.

- Law enforcement agencies across the country must implement a standard disciplinary system in order to control and prevent police abuse of power.

R.E.A.L. Sites

Site name: National Criminal Justice Reference Service

URL: http://www.ncjrs.org/lehome.htm

Why is it R.E.A.L.? This site contains online documents on various issues affecting law enforcement today. In addition, it offers a comprehensive list of law enforcement web sites and numerous links to police-related listservs, where an individual is offered the opportunity to participate in on-going discussions.

Try this: What are some of the advantages and disadvantages of community policing? What are some of the most important issues being discussed about policing in rural and small-town America?

Key topics: community policing, firearms, campus law enforcement, DNA, D.A.R.E., use of force

Site name: Bureau of Justice Statistics (Law Enforcement Statistics)

URL: http://www.ojp.usdoj.gov/bjs/lawenf.htm

Why is it R.E.A.L.? This page provides publications, information, and statistics on federal, state, and campus law enforcement.

Try this: Describe the various characteristics of campus law enforcement agencies. Discuss some of the findings derived from the 1996 census of state and local law enforcement agencies.

Key topics: law enforcement statistics, officers killed, census of law enforcement agencies

Site name: National Institute of Justice

URL: http://www.ojp.usdoj.gov/nij/

Why is it R.E.A.L.? This site is provided by the research and development branch of the U.S. Department of Justice. It provides information on funding opportunities, programs, and numerous issues affecting policing. It also refers to several related links.

Try this: What are the key issues affecting police overtime? What are the lessons left by an observational study regarding community policing?

Key topics: gang violence, violence against women, police body armor

section 2

Learning Objectives

After studying this section, you will know

- that appellate courts often make decisions on outcomes of cases prior to hearing contrary facts.

- that adult courts should not make decisions or impose sentences in juvenile criminal cases.

- that the United States Supreme Court hears only a small portion of the cases it is asked to review.

- that juries have become less responsible in making moral judgments.

- that courts should adhere to the basic constitutional requirements in an attempt to settle the dispute between the conservative and liberal positions on punishment.

- that campus-run courts are facing public pressure to give access to campus newspaper officials.

 **WiseGuide Intro** The adjudication process plays a crucial role in determining the outcome of a case. This process is perhaps the most often confused by the public. Many people, after watching publicized cases such as the O. J. Simpson trial, may come to believe that all criminal defendants not only enjoy the benefit of having well-regarded defense attorneys on their side but also enjoy the full benefit of a criminal trial by a jury of their peers. Unfortunately, reality as told to us by statistics shows a different image of the adjudication process. Specifically, statistics suggest that most defendants dispose of their criminal charges through a process called plea bargaining. In this process, the defendant usually admits to being guilty of a less serious charge in return for a less punitive sentence. Supporters of this process argue that all of the courtroom actors benefit from this process—the prosecutor adds one more conviction to her record, the judge reduces her case load, the defense attorney receives compensation for her services, and the defendant receives a less severe punishment. However, there are those who argue that this process deteriorates the quality of the adjudication process by almost forcing defendants to make a deal in order to reduce the possibility that they would be found guilty in a jury trial.

In order to formulate a more solid understanding of the argument provided by supporters and critics of the plea bargaining process, we must refer to the models suggested by Herbert Packer. His two models—crime control and due process—can be used to address the heart of the plea bargaining debate. In the 1960s, Packer described the crime control model as one where the courts place emphasis on the expediency of case processing. In other words, the adjudicatory process emphasizes that all cases be processed rapidly, so the case load is kept under control. As you may have already guessed, the due process model adheres to a distinct set of norms. Packer described the due process model as one in which the emphasis is placed on the rights of the individual being accused of a crime. In other words, the courts that follow this model place greater emphasis on the legal hurdles that guard against unfair adjudication. Some of these hurdles include the prosecution's difficult-to-accomplish burden of proof (i.e., beyond a reasonable doubt) and the admissibility of evidence provisions.

Even though the crime control and due process models are different from one another, we often find evidence suggesting that courts, and the system of justice at large, follow both models simultaneously. Despite this, some argue that courts usually give preference to one model over the other, depending on their jurisdiction and time in history. As you will notice, Packer's crime control and due process models are of particular relevance to some of the issues addressed in the articles selected for this section. Remember that, although these models were created in the 1960s, they can still be applied to today's judicial process.

Questions

Reading 8. Do appellate courts cheat? If so, how could we fix this problem?

Reading 9. Do you think we should try juveniles in adult courts? Explain your answer.

Reading 10. Explain why only a few cases are decided by the U.S. Supreme Court.

Reading 11. Do you think that juries have become less responsible in making moral judgments? Justify your response.

Reading 12. How do courts administer criminal justice while upholding the rights of inmates?

Reading 13. Do you think college-run courts should give access to campus newspaper officials? Explain your reasons.

Do appellate courts cheat? If so, how could we fix this problem?

Do Appellate Courts Regularly Cheat?

M. B. E. Smith

It probably will not surprise you to be told that the practice of law is almost entirely remote from its philosophy. Lawyers and judges are not much interested in jurisprudence—as indeed, not many mathematicians or scientists are much interested in the philosophies of their respective disciplines. (For that matter, philosophers are not much interested in the philosophy of what they do either.) But I have had one jurisprudential question set for me by my appellate practice, which has been almost entirely as a criminal defender. I have found in a substantial number of my appellate cases that I was left at its end with the distinct impression that the court had "cheated" in reaching its decision: that in considering the case it had early on made up its collective mind what this would be and that it had thereafter ignored contrary facts or legal principles, however weighty those might have been. And I believed in some of those cases (albeit not all) that the court had as a result come to a clearly incorrect legal conclusion—with

unfortunate consequences to my client. In talking shop with other appellate attorneys I frequently ask whether they too have often been left with the same impression, and their invariable response is: "Sure, let me tell you about. . . ." So I found that I and other practitioners believed that appellate courts frequently fail to follow the law—at times, as it seemed to us, deliberately so. (Because we had clearly brought those inconvenient facts and arguments to the court's attention!) This raised two significant questions: one seemingly empirical (Is it true that courts regularly `cheat' as so described?) and another straightforwardly jurisprudential (Is it proper—that is, consistent with true principles of political morality—for courts so to cheat?)

Somewhat surprisingly, the first question—do courts often cheat?—is the least tractable. It assumes a controversial jurisprudential hypothesis, namely, that at least some propositions of law have a determinate truth value. (If none do, then there is nothing for courts to follow, no way that they could cheat.) Champions of

indeterminacy—by whom I understand philosophers who deny that there is determinate truth in domains wherein we commonly suppose we have knowledge: that is, the physical sciences, the social sciences, morality—have also been very influential in jurisprudence. Holmes, one of our greatest judges, famously remarked in his essay *The Path of the Law* that law is only "the prediction of the incidence of public force through the instrumentality of the courts."[1] Legal realists in the 1930s, and Critical Legal Theorists today, agree that decisions in concrete cases are never deductions from facts and pre-existing law, but rather are mere expressions of judges' political ideologies. The point is sometimes made by saying: "The law is only what the judge had for breakfast." So one might quite reasonably, block my first question (Do courts often cheat?) by saying, "Courts can't cheat because they are not bound by anything at all."

Despite the attractive simplicity of the skeptics' answer, I suggest that we not make such short shrift of an interesting ques-

From M.B.E. Smith's "Do Appellate Courts Regularly Cheat?" as appeared in *Criminal Justice Ethics*, Volume 16, Number 2 (Summer/Fall 1997), pp. 11–19. Reprinted by permission of The Institute for Criminal Justice Ethics, 899 Tenth Avenue, New York, NY 10019–1029.

tion. (Indeed, the best argument against legal skepticism, and against skepticism generally, is that it makes every interesting philosophical question seem boring.) And legal skepticism, while now much in fashion in the law schools and the law reviews, is not the dominant view among scholars who specialize in the philosophy of law. Certainly it is not the dominant view among lawyers—to the extent that they count as having jurisprudential views. Legal scholars often say that legal skepticism is the lawyer's view of the law,[2] but it is more plausibly styled the law professors'. Legal education is still dominated by the case method, which focuses primarily upon appellate cases published in the official reporters. Compilers of casebooks tend to look for those signs of doctrinal embarrassment that prefigure changes in the law: where there is no convincing theoretical justification for an established rule or where such a rule frequently works an injustice. They concentrate upon hard, controversial cases: those about which superb lawyers and judges may reasonably disagree as to which party should win. Law teachers find boring the vastly more numerous "easy," cases, and so they tend to ignore them. When one's entire professional diet comprises controversial cases, it is easy to believe that every legal rule is "squishy," that legal reasoning can never produce determinate outcomes, and that every legal decision is at bottom only an exercise of raw power.

Unlike law professors and perhaps judges, we lawyers have no such sense of freedom. Our experience is that we are everywhere hedged 'round by rules. (This is frequently irksome but still more often reassuring: the

rules offer safe harbor—protection against professional discipline and malpractice suits.) We regularly experience factual indeterminacy. (In every case I have tried I would have had no doubt about its outcome had I but known which witnesses the jury would believe.) But in the vast majority of cases the governing law is quite clear to both sides. (That is surely the most important reason why 85 to 90 percent of both civil and criminal cases are settled short of trial.) So let us then hew to the lawyers' view of the law and reject legal skepticism. We thereby suppose that it is possible for appellate courts to cheat. How might we know whether they often do?

The disappointing answer is that we obviously cannot—at least not by the usual canons of empirical proof. Appellate cases are simultaneously wholly public and deeply hidden. All the papers—the trial transcript, the briefs, the exhibits, the decision—are public records. But in a case of even moderate complexity, these documents will comprise scores—perhaps hundreds—of pages, much of it exceedingly difficult for nonlawyers to comprehend. And there are thousands of appellate cases decided each year. (The cases in the official reporters are only the iceberg's tip: as in most large states, in Massachusetts about 80 percent of cases are disposed summarily, by a short decision that is circulated only to the parties and which has no weight as precedent.) So one is left to recounting experiences, to telling stories.

Efrain's Case

I recently argued Efrain's appeal after he had been convicted of trafficking in cocaine having a

street value of around $800,000. An element of this crime is that a defendant knowingly possess for distribution to others some quantity of three categories of controlled substances.[3] (He need not know exactly which one.) The sole evidence offered in the Commonwealth's case was that Efrain was observed to have parked his car outside a house where police were stationed who were expecting to intercept a delivery of cocaine. Carrying an open brown grocery bag under his arm, he walked to the back of the house, went upstairs to the door of a second-floor apartment, knocked upon it, and was then surprised to find himself confronted with six armed men, who promptly placed him under arrest. The brown bag contained eight plastic bags of "white, comprised powders" which chemical examination proved to be cocaine. That exhausted the evidence offered to show that he had had guilty knowledge. Many readers will think it exceedingly thin. Some may ask, "Had I been on that jury, would this really have been enough to persuade me beyond a reasonable doubt that Efrain was not an innocent dupe?" Notwithstanding, he is serving a sentence of fifteen to twenty years in state prison.[4]

I must now explain a fine point of Massachusetts criminal appellate procedure. Since victory promises a directed verdict on the issue instead of being placed once again in jeopardy at a new trial, appellants frequently attempt to show that the prosecution in its case in chief offered insufficient evidence to sustain the conviction. Success is rare because the standard is stringent: a convict will win only if the court finds that, when the evidence is viewed most favorably to the prosecution (for example, all conflicts in testimony resolved for it), no reasonable finder of fact could have been persuaded beyond a reasonable doubt that he was guilty.[5] As with virtually all other grounds for appeal, the issue must be preserved by a motion at trial—in this case a so-called Rule 25 motion, a motion for a required finding of not guilty.[6] Its timing is critical to a defendant's appellate rights. The motion may be offered either at the close of the prosecution's case or at the close of all evidence. (Experienced attorneys reflexively make it at both places.) If offered at the first point, it freezes the defendant's right to have the appellate court consider only the sufficiency of the prosecution's evidence and to have it ignore any weaknesses in his case that his evidence might expose.[7] But if the motion is first made later, at the close of all evidence, then when deciding whether the evidence was sufficient, the appellate court considers it all, including any introduced by the defendant.[8]

Upon reading the transcript I soon found a serious mistake made by Efrain's lawyer. He failed to make his Rule 25 motion when the prosecution rested; and he had Efrain testify, who then made a number of admissions that were very damaging to his credibility: in particular that he was promised $100 by an acquaintance to deliver a package to a certain address but was not told what the parcel contained. (On cross examination, he estimated that his errand would have taken fifteen minutes, exposing himself to the prosecutor's mocking question of how often he has been paid at the rate of $400 per hour.) But an odd thing happened. After closing his case, Efrain's attorney finally got around to making his Rule 25 mo-

tion. The trial judge acknowledged the motion and then "deemed" it also to have been made earlier, at the close of the Commonwealth's case. (He did not explain why he did this, but perhaps it was to forestall a later ineffective assistance of counsel claim. In any event, the trial prosecutor made no objection.) Then the judge promptly denied the defense motion.

This opened a window for me on appeal. Remember that the trial prosecutor made no objection to the judge's "deeming." Now, there is no more entrenched rule in appellate procedure than this: An error by a trial court will not be reviewed on appeal unless the issue is properly preserved at trial by a timely objection. The rule is stringently enforced against criminal defendants. In reading criminal appellate reports one continually runs across issues raised by defendants on appeal that were not properly raised below; and one finds them dismissed out of hand, except in the rare cases that falls under one of the exceptions to the contemporaneous objection requirement, for example, where the court believes that to ignore the issue would create a "substantial risk of a miscarriage of justice."[9] (This phrase is usually understood to signal one of those rare cases in which the reviewing court suspects from reading the transcript that an appellant might well be actually innocent.) So I claimed the benefit of the Rule 25 motion's having been made at the earlier point; and I excluded all mention of Efrain's testimony in my Brief. I then argued that the Commonwealth's evidence was not sufficient and that Efrain should therefore be discharged. And indeed the prosecution's Brief fell in with my strategy: it did not at-

tack what the trial judge had done; and it too made no mention of my client's testimony. It argued (without much conviction) only that the Commonwealth's evidence had been sufficient. I employed the same strategy at oral argument, and the prosecutor again followed my lead. The appeals court too focused upon the issue of whether the prosecution's evidence alone was sufficient to sustain the conviction, except that they were plainly made restive by what the trial judge had done.

When the appeals court finally issued its decision, it summarily dismissed the appeal, which did not surprise me. What flabbergasted me, however, was that in pronouncing the evidence to be sufficient the court considered both the Commonwealth's and the defendant's evidence.[10] (It also held, after the most perfunctory analysis, that the Commonwealth's evidence had been sufficient, but this seemed to me clearly pretextual.[11] In ten years of appellate practice I had never heard of a court doing any such thing: namely, on its own motion the appeals court corrected what it took to be judicial error below without citing any authority, without being requested to do so by a party to the appeal, and without soliciting argument from either side. I then prepared an application for further appellate review to the Supreme Judicial Court (SJC) in which I indignantly huffed and puffed. I asked the SJC to correct what I called "an extraordinary act of procedural injustice"; and I complained that the appeals court maintains an unfair and one-sided standard of review. It holds criminal defendants to a stringent gateway standard, vigorously enforcing the requirement that there be a timely objection at trial; but then it effectively holds the prosecution to no standard at all.

As I expected, the SJC turned down my application for further review without comment or explanation. I nonetheless firmly believe that the appeals court "cheated." It is a fundamental principle of appellate practice that issues not briefed or argued are deemed waived.[12] The appeals court ignored its usual procedural rules in order to obtain a particular result—or rather two results, for in addition to ratifying my client's conviction it also chastised the trial judge, telling him ". . . it behooves trial judges to follow the strict mandates of the Massachusetts Rules of Criminal Procedure."[13]

George's Case

Criminal defendants very often try to delay trial dates for as long as possible, perhaps hoping that the charges against them will somehow mysteriously disappear. A common tactic is to complain shortly before trial that one's attorney is incompetent or has some conflict of interest, and to demand that she be replaced. If successful, the tactic greatly inconveniences prosecutors, who must reopen negotiations with a new defense attorney and hope that their witnesses will still be available in a month or more. It is even more troublesome to judges with crowded trial calendars, who must strike a reasonable compromise between the values encapsulated in the old adage, "Justice delayed is justice denied," and those that underlie the sixth amendment right to counsel.

Their task is greatly complicated by the supreme importance that this right commands. It is one of the vanishingly few consti-

tutional rights exempted from the "harmless error" rule of *Chapman v. California*.[14] Lay people are often greatly surprised to discover that appellate courts frequently recognize that criminal convictions were infected by fundamental constitutional errors but yet refuse to reverse them. So long as an appellate court is satisfied beyond a reasonable doubt that a garden-variety constitutional error did not affect the trial's outcome—that a reasonable jury would yet have convicted even had that error not occurred—an appeal will fail. The Supreme Court has struggled often over the indicia of harmless error. Despite sharp protest from dissenting Justices, it has continually widened the rule's scope.[15] But it has consistently held that there are two paramount exceptions: the right to counsel and the right to an impartial tribunal. Justice Powell once opined for the Court that "if the defendant had counsel and was tried by an impartial adjudicator, there is a strong presumption that any other errors that may have occurred are subject to harmless error analysis."[16] Chief Justice Rehnquist has recently said of the right to counsel that its deprivation "requires automatic reversal of the conviction because [this infects] the entire trial process"[17] It is a "structural defect in the constitution of the trial mechanism, which def[ies] analysis by `harmless-error' standards."[18]

George was a dilatory defendant even though he was held on bail pending trial. (His lengthy probation record comprises convictions of many serious crimes and a generous sprinkling of defaulted court appearances.) When I came to represent him, he was appealing from convictions in su-

perior court of unarmed robbery, of assault and battery by means of a dangerous weapon (shod foot), of stealing a motor vehicle, and of operating a vehicle to endanger. He was sentenced to a term of fifteen to twenty years in state prison for the robbery and received lesser sentences for the other crimes. The evidence against him had been overwhelming. On several occasions the robbery victim firmly identified George as his assailant. Worse still, about three hours after the robbery and thirty miles away from it, George drove the victim's car through a red light into another vehicle, and he was taken to a hospital and from there to a jail. But the weight of the evidence was not important in his appeal. What gave George's case interest were his gyrations over counsel.

At his arraignment in superior court on January 25, the supervising attorney of the local public defender's office,[19] Michael H., was appointed to represent him. Trial was later set for March 26. However, on that date the trial was put off until April 6 by mutual agreement: a police witness was unavailable until then; and George announced to the court that he needed time to hire another attorney. He mentioned a Rhode Island attorney, C. In granting the continuance, Judge T. instructed George that C. or any other substitute attorney must file an appearance in the case by April 5th.

When George's case was called before Judge M. on the morning of April 6, no other counsel had appeared. George promptly requested a further continuance to obtain other counsel, again mentioning C. George complained that he and Michael were not "getting along at all" and that

Michael was trying to force him to plead guilty. Judge M. rejected George's request as a "paradigm 11th hour motion,"[20] and ordered trial to begin that afternoon. He further specified that, unless substitute counsel appeared by 2:00 P.M., George must either represent himself or be represented by Michael.

No substitute having appeared, Judge M. began the afternoon session by asking what George would do about counsel. He first heard and calmly dissected George's lengthy complaints about Michael, and he again offered George the options of representing himself or of being represented by Michael. George refused both. Michael then asked to be discharged from the case because during the lunch hour in the courthouse holding tank George had become "increasingly agitated," had yelled at him, "Get out of here; get away from me!," and had thrown something at him which shattered against the bars. At this point Judge M. briefly recessed, saying, "I must confess that I haven't encountered this precise problem before; but there may be a solution to it and I will find one." On return he announced that the trial would begin the next morning. He denied for the time being Michael's motion to withdraw. Judge M. warned George that, if tomorrow he continued to reject Michael and no successor had appeared, his election would be treated as an implied waiver of his right to counsel and he would be forced to proceed pro se. He stressed that self-representation was "a difficult and risky undertaking" and was "dangerous and unwise." George responded, "Sir, I don't want Michael to represent me, nor do I want to be forced to go pro se."

The court clerk's first business on the morning of April 7. was to determine whether Attorney C. would in fact appear. After several phone calls he was found to be unavailable: George's brother had spoken with him but had not yet paid him a retainer; and C. in any event sensibly declined to be placed on trial the very day that he first appeared in a case. After recognizing George's renewed motion to discharge Michael, Judge M. held a colloquy with the two concerning George's complaints that lasted almost an hour. He probed into Michael's case preparation, discovering that Michael was prepared to go forward with three witnesses. After concluding the colloquy, he repeatedly warned George that if Michael were discharged, he would be forced to represent himself, and he carefully instructed him about the manifold difficulties of self-representation. Judge M. then made findings of fact for the record, including inter alia that Michael was prepared for the trial, that George's account of why he sought to discharge Michael was untrue, and that a breakdown in communication between Michael and George had happened but was engineered by George to prevent the trial from going forward. He also found that George understood that an election to discharge Michael constituted "a knowing, free and voluntary waiver" of Michael's services and of his right to counsel. Judge M. then granted George's motion, but ordered Michael to remain in the courtroom as standby counsel and to assist George if requested. When allowed to speak, George said with surprising dignity, "I do not wish to relinquish my right to counsel or any of my rights afforded me."

The trial that followed was unlike any I have ever witnessed or imagined. Judge M. continually invited George to participate, and he even offered brief instruction at the various stages of the trial. With an equal grave courtesy George steadfastly refused to take any part, insisting that he did not understand what he was supposed to do and asking repeatedly for some attorney other than Michael.[21] Judge M. did all that he could to safeguard George's trial and appellate rights: at the end of the Commonwealth's case, he deemed a Rule 25 motion to have been made which he then denied; after instructing the jury he deemed "an objection to have been made to every sentence of the charge"; and after sentencing George he ordered appointment of appellate counsel. But of course, Judge M. could not be George's lawyer.

While reading the transcript I identified sympathetically with Michael, and I greatly admired Judge M.'s patient resolve to find a just solution to the difficult problem George had posed. However, my immediate gut-hunch was that his answer could not possibly have been correct. George had a constitutional right of absolute weight to be represented by counsel, a right that a court must respect unless it is validly waived. Judge M. had found that George's election to discharge Michael was a waiver of his right to counsel. But I did not see how his finding could possibly be true. The concept of waiver is a root legal notion familiar to every first-year law student, and it is everywhere defined as "the intentional [or voluntary] relinquishment of a known right."[22] George had said he did not wish to "relinquish" his right to counsel—using the very word of the black-letter definition! Throughout his trial he had continually asked for a lawyer and declined even to try to defend himself. How could he have voluntarily relinquished a right when he continually insisted in evident sincerity that he was not doing any such thing? How can anyone intentionally give up a trial right while being forced over one's protests to proceed without it?

Confident that I had a sure winner, I turned to the cases. I soon found an interesting Massachusetts decision, *Commonwealth v. Tuitt*[23] and its companion in the First Circuit Court of Appeals, *Tuitt v. Fair*,[24] which denied Tuitt's petition for habeas corpus after his direct appeal had failed. Despite important differences Tuitt's cases fitted oddly well with George's. Like George, Tuitt had attempted to discharge his appointed attorney on the eve of trial and had demanded that other counsel be furnished to him. Unlike George, Tuitt also demanded that he be permitted to serve as his own attorney. Tuitt's judge responded by ordering him to proceed with his original appointed attorney.

When Tuitt appealed and petitioned for habeas corpus, he gave up railing against trial counsel. He instead argued that he had wrongly been denied his right of self-representation, a fundamental constitutional right first recognized by the Supreme Court in *Faretta v. California*.[25] To counter the obvious rejoinder that one cannot simultaneously have the right to be represented by an attorney and to represent oneself, Tuitt ingeniously argued that he had waived his right to counsel. Quoting from a Massachusetts decision, *Commonwealth v. Appleby*,[26] and an earlier First

Circuit decision, *Maynard v. Meachum*,[27] Tuitt claimed that he fell within the recognized principle of law that "a refusal without good cause to proceed with able, appointed counsel is a `voluntary' waiver." Tuitt's argument was bold and brash but unavailing. The SJC retorted, "This [principle of implied waiver] is generally true, except in those situations where refusal to proceed with counsel is accompanied by an explicit refusal to waive one's right to counsel."[28] The First Circuit agreed, saying:

[T]he right to an attorney is in effect until waived, while the alternative right to self-representation is not in effect until asserted. Where the two rights are in collision, the nature of the two rights makes it reasonable to favor the right to counsel which, if denied, leaves the average defendant helpless.[29]

Tuitt remained in state prison. But the principles articulated in his cases gave powerful support to George's demand for a new trial. George did explicitly refuse to waive his right to counsel; Tuitt holds that such a refusal precludes waiver; therefore, George could not have waived this right. The facts of George's case and the holding of Tuitt strictly imply the conclusion. (Logicians call this argument form modus ponens.)[30] Clearly then, Judge M. had been mistaken. What he should have done was to hold Michael in the case for as long as George demanded counsel. Forcing George to trial pro se had deprived him of his right to counsel, which "requires automatic reversal of [his] conviction."[31]

The nub of my argument was now nearly complete, except for an awkward case that had to be met head on: *Commonwealth v.*

Moran,[32] which came down from the appeals court two years before Tuitt was decided by the SJC. Moran's facts were in all relevant respects identical to George's: Moran too had made unreasonable complaints against assigned counsel, had demanded another attorney, and had been unwillingly forced to trial pro se. The appeals court affirmed Moran's conviction. Quoting the *Appleby/Maynard v. Meachum* principle of implied waiver (to which Tuitt later grafted an exception), the court held that Moran had waived counsel. In my Brief I acknowledged that the Truitt court did not announce the impact of its holding on Moran, but I pointed out that the later decision from the higher court had evidently overruled the earlier case by implication.

The Commonwealth's Brief had no effective counter to Tuitt. It did what lawyers have to do at such times: attempt to confuse the issues in the hope of softening the weaknesses of one's arguments. Pointing out that a valid waiver must be "knowing and intelligent," the Brief argued at length that Judge M. had carefully explained to George all that he really needed to know. It even included George's lengthy probation record in an appendix to show George's "familiarity with the criminal justice system"—perhaps suggesting that a criminal gains the functional equivalent of a law license by being many times convicted. Since the ground of George's appeal was that his alleged waiver was involuntary, not that it was "unknowing," I thought that his position had emerged unscathed. Nonetheless, I fired off a short Reply Brief to highlight the weaknesses of the Commonwealth's arguments.

About two months later I was disappointed to discover that the appeals court had placed George's case on their Summary List. I had hoped out of simple vanity that it might merit a published opinion. (It is nice to have one's name appear at the head of a case report as the winning counsel of record.) But I also thought that the case posed an important issue. The problem of dilatory defendants is recurring. *Tuitt and Tuitt v. Fair* specify precisely what judges should do with them. Nonetheless, despite his evident judicial competence Judge M. did not know what the right answer was—as indeed he might not have known, with such a case as Moran outstanding to confuse him. And I thought that there must be many other Massachusetts judges who shared Judge M.'s ignorance on this point of law, and what better case to instruct them than mine? Still, I consoled myself by thinking that the appeals court had found Judge M.'s error to be as obvious as I had, and I expected a summary reversal. The appeals court does not often so dispose of criminal convictions, but it does happen. (Two of my winners have come in this way.)

I therefore approached oral argument confidently. I spent most of my time puffing up the importance of the issue raised by George's case, and I urged the court to take it off the Summary List and to give it full-dress treatment. The three judge panel did not look at all pleased by me— but then appellate judges usually do seem vaguely disapproving of counsel at oral argument and never signal which way they will vote. The prosecutor made his pitch into the same somber judicial air, and then we attorneys went home.

The reader will have long since guessed that my confidence was wholly misplaced. In almost twelve full pages—which I believe is expansive for a Memorandum and Order in a summary disposition—the appeals court affirmed George's conviction. I was shocked by the opinion: I greatly respect the Massachusetts judiciary, and I did not want to believe that the appeals court would emit such slovenly reasoning. After expending half its pages reciting the procedural history and most of the essential facts, the court began its legal analysis by noting that George's appeal was based on Tuitt. It even quoted the Tuitt exception to the doctrine of implied waiver. But then the court straight-away turned to *Commonwealth v. Moran.* After describing this case and its holding at some length, the court abruptly announced: "We conclude that the present circumstances are controlled by the Moran opinion." It made no attempt to show that George's waiver of counsel had been voluntary or intentional; neither did it articulate a concept of unintentional or involuntary waiver. Apparently the court would have conceded—the Transcript made the fact undeniable—that George had continually voiced his demand for counsel. But it made no attempt to distinguish Tuitt, to explain how Tuitt's demand for another attorney would preclude his waiving his right to counsel but not George's. Neither did the appeals court even mention the federal case, *Tuitt v. Fair.*

I trust that the fallacy in the appeals court's opinion is obvious: Tuitt and Moran are inconsistent holdings—by which I mean "inconsistent" in the logician's

sense of implying a contradiction. Moran stands for the proposition that a person may be forced to trial pro se over his express demand for counsel and yet still be counted as having voluntarily waived his right to counsel. Tuitt stands for the proposition that a defendant who expressly demands to be afforded counsel cannot be held to have waived the right to counsel. These propositions are flatly inconsistent; by the canons of logic they cannot both be true. Since Tuitt is the later decision and emerged from a higher court, it must prevail. Hence, Moran was overruled on the issue of waiver. Therefore, it cannot "control" George's or any other case on that issue.

The court did note in a footnote that George had claimed that Tuitt had overruled Moran, saying:

Contrary to the defendant's claim, *Commonwealth v. Tuitt* [cit om.] did not overrule the Moran case. Moran has been cited favorably in subsequent cases. See *Commonwealth v. Lee*, 394 Mass. 209, 216 (1985).

This footnote was perhaps the most disingenuous touch of all. Moran has been cited in post-Tuitt reported cases, but not once on the issue of whether a defendant's express refusal to waive counsel precludes his having done so. Tuitt even cites Moran— but again not on the crucial issue.[33] Lee cites Moran twice but always to support some other principle of law. As the appeals court well knew, the fact that Moran has been cited on other issues is no reason at all to hold it to be valid authority on the issue presented in George's case. The court's fallacy was too blatant to have been accidental, which I took to be decisive evidence that it had deliberately cheated. It had made up its collective mind that

George would not get a new trial, and it would enforce that result regardless of what the Constitution requires.

I made these criticisms and more in a Petition for Rehearing addressed to the appeals court, and I tendered them all over again to the SJC in an Application for Further Appellate Review. Being still outraged my tone was at times intemperate—I accused the appeals court of deliberately ignoring settled law—and I worried somewhat that this might draw a rebuke. However, the Petition and the Application were each denied with a single short sentence. George's appeal died and he remained in state prison. I was left feeling ridiculous.

Jurisprudential Implications—A Sketch

Although my experience is almost entirely with the Massachusetts Appeals Court, I doubt that it is at all atypical, at least among courts that hear appeals as of right. (Courts such as the SJC or the U.S. Supreme Court, whose rules permit them to reject appeals without explanation, are perhaps less given to cheating as they need not entertain arguments that displease them.) Therefore, suppose with me that many appellate courts do regularly cheat. What should we make of this fact?

Here I shall offer only a sketch of an answer, which I begin by supposing that many readers will find my hypothesis shocking: that they will say appellate cheating is wholly inconsistent with democratic theory and with the principle that the citizenry ought to be ruled by laws and not by individual men or women. That was my initial re-

action when I first encountered the phenomenon, which also was mixed with the unreasonable feeling that I had wrongly been cheated of a victory. However, my indignation has since been tempered by the realization that, in all the appellate cases where I have thought I have encountered clear judicial cheating—some six or seven—only in one did I believe upon reflection that any real injustice had been done. As for Efrain, although he never confessed to me, I believed with the appeals court that he had known he was transporting cocaine and that he was in fact guilty. And, although I remain certain that George had a constitutional right to be represented by counsel at a new trial, I am also quite certain that securing that right would have been worthless to him. No attorney could have won an acquittal over the Commonwealth's proof. (I did not for a minute believe that George would have been saved by the three witnesses Michael had mentioned.) Moreover, since he was clearly guilty, justice would hardly have triumphed had George through some miracle won at a new trial.

Some years ago, in 1973, two brothers, Sanford and Mortimer Kadish, one a law professor and the other a philosopher, published a book called Discretion to Disobey, wherein they argued that many legal roles are what they called "recourse roles."[34] Such roles permit their holders to disregard parts of the law when this will better secure the role's end of doing justice than would strict compliance with it all. (The Kadishs' most immediately persuasive example is jury nullification in criminal cases: since Bushell's Case in 1670, Anglo-American juries have had power to acquit in the teeth of the law

and may not be punished for their verdict.[35] The Kadishs suggested that judging is also a recourse role: that judges have the legal power (and the moral right) to disregard the law when this leads to a better or more just result. I did not much like the notion of a recourse role when I first encountered it, and I reviewed the book somewhat disparagingly in the *Yale Law Journal*[36]—to my regret soon after because I became friendly with Sandy Kadish, who was dean of my law school and a bit of a mentor to me. But now I regret my unkind words even more keenly, because I have come to believe that something akin to Sandy's theory must probably be right.

Notes

1. Holmes, Jr., The Path of the Law, 10 Harvard. L.R. 457 (1897).
2. See, e.g., Pepper, The Lawyer's Amoral Ethical Role: A Defense, A Problem and Some Possibilities, 4 Am. Bar Foundation Research J. 613, 624–26 (1986); Wilkins, Legal Realism for Lawyers, 104 Harv. L.R. 469,478–99 (1990).
3. Commonwealth v. Rodriguez, 415 Mass. 447, 614 N.E. 2d 649 (1993).
4. The mandatory minimum punishment for trafficking in over 200 grams of cocaine is fifteen years in state prison. Mass. Gen. L. c. 94C [sections] 32E(b)(4).
5. Jackson v. Virginia, 443 U.S. 307, 318–19 (1979); Commonwealth v. Lattimore, 378 Mass. 671, 677, 393 N.E.2d. 370 (1979).
6. Mass. R. Crim. P. 25, 378 Mass. 896 (1979).
7. Cf. Commonwealth v. Sheline, 319 Mass. 279, 283, 461 N.E.2d. 1197, 1201f (1984). If the motion is made at close of the Commonwealth's case, the reviewing Court only considers the defendant's evidence to determine whether its "position as to proof deteriorated after it closed its case," Id.
8. Commonwealth v. Torres, 24 Mass. App. Ct. 317, 508 N.E.2d 877 (1987).
9. Objections to trial rulings by either party are governed by Mass. R. Crim. P. 22,378 Mass 892 (1979) See

Commonwealth v. Miranda, 22 Mass App. Ct. 495, 490 N.E.2d 1195 (1986) for discussion of the five rarely-applicable exceptions to the contemporaneous objection requirement. For an arguably draconian insistence in a high-profile case upon the necessity of such objection, see Commonwealth v. Amirault, 424 Mass. 618, esp. 645–53, 677 N.E. 2d 652, 670–74 (1997).

10. The last sentence of the unpublished opinion reads, "Moreover, at the close of all of the evidence the Commonwealth's case was strengthened by the defendant's testimony that he was paid $100 to merely deliver a bag to a person and address unknown to him." Technically, however, these admissions count only against the defendant's credibility and were not evidence of his guilt. It is a fundamental principle of the law of evidence that disbelief of testimony does not constitute proof of opposing facts required to sustain a finding. Morse v. Board of Selectmen of Ashland et al., 7 Mass. App. Ct. 739, 401 N.E.2d 379 (1980)

11. This finding forestalled a motion for a new trial based upon ineffective assistance of counsel, since it foreclosed the claim that counsel's error deprived the defendant of "an otherwise available, substantial ground of defense." Commonwealth v. Saferian, 366 Mass. 89, 96, 315 N.E.2d 878 (1974)

12. Massachusetts cases, like those of every other jurisdiction, continually recite this principle. See e.g., Brown v. Fairhall, 213 Mass. 290, 100 N.E. 556 (1913); Budish v. Daniel, 417 Mass. 574, 631 N.E.2d 1009 (1994).

13. This is taken from the unpublished Memorandum and Opinion of the appeals court in Efrain's case, on file with the Institute for Criminal Justice Ethics.

14. Chapman v. California, 386 U.S. 18 (1967).

15. Chapman offered three illustrative examples of constitutional error that required automatic reversal: the positive rights to counsel and to an impartial judge, and the negative right that a defendant's coerced confession not be admitted into evidence against him. Id. at 24 n8. The last right was pared from the list in Arizona v. Fulminate, 499 U.S. 279 (1991)

16. Rose v. Clark, 475 U.S. 570, 579 (1986)

17. Brecht v. Abrahamson, 507 U.S. 619, 629f. (1993)

18. Id. at 629., quoting Arizona v. Fulminante, 499 U.S. 279, 309 (1991).

19. In Massachusetts, a state agency called the Committee for Public Counsel Services is the public defender. It has two main branches: public counsel (such as Michael), comprising the Committee's staff attorneys, and private counsel (such as myself), who are independent attorneys under contract with the Committee. I do not know Michael, but my experience with public counsel is that they are excellent attorneys who are fiercely devoted to indigent criminal defense.

20. All quotations from George's case are taken from official records on file with the appeals court and in the possession of the author. The specific sections cited in this article are on file with the Institute for Criminal Justice Ethics.

21. George's mien reminded me most of Melville's Bartleby the Scrivener who, as disasters piled on, kept saying to his would-be helper (the narrator of the story), "I would prefer not to."

22. Rose v. Regan, 344 Mass. 223, 999, 181 N.E.2d 796, 800 (1962). Accord: Brady v. United States, 397 U.S. 742, 748 (1970)(A waiver of a constitutional right must be voluntary.) To see the ubiquity of this definition of waiver, see its entry in any edition of Black's Law Dictionary.

23. 393 Mass. 801, 475 N.E.2d 1103 (1985)

24. 822 F.2d 166, 174 (1st Cir. 1987).

25. 422 U.S. 806 (1975).

26. 389 Mass. 359, 366–67, 450 N.E.2d 1050, 1076 (1983)

27. 545 F.2d 273, 278 (1st Cir. 1976)

28. 393 Mass. at 808, 475 N.E.2d at 1109. We may call this the Tuitt exception to the doctrine of implied waiver. Note that the exception was not mere dicta, but was essential to the holding of the case. Since Tuitt expressly demanded his right of self-representation, the Court could only escape the conclusion that he was denied it by holding that the right had never "clicked in," on the ground that he had never waived the right to counsel.

29. Tuitt v. Fair, 822 F.2d at 174.

30. The argument's formal structure is: If p [George refused to waive his right to counsel] and if p then q [If a defendant refuses to waive counsel, then he has not waived it.], then q [George did not waive counsel].

31. See note 18 supra.

32. 17 Mass. App. Ct. 200, 457 N.E.2d 287 (1983).

33. 393 Mass. at 806, 475 N.E. 2d at 1109.

34. S. Kadish and M. Kadish, Discretion to Disobey: A Study of Lawful Departures from Legal Rules (1973). For a somewhat similar view, see Frederick Schauer's defense of "presumptive positivism" in his Playing by the Rules: A Philosophical Examination of Rule-Based Decision Making in Law and in Life, esp. ch. 8 (1991). For argument by a sitting judge that may fairly be read as asserting a right to cheat (as that word is used here) in constitutional cases, see R. A. Posner, What am I? A Potted Plant?, in his Overcoming Law, ch. 8 (1995).

35. 124 Eng. Rep. 1006 (C.P. 1670). This case ended the practice of punishing juries that acquit against the law. The jury had found William Penn and William Mead not guilty of unlawful assembly. The trial judge then locked them up without food for two days and fined them for their final verdict. The jurymen's case was taken up on a petition for habeas corpus; and they were discharged. A wall-plaque in the Old Bailey says inter alia of their case, "This plaque commemorates the courage and endurance of the jury." S. Kadish & M. Kadish, supra note 34, at 46n.

36. Smith, Concerning Lawful Illegality, 83 YALE L. J. 1534 (1974).

Article Review Form at end of book.

Do you think we should try juveniles in adult courts? Explain your answer.

Juvenile Offenders

Should they be tried in adult courts?

The "get tough" approach to dealing with young law violators seen throughout the criminal justice system is society's reaction to violent, uncaring youths.

Michael P. Brown

Dr. Brown is professor of criminal justice, Ball State University, Muncie, Ind.

Children have been described as our future, our greatest resource, and our hope for a better tomorrow. For many Americans, though, children invoke fear. They represent violence, a segment of society lacking in self-control and devoid of ethics and morals, and the failure of the family to instill traditional values—chief among them being the value of human life and respect for others.

Fear of crime, especially random violence perpetrated by young Americans, is among the nation's greatest concerns. It has served as the motivation for countless numbers of people to change their lifestyles, take self-defense classes, install home security systems, and carry handguns for protection. Moreover, fear of crime has influenced politicians and laypersons to adopt the position that a conservative justice system, which seeks to punish and deter, holds the most promise in curtailing juvenile crime. Waiving juveniles to criminal (*i.e.*, adult) court and imposing criminal penalties, according to the conservative position, are effective ways for society to express outrage for the transgressions of "out-of-control" youth and to placate its desire for retribution. Others, however, contend that treating juveniles as adults is going too far. Although many of these juveniles are incarcerated for their crimes, which the law allows, they often are the easy victims of homosexual rape and other forms of violence at the hands of hardened adult criminals.

The criminal sanctioning of juvenile offenders is not a contemporary phenomenon. Juveniles have been punished as adults for centuries. Prior to the 17th century, for instance, children were seen as being different from adults only in their size. Hence, they were held essentially to the same behavioral standards as adults. Youngsters were perceived of as being miniature adults and, therefore, subject to the same punishments as offenders who were decades their senior. Childhood was considered to end at about age five.

It was not until the 17th century that European church and community leaders successfully advanced the notion that children were weak and innocent and in need of the guidance, protection, and socialization of adults. Consequently, childhood was prolonged, education became a priority, and societal norms emerged specifying age-appropriate behavior. Youngsters no longer were viewed as miniature adults. For the first time in recorded history, they were a separate and distinct group.

Reprinted by permission from *USA Today* Magazine, Jan. 1998, Vol. 126, No. 2632, pp. 52–54.

By the 18th century, English common law characterized those under the age of seven as being incapable of forming criminal intent. For an act to be considered criminal, there must be *actus reus* (the criminal act itself), *mens rea* (the intent to commit the criminal act), and *corpus delecti* (the interaction between the act and the intent to commit it). Therefore, since youths were considered to be incapable of forming *mens rea,* they were legally unable to commit a crime or be criminally sanctioned. Between the ages of seven and 14, children were presumed to be without criminal intent unless it could be proven that they knew the difference between right and wrong. At age 14, they legally were considered adults, capable of forming criminal intent and therefore justly sentenced to serve time in jail and prison alongside other adults.

By the early 1800s, there was the belief that juvenile and adult offenders should be incarcerated separately. At that time, special correctional institutions for youthful offenders were established in the U.S. It was not until 1899, though, that the first juvenile court was established. This uniquely American institution was based on the premise that youthful offenders should be treated differently than their adult counterparts. Instead of deciding guilt or innocence, the court would ascertain whether youths were in need of treatment. Under the driving philosophy of the new court, *parens patriae,* it would serve as the benevolent parent—all-knowing and all-loving, wanting only that which is in the best interest of children. Consequently, instead of harsh, punitive sanctions that sought to deter, the court would seek long-term behavioral change by pro-viding the guidance youths so woefully lacked from their natural parents. Sentences were to be customized to meet the needs of each juvenile so as to optimize the rehabilitative effects of court intervention.

For most juveniles, the *parents patriae* doctrine still serves as the foundation upon which their sentences are based. Such an orientation is not deemed appropriate, however, for those juveniles waived to criminal court. Provisions that allow juveniles to be waived are, on the one hand, in contrast with the original intent and purpose of the juvenile justice system. On the other, they are consistent with the manner in which youthful offenders were sanctioned in the past.

The present-day controversy surrounding waivers appears to be a consequence of at least two factors converging. First, the definitions of childhood and age-appropriate behavior are in a state of flux. Young people are said to be more predisposed toward violence today than they were in the past. National crime data sources seem to support this notion. Violent juvenile crime has increased by nearly 70% since 1986. Moreover, the violence perpetrated by juveniles is portrayed by the mass media as being more heinous than at any other time in history. People are fearful of falling victim to a generation that seemingly holds beliefs and values that diverge drastically from those of normative society.

Second, the "get tough" approach to dealing with law violators—as seen throughout the criminal justice system—increasingly is being applied to juvenile offenders as well. Although a conservative approach to juvenile crime is not new, it is in sharp contrast to the predominant way in which the juvenile justice system has responded to youthful offenders in the U.S. for nearly 100 years. While it is true that waivers have been in existence for more than 70 years, they are used more today than in the past. This has drawn attention to how society's response to juvenile offenders is changing from primarily being oriented toward rehabilitation to increasingly becoming prone to subjecting juveniles to conservative criminal court practices.

"Legal Adults"

Every state and the District of Columbia have at least one provision (some states have as many as three) to waive certain juveniles to criminal court. Juveniles may become "legal adults" through judicial waiver, prosecutorial discretion, or statutory exclusion. A judicial waiver involves the juvenile court waiving jurisdiction over a case and sending it to criminal court for prosecution. In all but three states, juvenile court judges have been entrusted with the power to waive juveniles to criminal court. Prosecutorial discretion (also known as concurrent jurisdiction) refers to the prosecutor deciding in which court—juvenile or criminal—charges will be filed. Ten states and the District of Columbia give prosecutors this authority. Statutory exclusion involves state legislatures designating certain offenses for which criminal prosecution is required. Thirty-six states and the District of Columbia have enacted legislation that excludes certain offenses from juvenile court jurisdiction.

Age and offense seriousness traditionally have been the criteria by which juveniles are waived to criminal court. Twenty-one states and the District of

Columbia have no minimum age requirements for transferring juveniles to criminal court. Among the remaining 29 states, minimum age requirements range from seven to 16. The largest proportion of cases waived to criminal court are serious crimes such as murder; offenses involving serious personal injury (such as aggravated assault); property crimes; public order offenses (such as disorderly conduct, obstruction of justice, and weapons offenses); and drug offenses. Additionally, some minor offenses (such as fish and game violations), which do not fall within the jurisdiction of the juvenile court, are tried in criminal court. Moreover, some states permit juveniles to be waived if their current charge is a felony and there is evidence of prior felony convictions. Furthermore, most states have a provision that allows juveniles to be waived to criminal court if there is reason to believe that offenders are not amenable to treatment.

Using the most recent available data, the Office of Juvenile Justice and Delinquency Prevention (OJJDP) reports that, from 1985 to 1994, the number of delinquency cases waived to criminal court rose from 7,200 to 12,300, a 71% increase. Despite this growth, the percentage of cases waived to criminal court during this 10-year period remained relatively constant, ranging from a low of 1.2% to a high of 1.5% of all formally handled delinquency cases.

Over this span, the types of offenses waived to criminal court have changed considerably. While 54% of the cases waived in 1985 were for property crimes, the percentage dropped to 37% by 1994. Cases involving murder and personal injury rose from 33 to 44%.

The percentage of drug offenses more than doubled, from five to 11%. Public order offenses remained relatively constant—nine percent in 1985 and eight percent in 1994.

The percentage of cases involving youthful offenders under the age of 16 increased from six to 12%. Males consistently have comprised the majority of cases waived to criminal court—95% in 1985 and 96% in 1994. Of the juveniles waived to criminal court in 1985, 57% were white, 42% black, and two percent of other racial and ethnic groups. By 1994, the percentage of white and black juvenile offenders became more similar (49 and 48%, respectively), and youths from other racial and ethnic groups increased to four percent. (Figures have been rounded off to nearest full percentage point.)

Waiving juveniles to criminal court often is justified on the grounds that they are deserving of more punitive criminal court sanctions and that the "get tough" approach to fighting crime will serve to deter future criminal conduct. Decades of research has yielded mixed findings regarding whether juveniles are sentenced more harshly by criminal courts and are less likely to recidivate. Most studies indicate that juveniles waived to criminal court do not receive substantially more punitive sanctions. In fact, many studies have reported that juveniles are more likely to receive probation instead of incarceration. Of those incarcerated, most receive terms of confinement comparable to those imposed in juvenile court. Moreover, research has revealed that juveniles waived to criminal

court are no less likely to recidivate than those sanctioned in juvenile court.

The methods by which the justice system responds to unlawful conduct are not determined in a vacuum. They are a reflection of societal attitudes. In the past, waiving juveniles to criminal court was considered an option after all other avenues of treatment in the juvenile court had been explored. Today, the situation is drastically different. The conservative environment that currently exists not only makes it more acceptable, it is an expectation that judges and prosecutors will act decisively by waiving certain juveniles to criminal court. Hence, waivers no longer are viewed as a last resort. In fact, the use of waivers has been expanded to include first-time juvenile offenders. The establishment of exclusionary statutes, requiring certain juveniles to be waived automatically, eliminates the possibility of the exercise of discretion by those who know youngsters best—juvenile court judges and prosecutors. It is estimated that exclusionary statutes have resulted in more juveniles waived to criminal court than judicial waivers and prosecutorial discretion combined.

Waiving juveniles to criminal court is not the answer to the crime situation. At best, waivers are a short-term solution to a complex social condition that will not be simplified by transferring juveniles to the jurisdiction of the criminal court. At best, they merely serve to mollify the public's desire for retribution. After all, the majority of those juveniles waived to criminal court will re-enter society stigmatized by their

". . . The majority of those juveniles waived to criminal court will re-enter society stigmatized by their criminal label. . . ."

criminal label and, in all likelihood, more dangerous than they were before being sanctioned as adults. This is especially true of youths who have served time in prison alongside adults.

Nevertheless, it is unlikely that waivers will be repealed. Therefore, it is incumbent upon decision-makers to make an informed, socially responsible use of waivers. In so doing, they would be restricted to those who pose the greatest risk to the safety and security of society—violent youth such as murderers, rapists, and robbers who show no apparent promise for reformation.

As for the others, juvenile court intervention holds the most promise for transforming troubled youths into productive, law-abiding adults. The OJJDP, based upon the results of numerous studies, has proposed a multifaceted strategy for dealing with youthful offenders:

Strengthen the family unit. Parents are primarily responsible for instilling in their children socially redeeming morals and values. Parenting classes may be necessary when mothers and/or fathers lack the skills, abilities, and maturity to socialize their offspring properly. When a functional family is nonexistent, a surrogate one should be established to fill that void in a child's upbringing.

Support core social institutions. Capable, productive, and responsible youths are influenced positively by schools, religious institutions, and community-based organizations. Social institutions impart law-abiding beliefs and values and offer youths legitimate opportunities for economic gain.

Promote delinquency prevention. Communities must be proactive by responding to children who are at risk of committing delinquent acts. Although youths have a responsibility to live within the boundaries of the law, social institutions have a similar responsibility to engage youngsters in activities that encourage productive, law-abiding behavior.

Encourage an effective and immediate justice system response to delinquency. When delinquency occurs, the justice system must respond immediately to prevent future such actions and suppress escalation in their seriousness. The justice system should act in concert with conventional social institutions to enlist the influences that the family and religious organizations, for instance, have on the lives of youths.

Identify and control those youths who already are serious offenders. Youths who have not responded to traditional juvenile court intervention efforts or have demonstrated an unwillingness to abide by the rules of nonsecure community-based treatment efforts should be isolated in secure juvenile facilities for the protection of society. Deviating somewhat from the OJJDP's proposal, this intervention effort would be restricted to nonviolent offenders.

The alternative to waiving juveniles to criminal court is a comprehensive community response to juvenile unlawfulness that views juvenile and criminal justice as components of a larger whole—society. Moreover, it sees crime as a community problem with a community solution, instead of viewing it solely as a justice system problem with a justice system solution.

Many people will resist the notion of instituting alternatives to criminal court waivers. A community response to juvenile crime requires the commitment of the entire society. Therefore, it needs more effort than simply waiving juveniles to criminal court. Nevertheless, it holds the promise of returning children to their natural and rightful position as our future, our greatest resource, and our hope for a better tomorrow.

 Article Review Form at end of book.

Explain why only a few cases are decided by the U.S. Supreme Court.

The Jurisdiction of the Supreme Court

Harold J. Spaeth and Edward Conrad Smith

Although losing litigants commonly pledge to take their cases all the way to the U.S. Supreme Court, such action does not depend on the persistence of parties who have lost their cases. The Court may only decide such cases as the Constitution and Congress authorize it to hear. Vast areas of the law are the exclusive purview of the state courts: most criminal offenses, personal injuries, commercial activities, and property disputes. Moreover, only a handful of the cases that are grist for the federal courts are decided by the Supreme Court because the justices are free to pick and choose among the cases that properly land on the doorstep of its marble palace.

How Cases Reach the Supreme Court

Except for a handful of cases between states or between a state and the federal government (in which the Supreme Court functions as a trial court), the Court hears cases under its appellate jurisdiction after they have been decided either by a lower federal court (usually a circuit court of appeals) or by the highest court in a state that has jurisdiction to try the particular case. The justices strictly limit access to the Court, accepting for review no more than 1 to 2 percent of the cases losing litigants bring to their attention.

Federal Questions

With a few relatively unimportant exceptions, the federal courts may decide only "federal questions"— those that pertain to the meaning of an act of Congress, a treaty of the United States, or a provision of the Constitution. Disputes about property, contracts, or personal injuries rarely have such a component. Hence, judicial resolution of these commonplace matters is the province of the state courts.

Writ of Certiorari

Most cases come to the Supreme Court on a writ of certiorari, which Congress authorized in 1925. It is a petition that a losing litigant files with the clerk of the Court requesting the justices to review the lower court's decision. If four justices vote to grant the petition, the Court will hear and decide the case. The usual grounds for granting the writ are the presence of a fundamental constitutional issue, an issue of general importance, an important private right, a federal statute not previously interpreted by the Court or conflicting decisions by lower federal or state courts on a particular federal question.

How the Court Operates

The justices examine lower court records of the case, study the briefs of the attorneys who represent the litigants, and, if the petition to review the case is granted, hear oral arguments. A majority vote determines the outcome of the case. If because of nonparticipation a tie vote results, the decision of the lower court stands. When he votes with the majority, the chief justice assigns the writing of the Court's opinion. Otherwise, the senior associate justice who voted with the majority makes the assignment. A justice who disagrees with the decision of the court may write a dissenting opinion. If a justice agrees with the decision but not with the reasons given in the opinion of the court, he or she may write an opinion concurring in the result. Such opinions, especially dissents, sometimes foreshadow changing interpretations of constitutional law.

The Effect of Precedents

Constitutional precedents set by the Supreme Court bind all lower courts, state and federal. The Supreme Court, interestingly enough, need not follow its own precedents, but it usually does so. Frequent overruling of precedents would make the law uncertain and the outcome of later cases unpredictable.

On the other hand, slavish adherence to a specific line of precedent may retard adaptation of the law to changing circumstances and conditions. The Court has several options. It may follow precedent. It may distinguish the case before it from earlier cases and apply a different set of precedents to its resolution. It may specifically overrule the precedent. It may ignore the precedent, in effect overruling it sub silentio. It may label an issue a "political question" to be decided by Congress or the executive branch. Whatever it chooses to do, the Court's decision becomes the law of the land.

Formal Alteration of Precedent

During the thirty-six terms from the beginning of the Warren Court in 1953 through the end of the 1988 term, the Court overruled or otherwise formally altered precedents in ninety-five opinions, an average of less than three per term. The total number of precedents these ninety-five

cases overturned (eighty) or formally altered (fifteen) cannot be specified with precision because the Court does not always indicate how many precedents its opinion has voided. The vast majority, however, only pertained to a single precedent.

During these same thirty-six terms, the Court declared 396 state laws and local ordinances unconstitutional—356 of the former and forty of the latter, along with 55 acts of Congress. The Court, therefore, was more than four times as likely to overturn a statute as it was to formally alter a precedent. The Court voided an average of 11 state and local laws on constitutional grounds per term, along with an average of 3 acts of Congress every two years.

Federal Court Jurisdiction

Notwithstanding the authoritative character of its decisions and its policy-making capabilities, the Supreme Court does not sit to right every wrong—popular belief to the contrary. The often-heard vow of losing litigants that they will take their cases all the way to the Supreme Court may represent their sense of injustice, but it most assuredly does not reflect reality. The Supreme Court, along with the other federal courts, are courts of limited jurisdiction in the sense that they may not hear any case or controversy unless it falls within the grant of power contained in Article III, section 2 of the Constitution. Moreover, as section 2 also makes clear, with a few minor exceptions, Congress must enact legislation authorizing the Court to hear various types of cases. This dependence of the federal courts on Congress for their jurisdiction is the major control that Congress

has over the judiciary. Although Congress has rarely used this power to check Supreme Court policy making (the last major instance occurred in 1932 when Congress forbade the federal courts to issue injunctions at management's request in labor disputes), its exercise can deprive the courts of their ability to resolve disputes in sensitive areas.

Federal Questions

Federal questions are the heart of federal court jurisdiction. Article III defines them as "all cases . . . arising under this Constitution, the Laws of the United States, and treaties." To invoke federal-question jurisdiction, a plaintiff must demonstrate to the court's satisfaction that the case substantially involves a constitutional provision, an act of Congress or administrative action pursuant thereto, or a treaty of the United States.

Other Subjects of Federal Jurisdiction

Of lesser importance are disputes to which the United States is party, those between states, admiralty and maritime matters, cases concerning foreign diplomatic personnel accredited to the United States, and those between residents of different states. Virtually all cases to which the United States is party contain a federal question. Except for an occasional interstate controversy, which usually concerns a boundary dispute or water rights, these other types of cases rarely reach the Supreme Court.

Access to the Federal Courts

The mere fact that parties seeking access to the federal courts can show a federal question does not guarantee that their cases will be heard. Plaintiffs must also meet a set of constitutional and Court created criteria known as "standing to sue." An actual dispute must exist between two or more persons. Federal courts will not decide hypothetical cases or render an advisory opinion. Neither will they hear a case in which the parties' interests do not conflict; e.g., a stockholder suing a corporation to prevent the payment of a tax.

Elements of Standing to Sue

The dispute, moreover, must concern a legal injury—rights and interests that have statutory or constitutional protection. Ordinary commercial competition, for example, does not have such protection. The injury that plaintiffs allege must be one they personally suffer. Unless the injured person is incapable by reason of death or incompetence, a third party may not initiate litigation in the federal courts except for prosecutors and others charged with enforcing federal law.

Cases that otherwise lie within the jurisdiction of the federal courts will not be decided if they are "political questions." While the short definition of a political question is whatever the Supreme Court says it is, such cases concern matters that the Court prefers the other branches of government resolve. Examples include the ratification of a constitutional amendment, the legitimacy of competing state governments, and the occupation of enemy territory.

The Supreme Court has instructed the federal courts to refuse to resolve issues if the judicial decision lacks "finality"; if the matter is one Congress has authorized a nonjudicial official or agency to authoritatively decide. The classic example concerns the eligibility of veterans for pension and disability benefits. Federal courts will not touch this matter because any action they take can be overturned by the Veterans Administration, whose decision is final and binding. In other words, if a court's decision is susceptible to review by a bureaucrat or by an administrative agency, it lacks finality.

With rare exceptions, courts also refuse to rehear a case they have decided. In short, litigants are entitled to only one bite of the apple. Once a court has entered a final judgment on the merits of a controversy, res judicata bars the same parties from relitigating the same claim in a second lawsuit. Similarly, collateral estoppel prevents a party from relitigating an issue that was actually decided in an earlier proceeding, as long as that issue had to be decided in order to resolve the original dispute. Thus, if a competent court authoritatively establishes that the negligence of Airline X caused a plane crash, Airline X may not deny its negligence in a lawsuit brought by another victim of the same crash.

Finally, if Congress has prescribed administrative procedures for resolving certain kinds of disputes—such as unfair labor practices, sex discrimination, the amount of taxes owed—litigants must exhaust these remedies before accessing the federal courts.

This chapter outlined the procedure whereby cases reach the Supreme Court. Most such cases contain a federal question. If four or more of the justices vote to hear the case, the Court will decide the matter. Very few cases pass through this screen—by and large, only those that raise an important unresolved question that concerns an act of Congress or a provision of the Constitution.

Apart from the foregoing factors, the federal courts will not hear a case unless the plaintiff—the party who seeks access to the court—who initiates the lawsuit—has standing to sue. By determining whether a litigant is a proper party the federal courts limit the types of disputes that they will hear. They do so in order to avoid hypothetical and redundant controversies, and to avoid unnecessary conflict with other decision makers.

 Article Review Form at end of book.

Do you think that juries have become less responsible in making moral judgments? Justify your response.

Lack of Conviction

The culture of victimhood enters the jury room.

Virginia I. Postrel

Americans are worried—and increasingly angry—about violent crime. They want more prosecutions and tougher sentences. They demand capital punishment for murder and more cops on the street. "The attitude of ordinary people indeed is essentially vindictive: They desire revenge," writes Paul Johnson in The Wall Street Journal.

That's the story you get over and over, in magazine cover features and in newspaper headlines, in made-for-TV movies and in campaign commercials, in opinion articles and in television news specials. There is truth to the story. Americans are scared, and they are angry. They do want tougher laws. But only in the abstract.

Put 12 ordinary people in a courtroom, present them with a real, live defendant, give the defendant a good lawyer, and those ordinary Americans will forgive just about anything. "Beyond a reasonable doubt" has been superseded by "beyond any shred of an excuse."

When a jury acquitted the cops who beat Rodney King, critics blamed racism. But the jury seemed swayed less by race than by the argument that police work is risky, that the police stand as the "thin blue line" between law-abiding citizens and criminals, that King's behavior was frightening. The police, the jury reckoned, had a good excuse.

When another jury acquitted four defendants of all serious charges in connection with the savage beatings of Reginald Denny and others, critics said the jurors were afraid of another riot. What else would explain their decision that smashing someone's head with a brick constitutes neither attempted murder nor felony mayhem? But the jury seemed swayed less by fear than by the argument that the defendants were caught up in the moment, that they'd lost their heads in mob violence, that under the circumstances, the attacks were understandable. The defendants, the jury reckoned, had a good excuse. Those were politically and racially charged trials, and they were analyzed as such. But they weren't, it seems, unique. Lyle and Erik Menendez plotted and schemed and blew away their rich parents with shotguns. There was nothing political about that act; it had no racial significance.

Yet the Menendez brothers' entire trial has been about whether they had a real excuse, about whether their parents abused them and therefore deserved to die. At this writing, Lyle's jury has been out for 22 days. Erik's has deadlocked, and the judge has declared a mistrial. It looks as though someone, at least, reckoned Lyle and Erik Menendez had a good excuse.

In Virginia, Lorena Bobbitt is on trial, with cheering supporters lining the walkway to the courtroom. We used to see cutting off genitals as the ultimate sign of barbarity, whether documented in Amnesty International reports or in the history of medieval tortures or American lynching. Now it makes you a heroine, at least if you have a good excuse. The central issue in Bobbitt's trial, as in the Menendez brothers', is whether her excuse is true, not whether it is valid, not whether her act deserves punishment.

Communitarians like to point to jury duty as proof that Americans want rights without responsibilities—the right to a jury trial without the responsibility of serving on a jury. But that's mostly nonsense. If Americans are shirking their responsibilities toward jury service, they aren't doing it by not showing up.

After two weeks on jury duty, including five actual days waiting around in courthouses and not a single second hearing a case, I've met lots of Americans who would love to serve on a jury. They just don't like the way the system treats them as chattel whose time is worth nothing. They start off enthusiastic and get worn down by the waiting. If you're not actually going to be put on a jury, many people reason, why bother to waste your time hanging out in jury rooms? (Victims and witnesses get the same abusive treatment, with no two-week time limit.)

The communitarians forget that you don't exhibit "responsibility" by complying with a court order backed by criminal penalties. Responsibility doesn't exist without choice. And it is the choices juries make that are disturbing. Juries are shirking their responsibility to make moral judgments. It is easier to make excuses.

We have come to the logical extension of the politics of victimhood, a politics that pervades not only high-brow opinion magazines and academic seminars but also the talk shows and advice columns that reflect and direct mass opinion. Bombard ordinary Americans with the notion that everyone is a victim, and a lot of people will start to believe it. The implication of universal victimhood is universal innocence. No one is guilty, no matter how heinous the crime. And to fundamentally alter the criminal justice

system, it isn't even necessary for everyone—or even most people— to believe in universal victimhood, only for the concept to be pervasive. On a criminal jury, you don't need a majority; you need unanimity. A good defense lawyer will screen out potential jurors obviously willing to make moral judgments. The dynamics of the jury room, and of American culture, will take care of the rest. Portia teaches mercy, Perry Mason innocence. Twelve Angry Men said nothing about holding out for conviction. Paradoxically, the only crimes not subject to the victimhood defense are those that have no victims. If you're carrying illegal drugs, it doesn't matter if you were an abused child or a member of an oppressed racial group. You can't argue that the drugs deserved to be used or that you had a good reason for taking them. No sympathy is allowed. The drugs speak for themselves. Case closed. Many people who oppose drug laws argue for giving juries explicit discretion to ignore them. They say that juries used to be considered judges not merely of the facts but also of the law, that juries can and should have the power to deem laws too odious to enforce.

I am sympathetic to this position and certainly to its goal of curtailing the punishment of consensual acts. But encouraging jurors to rewrite the laws is wrong. Justice requires objectivity. It entails a promise that everyone is equal before the law, that a defendant's sob story or a victim's obnoxious personality won't determine the outcome of a case.

It demands that juries decide not with their hearts but with their minds. Binding juries to honor the law—as the judge in the Menendez trial did when he told jurors that the evidence precluded acquittal—makes it more likely that jurors will fulfill that responsibility. It helps jurors check their prejudices and emotions; it forces them to give reasons for their decisions.

But it is not a fail-safe device, only a help. A government of laws cannot stand against a people who can see only victims, against jurors who believe neither in criminals' responsibility nor in their own. Once, runaway juries driven by rage gave us legal lynching, a complement to the illegal kind. They would not reason, so they could find no reasonable doubt.

Today, their successors feel not rage but pity, not hatred but empathy. They, too, do not reason, but neither do they doubt. They can look at proof of guilt and still find innocence— innocence in the victimhood of the victimizer.

Many of the ordinary people who make up juries desire neither justice nor revenge. They desire absolution, the obliteration of all responsibility. We have created a culture of excuse, and it has conquered our courtrooms—not by judicial fiat but by the most democratic of means. Our juries have gone soft on crime.

 **Article Review Form at end of book.**

How do courts administer criminal justice while upholding the rights of inmates?

Courting the Middle Ground

Daniel Pollack

Attorney Daniel Pollack is a member of the faculty at the Wurzweiler School of Social Work, Yeshiva University. Prior to joining the staff in 1992, he was executive assistant to the governor of Ohio, administrator for the Ohio Department of Youth Services, deputy director for Maryland's Social Service Administration and assistant legal counsel for the Ohio Department of Human Services.

The number of lawsuits brought by and on behalf of inmates has grown to unmanageable proportions. Some decry this trend as an epidemic of frivolity. Still, the ultimate deprivation of liberty—prison—naturally invokes the ultimate legal sanctuary: the Constitution.

In the middle of the liberal notion of rehabilitation and the conservative mantra of "lock 'em up and throw away the key" are the courts. We expect them to reflect our increasing impatience with any expansion of inmates' rights. Weightlifting equipment and cable television are being removed. They are being replaced by a political and judicial consensus articulated by one Texas court: "It is our very strong feeling that comfort and convenience are not elements that should be

supplied by society to prison inmates. If the prison system were made less comfortable and convenient, the recidivism rate . . . would diminish proportionately" [Johnson v. Ozim, 804 S.W. 2d 179, 181 (1991)].

Like inmates and corrections officers, no two lawsuits are the same. For each case, a court's job is to decisively frame the legal issues and apply the relevant law. The characteristic feature of each case lies in the court's desire to find current practice solutions to paradoxes brought about by having to deal simultaneously with the U.S. Constitution and the realities of corrections. Dilemmas in correctional practice create opportunities for new court precedents.

Judges are adamant that good correctional practice cannot be derived solely from their deductions; rather, they admit that the experience of corrections officials also must influence this evolving field of law.

Courts constantly reiterate their hesitation to engage in independent speculation and second guessing of corrections administrators. Their business is interpreting policy and procedure, enforcing a sense of order and in-

culcating respect for the law. Only when clear abuses occur do courts intervene.

Judges are aware that corrections is a job, not just a philosophy. It is the responsibility of the courts to discuss and describe minimum Constitutional requirements and allow corrections administrators to adapt their programs and facilities accordingly. With more than five million people either incarcerated or under some form of correctional supervision, courts simply are not interested or able to engage in microscopic oversight.

The Bible says, "Depart from evil—then do good" (Psalms 34: 15). First, it is necessary to separate the perpetrator from society; then, rehabilitation is possible. This, it seems, is the current state of mind in our courts. This new thinking also suggests a vehement interest in reducing ideology to a fact—incapacitation.

Prison may help to rehabilitate, degrade, humiliate, chasten, demoralize or repair. Incarceration is an opportunity for society to restrain and for the perpetrator to repent. Rehabilitation, if it does occur, is ultimately the choice of the perpetrator. Thus, punish-

Reprinted with permission from *Corrections Today*, April 1996, Vol. 58, No. 2, pp. 18–19.

ment and rehabilitation are not necessarily incompatible.

Since colonial times, law and corrections have intersected in various ways. As these overlapping interests evolved, corrections concerns became legal concerns. Given the breadth of this interaction, some corrections professionals may argue that the boundaries of law have encroached upon the domain of corrections.

The accuracy of this assertion will not be debated here. It is enough to acknowledge that significant controversies exist. The balance between judicial intrusion and neglect is ultimately left for the courts themselves to decide. Their power is rooted in their authority to rule on the constitutionality of all laws and policies proposed by the other branches of government.

The correctional system must always be seen from the perspective of the larger judicial system. There may be considerable dissonance between judicial pronouncement and corrections behavior. But then, as surely as law is more than the Constitution, so corrections is more than locks and bars.

 **Article Review Form at end of book.**

Do you think college-run courts should give access to campus newspaper officials? Explain your reasons.

Private Courts Face Public Scrutiny

Allan Wolper

Wolper, professor of journalism at Rutgers University, Newark, N.J., covers campus journalism for E&P.

The rumors were flying all over the University of North Carolina campus at Chapel Hill. A woman reported that she had been sexually assaulted.

But there was no police report. No victim on record. No perpetrator. No verdict. And no way to find out what had happened.

The case was tried four years ago in UNC's student-run Honor Court, which holds hearings when students are charged with violating campus codes of conduct.

After the student judges had rendered a decision, records of the sexual assault case were destroyed.

"It was so damn frustrating," said Kevin Schwartz, general manager of the *Daily Tar Heel*, the student newspaper. "We knew something had happened, but we never could pin it down. No one was willing to go on the record."

The Chapel Hill Honor Court, like other campus disciplinary systems, was set up to pre-

side over academic crimes like cheating and plagiarism. But university courts nationwide are increasingly being asked to handle cases involving theft, robbery, drugs, rape, and arson.

The Chapel Hill court is run by students, but other university judicial systems include faculty members and administrators. Penalties include censure, probation, suspension, expulsion or referral to campus or town police for prosecution.

Students' press tries to open up campus courts—and the crimes they hide in the name of student privacy.

The *Tar Heel's* inability to track down the sexual assault story haunted the student newsroom from one academic year to the next. Student journalists waited for the right moment to mount a legal attack on the school's secret disciplinary system.

On Feb. 16, the *Tar Heel* found the test case its attack on the school's secret disciplinary system had been waiting for: *Carolina Review*, a conservative magazine, published a cover story featuring a picture of Aaron Nelson, a candidate for student president, with horns and a pitchfork protruding from his head.

The magazine, distributed the day before the election, was branded anti-Semitic, but the content debate was muted because the magazine's 1,500 copies were stolen the next morning, before balloting began.

Nelson won the election, but two of his fraternity brothers were charged with infringing on the free speech rights of students by stealing the *Review*.

Two months later, Thanassis Cambanis, then *Tar Heel* editor, went to cover the frat brothers' disciplinary hearing. University officials barred him, saying the hearing was closed in compliance with the Family Educational Rights Privacy Act, known as the Buckley Amendment, which forbids the release of student education records without their consent.

The *Tar Heel* immediately filed suit in Orange County Superior Court charging the university with violating the state's open meetings laws.

While the paper's lawyers argued in Superior Court, the student-run Honor Court acquit-

Discrete Court for Sex Cases

Should the accuser and the accused in sexual assault cases be identified in press reports of college and university disciplinary hearings?

The question worries the people who want to see college courts opened as much as those who say they should remain closed.

Police officials believe that some women victims take their accusations through the college's private system because they're afraid their parents will find out if they go to police.

"One of the strengths of the school system is that it can offer victims a pretty confidential way of confronting the person who assaulted her," said Douglas F. Tuttle, recent past president of the International Association of Campus Law Enforcement Administrators (IACLEA).

Tuttle, the director of public safety at the University of Delaware, supports limited disclosure about sexual misconduct cases.

"The standard of proof in college courts is much lower than the criminal court," Tuttle said. "Still, if I had to choose, I would identify the accused only in situations in which he was found guilty."

The call becomes even tougher when the accused and the accuser were at a party.

"The worst situations are those in which both parties have been drinking and disagree on the intent of the evening," Tuttle said. "In that case, the press will name the accused even though he hasn't been arrested."

He agreed that victims of sexual attacks use the college system in order to keep their pain as private as possible.

"If a woman knows the case is open, she may not want to report anything," he continued. "You wouldn't want your mom to read in the campus newspaper that something like that has happened to you."

In addition, the slow pace of the criminal justice system effectively denies victims a chance to rid themselves of the nightmarish encounter and get on with their lives.

"It is especially difficult when they are living in the same residence, attend the same classes," Tuttle said. "On a campus, that can be handled right away."

Susanna Matsen, the chairwoman of the University of North Carolina Honor Court, says the student court process provides a safety net for sex crimes victims, and for those falsely accused.

"They won't be able to function on campus if the newspapers get a hold of it," Matsen insisted. "The right of the public to know has to come second to the rights of the people involved.

"The trials are very traumatic. And very heart wrenching. If the student newspapers publicize them, even the people who are found innocent will have their reputation ruined."

Jeanne Furgate, editor of the *Daily Tar Heel*, sees the debate over sexual assault coverage as a reprise of complaints against the mainstream press.

"It is a judgment call about whether to publish a victim's name," Furgate said. "But it is obvious that we would handle a sexual assault case differently than one involving cheating."

Closing a hearing to protect a child's parents is simply wrongheaded, the editor contended.

"All we have now are rumors, which tend to be unreliable and controversial," she said.

"I would think that parents would want to send their children to a university that upholds the principles of free speech, one that would uphold the principles of a free and open court."

—Allan Wolper

---

ted the frat brothers of charges of stealing magazines.

But the Superior Court also ordered the records of the student disciplinary hearing to be kept intact until it decides whether the public should have access to them. The legal skirmish is expected to conclude by mid-October, but it seems certain that the loser will appeal to the North Carolina Supreme Court.

Mark Goodman, executive director of the Student Press Law Center in Arlington, Va., sees the case as a test of a 1995 federal ruling suggesting the legal curtain be lifted on campus disciplinary hearings.

The Department of Education has ruled that the Buckley Amendment does not prevent the opening of campus disciplinary proceedings. But it also said that educational records are private—an invitation to a court fight.

"The education department said the disciplinary hearings should be open," said Goodman. "But they haven't said which tes-

> **"People are aghast when they find out that students are acting as judges and juries in criminal cases"—Kevin Schwartz, <u>Daily Tar Heel</u> general manager**

timony would be considered public and what is not."

The University of North Carolina and other institutions have argued that they would lose tens of millions of dollars in federal grants if they violate the privacy terms of the Buckley Amendment.

The Department of Education, which is supposed to monitor Buckley Amendment violations, can cut off grants to universities found in contempt of it.

But the *Red And Black*, the University of Georgia student newspaper, seemingly scuttled that argument when it convinced the state Supreme Court in 1993 to open disciplinary hearings.

That suit provided the public a front-row view of a case involving a 19-year-old student who nearly died in a fraternity hazing incident. But the groundbreaking Georgia decision hasn't persuaded the Department of Education to cut funding to the Athens, Ga., campus.

"No one has ever lost funding for violating Buckley," said Doug Tuttle, the recent past president of the International Association of Campus Law Enforcement Administrators. "There has never been a sanction against any university."

Tom Ziko, a special state deputy attorney general defending the University of North Carolina, says he plans to "make certain" the Buckley Amendment is fairly applied. "The student Honor Court is not a court for purposes of constitutional law," he said. "It is an administrative body."

Amanda Martin, an attorney representing the *Tar Heel*, believes the student judicial system should not be shut off from the campus community it serves.

"The community has to know whether someone in power has gotten preferential treatment," she said. "The only way to know that is to open up the hearings. Right now, a lot of power is being entrusted to just a few students."

But Ziko will argue in Superior Court next month that making the disciplinary hearings public might force open disciplinary meetings in high schools or even elementary schools.

Both sides agree that Honor Court hearings can be opened at the discretion of the person charged. In sexual assault cases, the hearings are closed unless the accuser agrees to make them public.

The University of North Carolina recently began distributing summaries of disciplinary actions, but without names, addresses and witnesses, making it difficult to discern the seriousness of charges. For example, the Honor Court announced that 16 hearings last summer resulted in censures and suspensions for charges including drug possession, theft, plagiarism, forgery, as well as disorderly and obscene conduct.

Journalists fighting to pry open the doors to campus disciplinary hearings say that the people in charge are not qualified to handle the criminal cases they preside over.

Schwartz believes that students who are accused of criminal behavior should not be tried in a campus court.

"People are aghast when they find out that students are acting as judges and juries in criminal cases," said Schwartz, the *Tar Heel's* professional business manager.

But members of the school's Honor Court say they are well prepared.

"We go through a lot to get on the court," said David Huneycutt, a 22-year-old chemistry and political science major who serves as student attorney general for the Chapel Hill judiciary. "We are heavily screened and we must be confirmed by the Student Congress.

"I understand why it is so frustrating to people who don't know how we work. If people knew the truth, they wouldn't worry as much. It is so much better than what they imagine."

Tar Heel editor Jeanne Furgate says students should be given an opportunity to judge the process for themselves.

"The campus has a right to know what is going on in these hearings," Furgate insisted. "There are too many things that can happen behind closed doors. They could involve the quarterback of the football team or even the editor of a student newspaper.

"When parents send their children to a school, they would want, I think, for them to participate in a community that holds up the ideals of free speech in a democracy."

Susanna Matsen, a 21-year-old biochemistry and comparative literature major and chairwoman of the Honor Court judges, believes that close-knit campuses need student Honor Courts.

"A university is distinct from a town or a community," Matsen said. "The Honor Court is about integrity. It is about fostering an intellectual climate."

 Article Review Form at end of book.

WiseGuide Wrap-Up

- Although the juvenile crime problem must be addressed, adult courts should not be involved in this process.

- The U.S. Supreme Court hears only a handful of cases, since justices are free to choose which cases they wish to review.

- College newspapers are attempting to open up campus-run courts in order to gain access to information regarding campus crimes.

R.E.A.L. Sites

This list provides a print preview of typical **coursewise** R.E.A.L. sites. (There are over 100 such sites at the **courselinks**™ site.) The danger in printing URLs is that web sites can change overnight. As we went to press, these sites were functional using the URLs provided. If you come across one that isn't, please let us know via email to: webmaster@coursewise.com. Use your Passport to access the most current list of R.E.A.L. sites at the **courselinks**™ site.

Site name: National Criminal Justice Reference Service

URL: http://www.ncjrs.org/courhome.htm

Why is it R.E.A.L.? On this site, you will be able to find court-related documents, World Wide Web sites, and listservs. Topics include, but are not limited to, the feasibility of drug night courts, court security and transportation of prisoners, the drug court movement, and intermediate sanctions in sentencing guidelines.

Try this: Analyze recent juvenile court statistics. Outline the key legislative issues in mandatory sentencing.

Key topics: Alternative sanctions in Germany, restorative justice, civil jury cases, comparison of cases processing statistics, court appointed special advocates, court security, transportation of prisoners

Site name: FindLaw

URL: http://www.findlaw.com/casecode/supreme.html

Why is it R.E.A.L.? This site allows you to search for Supreme Court opinions by volume, year, party name, or citation. It also offers Supreme Court resources, including the Court's calendar, court rules, court news, and the justices' biographical information.

Try this: Search for a historical case and report the decision and highlights of the case to your class.

Key topics: U.S. Supreme Court opinions, Supreme Court news, Supreme Court resources

Site name: Legal Information Institute

URL: http://supct.law.cornell.edu/supct/

Why is it R.E.A.L.? This site contains all opinions of the United States Supreme Court since 1980. In addition, on this site, you can search for historic Court decisions, background of current cases being heard by the Court, and the schedule of oral arguments.

Try this: Are there any common characteristics found in the background of Supreme Court justices?

Key topics: opinions of the Court (since May, 1990), current Court calendar, schedule of oral arguments, background on current cases, gallery of current and past justices, glossary of terms

section 3

Learning Objectives

After studying this section, you will know

- the history of the federal parole system from 1910 to 1997.

- the ideological and political context of recent sentencing reforms, such as "three strikes and you're out."

- that a survey conducted by the National Institute of Justice revealed that there is no consensus on the definition of a supermax prison.

- that public support for the death penalty vanishes when an alternative is the option of life in prison without the possibility of parole coupled with a requirement of work and restitution.

- restorative justice seeks to heal the injuries that result from crime through the participation of correctional institutions, victims, offenders, and communities.

- that education in law is becoming popular among juvenile offenders and juvenile justice staff.

- that, after years of debate, the American Correctional Association's Community Corrections Committee has finally agreed to define *community corrections*.

- that convicted sex offenders are less likely than other convicts to be placed in community release programs, according to a study conducted by the Bureau of Justice Statistics (BJS).

- the experiences of a probation professional.

Corrections

 **WiseGuide Intro**

Corrections is the component of the criminal justice system concerned with the execution of the sentences issued by the courts. Contrary to popular belief, not all of these sentences include incarceration. Although most of us think of prisons when we talk about corrections, this component of the system encompasses a great deal more. In fact, corrections involves the supervision of not only offenders who are held inside prisons but also of those sentenced to a form of punishment outside correctional facilities. Statistics show that the most frequently used form of punishment is probation. Moreover, it is important to note that individuals sentenced to probation or another form of punishment, aside from imprisonment, are still under the supervision of correctional personnel. Thus, it is not hard to believe that corrections oversees a large number of individuals and is responsible for the operation of numerous programs.

The incarceration trends in the United States have increased to such levels that prisons are not being built fast enough. States often report their prison populations to be over their capacity levels. Furthermore, inmates are often transported from one jurisdiction to another in order to help relieve overcrowded prisons. Many critics argue that the overcrowding of prisons is the direct result of a growing movement to incarcerate offenders for their wrongdoings, even if these are not violent in nature. The recent sentencing trends show that a great percentage of the inmate population is presently incarcerated as a result of convictions of drug-related charges. This, coupled with the fact that the baby boom population is aging, results in a growing elder inmate population in prison. This means that a greater portion of the money allocated from taxpayers will be directed not only to pay for incarceration costs but also for expensive medical expenses likely to be incurred by older inmates. What is the remedy for this? No one really knows. All we know for certain is that the problem is growing and that the only solutions proposed by politicians are quick fixes involving the construction of more correctional facilities and the incarceration of more people.

In recent years, the correctional field has grown to such an extent that the emergence of private correctional facilities has taken place. These facilities are privately owned and operated, and they contract their services to the government in order to assist in the relief of overcrowded prisons. In recent years, the main problem associated with these facilities has been that they do not have the same standards as those owned and operated by the government. In some cases, states do not have an option but to send their inmates to these private facilities as they struggle to keep their prisons from being severely overcrowded with inmates.

When considering the power and important role of corrections in our system of justice, we must be reminded of the fact that the department of corrections is also responsible for the execution of offenders. Needless to say, the responsibility this burden carries is immense and perhaps unmeasurable. At the time of an execution, the system is materialized in the form of a needle, an electric shock, or perhaps a rope. Regardless of the form of execution, the mission remains to carry out the mandate specified by the court. In fact, many correctional officers answer to inmates, who constantly claim their innocence, that they are not judges or police officers but simply individuals who are instructed to make certain that the sentence is carried out completely, regardless of the status of the offender or the circumstances surrounding the offense. In this section, you will learn about various important issues surrounding the individuals that work for the correctional system, as well as the inmate population. It is my hope that the issues raised by the articles selected for this section will provide you with a deeper understanding of some of the complexities of the correctional field.

Questions

Reading 14. Describe the major historical developments of the federal parole system from 1910 to 1972.

Reading 15. Describe the major historical developments of the federal parole system from 1973 to 1997.

Reading 16. What are the consequences associated with the implementation of the "get-tough" sentences?

Reading 17. Provide a current overview of supermax prisons.

Reading 18. Why do legislators misread the opinions of their constituents regarding capital punishment?

Reading 19. What is the role of restorative justice in the criminal justice system?

Reading 20. Critique the implementation and role of law-related education (LRE) programs.

Reading 21. Explain some of the elements taken into consideration before community corrections was defined.

Reading 22. Describe the results of the Bureau of Justice Statistics (BJS) study regarding convicted sex offenders.

Reading 23. How does technology influence probation?

Describe the major historical developments of the federal parole system from 1910 to 1972.

History of the Federal Parole System

Part 1 (1910–1972)

Peter B. Hoffman, Ph.D.

Staff Director (Retired), United States Parole Commission

Introduction

As George Santayana (1863–1952) observed, "[t]hose who do not remember the past are condemned to repeat it." Stated differently, a solid grounding in history can be extremely useful to the legislator, administrator, or practitioner who wishes to improve a product or process by changing it, particularly if substantial change is involved. The field of corrections does not appear to be exempt from this principle. There have been substantial changes in the federal sentencing structure in recent years, including the abolition of parole release and the phasing down of the U.S. Parole Commission, the creation of the U.S. Sentencing Commission and the implementation of sentencing guidelines, a substantial reduction in authorized goodtime credits, and the reappearance of long, mandatory minimum sentences.

Given the recent passage of the Parole Commission Phaseout Act of 1996, it appears a particularly appropriate time to review the history of the federal parole system, as well as related sentencing and good-time provisions.

Historical Overview

Parole of federal prisoners began after enactment of legislation of June 25, 1910. There were three federal penitentiaries, and parole was granted by a board at each institution. The membership of each parole board consisted of the warden of the institution, the physician of the institution, and the Superintendent of Prisons of the Department of Justice in Washington, DC.

By legislation of May 13, 1930, a single Board of Parole in Washington, DC, was established. This board consisted of three members, serving full-time, appointed by the Attorney General. The Bureau of Prisons performed the administrative functions of the board. In August 1945, the Attorney General ordered that the

board report directly to him for administrative purposes. In August 1948, due to a postwar increase in prison population, the Attorney General appointed two additional members, increasing the Board of Parole to five members.

By legislation of September 30, 1950, the board was increased to eight members appointed by the President, with the advice and consent of the Senate, for 6-year, staggered terms. The board was placed in the Department of Justice for administrative purposes. Three of the eight members were designated by the Attorney General to serve as a Youth Corrections Division pursuant to the Youth Corrections Act.

In October 1972, the Board of Parole began a pilot reorganization project that eventually included the establishment of five regions, creation of explicit guidelines for parole release decision-making, provision of written reasons for parole decisions, and an administrative appeal process. By October 1974, five regions were operational with one member and a corps of hearing examiners

Reprinted with permission from *Federal Probation*, Sept. 1997, pp. 23–31.

assigned to each region. The chairman and two members remained in Washington, DC, at the headquarters office.

In May 1976, the Parole Commission and Reorganization Act became effective. This act retitled the Board of Parole as the United States Parole Commission and established it as an independent agency within the Department of Justice. The act provided for nine commissioners appointed by the President, with the advice and consent of the Senate, for 6-year terms. These included a chairman, five regional commissioners, and a three-member National Appeals Board. In addition, the act incorporated the major features of the Board of Parole's pilot project: a mandate for explicit guidelines for parole decisionmaking, written reasons for parole denial, a regionalized structure, and an administrative appeal process. The Youth Corrections Division of the Board of Parole was eliminated and its duties absorbed by the Commission.

The Comprehensive Crime Control Act of 1984 created a United States Sentencing Commission to establish sentencing guidelines for the federal courts. The decision to establish sentencing guidelines was based in substantial part on the success of the U.S. Parole Commission in developing and implementing its parole guidelines. On April 13, 1987, the U.S. Sentencing Commission submitted to Congress its initial set of sentencing guidelines, which took effect on November 1, 1987. Defendants sentenced for offenses committed on or after November 1, 1987, serve determinate terms under the sentencing guidelines and are not eligible for parole consideration. Post-release supervision, termed "supervised release," is provided as a separate part of the sentence under the jurisdiction of the court. The United States Parole Commission retains jurisdiction over defendants who committed their offenses before November 1, 1987.

The Comprehensive Crime Control Act of 1984 also provided for the abolition of the Parole Commission on November 1, 1992 (5 years after the sentencing guidelines took effect). This phase out, however, did not adequately provide for persons sentenced under the law in effect before November 1, 1987, who had not yet completed their sentences. Elimination of, or reduction in, parole eligibility for such cases would raise a serious *ex post facto* issue. To address this problem, the Judicial Improvements Act of 1990 extended the life of the Parole Commission until November 1, 1997.

The Parole Commission Phaseout Act of 1996 again extended the life of the Parole Commission for the same reason. This act authorizes the continuation of the Parole Commission until November 1, 2002. In addition, it provides for a reduction in the number of Parole Commissioners and requires the Attorney General to report to the Congress annually, beginning in 1998, on whether it is more cost effective for the Parole Commission to continue as a separate agency or whether its remaining functions should be transferred elsewhere.

Chronological History

Set forth below is a chronological history of the federal parole system. Significant events are shown corresponding to the date above each entry. At the end of the entry, an abbreviation for the source material used is shown in brackets; the full citation is given in the references at the end of the article. The few entries without a bracketed citation are based either on the source described in the entry itself or on the personal knowledge of the author.

The precursors of parole in the federal system were (1) the exercise of the Presidential power to commute sentences and (2) the reduction in the term of imprisonment by institutional officials for good conduct. In each case, the prisoner was released from imprisonment before the expiration of the sentence set by the court.

1867

The first statute providing for the reduction of sentences of federal prisoners because of good conduct was enacted. This statute authorized a deduction of 1 month in each year from the term of sentence of federal prisoners confined in state jails or penitentiaries, upon the certificate of the warden or keeper with the approval of the Secretary of the Interior. [AGSRP]

1870

The Department of Justice was created. [AGSRP]

The good-time statute was amended to provide that the good time specified in the act of 1867 applied only to institutions in which no other good-time credits were allowed. In all other cases, the deductions applicable to state prisoners were to apply. [AGSRP]

1872

The duties of the Secretary of the Interior relating to the imprisonment and discharge of federal prisoners were transferred to the Department of Justice. [AGSRP]

1875

The schedule of credits was changed so that federal prisoners in any state or territorial institution in which no system of good-time credits existed might earn a credit of 5 days for each month in which no charge of misconduct was sustained. [AGSRP]

1891

As part of legislation providing for the establishment of federal prisons, the Attorney General was given authority for the reduction of sentences for good behavior, but not to exceed 2 months for the first or any succeeding year of imprisonment. [AGSRP]

1902

A general revision of the good-time credit statute was made, placing all federal prisoners, wherever confined, on an equal basis. The schedule of good-time credits was made more liberal and graduated so as to increase with the length of sentence. The credits allowed per month follow: 5 days upon a sentence of not less than 6 months or more than 1 year; 6 days upon a sentence of more than 1 year and less than 3 years; 7 days on a sentence of at least 3 years but less than 5 years; 8 days on a sentence of at least 5 years but less than 10 years; and 10 days on a sentence of 10 years or more. In addition, a prisoner in a camp or employed in prison industry could earn an additional 3 days per month in the first year and 5 days per month in each succeeding year. [AGSRP]

Good-time credits are primarily under the control of the officials of the institution at which the prisoner is confined. Forfeitures for breach of institutional rules are determined by the warden after the prisoner has been given a hearing before a disciplinary board composed of three members of the prison staff with the deputy warden or disciplinary officer acting as chairman. The prisoner has the privilege of replying and may choose some member of the staff to represent him as counsel. This board thoroughly investigates the alleged misconduct, hears the prisoner and any witnesses he may wish to present, and the members individually recommend to the warden the extent of discipline. The Bureau of Prisons issues general policies concerning the administration of good-time deductions. [AGSRP]

The Attorney General is granted authority to restore credits lost because of misconduct of prisoners in any United States penitentiary upon recommendation and evidence submitted to him by the warden in charge. As to prisoners in state or territorial institutions, restorations are governed by the rules of the particular institution. [AGSRP]

There was no post-release supervision for persons released by good time. [HUSBP]

1910

The federal parole system was created with the passage of an act authorizing the parole of prisoners sentenced to terms of 1 year or more. Any such prisoners were made eligible for parole upon the expiration of one-third of their sentence. The power to grant and revoke parole was placed in the hands of the respective boards of parole established at the several penitentiaries and prisons. The board of parole at each penitentiary was composed of the superintendent of prisons in the Department of Justice and the warden and physician of the particular penitentiary. The board of parole at any federal prison other than a penitentiary was composed of the superintendent of prisons and such officers of the particular prison as the Attorney General designated. [AGSRP]

A parole officer was provided for each penitentiary to supervise parolees and to perform such other duties as the board of parole might direct. It was provided that supervision of parolees might also be devolved upon the United States marshals. [AGSRP]

The parole officer at each penitentiary served mainly as a clearing house for the volunteers and United States marshals who had personal contact with the parolees. [ARUSBP (1970–72)]

The Act of 1910 also provided that whenever any person has been convicted of any offense against the United States and sentenced and confined in any state reformatory or institution, that person becomes subject to the parole laws applicable to the inmates of such institution. [AGSRP]

The Act of 1910 further provided that no parole from either a state or federal institution became effective until approved by the Attorney General. [AGSRP]

Upon violation of parole, the warden or any member of the institutional board of parole was empowered to issue a warrant for the parolee's retaking. A revocation hearing was conducted by the board of parole at the institution soon after the parolee's return. Each institution employed a parole officer (at a salary not to exceed $1,500) to assist parole applicants in obtaining employment and supervise parolees after release. U.S. marshals were used as parole supervisors when needed. A system of monthly reports by parolees and their "first friends" was initiated. [HUSBP]

1911

The first Rules of the Board of Parole were promulgated. (HUSBP]

1913

The federal parole statute was amended so as to make prisoners serving a life term eligible for parole after the service of 15 years. [AGSRP]

No further amendments were made to the parole law until 1930. [AGSRP]

1930

The federal parole system was materially altered by legislation in 1930. In lieu of the several institutional parole boards, there was created a single parole board in the Department of Justice to be composed of three members appointed by the Attorney General. This board (the United States Board of Parole) was given power to grant parole without any requirement of approval by the Attorney General. Salaries for the three parole board members in 1930 were $7,500 per year each. [AGSRP]

Appointments to the parole board by the Attorney General were for an indefinite period. [HUSBP]

Eligibility for parole of persons sentenced to federal institutions with sentences of more than 1 year was set at one-third of the maximum sentence or 15 years in the case of a life sentence: "Every prisoner who has been or may hereafter be convicted of any offense against the United States and is confined in any United States penitentiary or prison, for a definite term or terms of over 1 year, or for the term of his natural life, whose record of conduct shows that he has observed the rules of such institution, and

who, if sentenced for a definite term, has served one-third of the total of the term or terms for which he was sentenced, or, if sentenced for the term of his natural life has served not less than 15 years, may be released on parole" if it appears to the Board of Parole "that such applicant will live and remain at liberty without violating the laws, and if in the opinion of the board such release is not incompatible with the welfare of society." [AGSRP]

A federal offender serving a sentence in a state institution was eligible for parole under the same terms and conditions and by the same authority as a prisoner committed to that institution by a state court, but all such paroles were subject to approval by the United States Board of Parole. Supervision within the state was provided by state authorities. If the parolee was permitted to return to his home outside that state, his supervision was devolved upon the United States marshal in the district in which the parolee resided. [AGSRP]

The legislation also provided for the transfer of the supervision of federal parolees to the probation officers that supervised probationers for the federal courts by providing that federal probation officers shall perform such duties with respect to persons on parole as the Attorney General shall request. The position of federal probation officer had been established by legislation in 1925 that for the first time authorized courts to impose probation in federal cases. As originally enacted, the probation statute required appointments for probation officers to be made by the judge of the particular district from the civil service register, but in 1930 the requirement for use of the civil service register was re-

moved. The Bureau of Prisons (which had general oversight responsibility for the probation system) promulgated general qualifications that appointees should possess. In brief, these provided that persons selected should have physical vigor and mental adaptability, at least a high school education plus 1 year in college or a year's experience in organized probation work, and thorough training in the technique of social investigation. General oversight of supervision activities with respect to persons on parole was provided by the parole executive whose office was attached to the Board of Parole in Washington, DC. [AGSRP]

Although the Federal Probation Act was passed in 1925, the first congressional appropriation to implement that act was in 1927, and five officers were appointed that year. Two more were appointed in 1928, including Richard A. Chappell, who was later to serve on the Board of Parole. [HUSBP]

Preparation for parole was the responsibility of institutional parole officers, who, as staff members in the several institutions, participated in classification procedures, developed social histories, prepared and assembled official reports, and were responsible for social casework involving the prisoner and the prisoner's family in the community. Under the original parole act, an institutional parole officer was appointed by the parole board at each institution. In 1930, this authority was transferred to the United States Board of Parole but was actually exercised by the Bureau of Prisons, subject to the satisfaction of the Board of Parole. In 1930, the salary of an institutional parole officer was set at $2,000 to $2,600 per year. [AGSRP]

The first offices of the Board of Parole were located in Room 201 of the Tower Building in Washington, DC. The first three parole board members entered on duty on June 13, 1930. An executive secretary was employed to act as the administrative officer of the board. [HUSBP]

1931

In the board's first year of operation, the board's three members traveled as a group to hold hearings in institutions. After a short experimental period in which they discovered that two-thirds of their time was spent in travel status, they began traveling singly to conduct hearings with the vote taken later at headquarters in Washington, DC. When traveling as a group, the board heard an average of 40 cases per day and made on-the-spot decisions about parole. The board also made decisions on federal prisoners serving sentences in state institutions. In these cases, a local board made recommendations to the Board of Parole. [HUSBP]

During the first year of operation, the board heard a large number of offenders who had violated the National Prohibition Act. In the year or two after the board was created, it paroled a large percentage of this type of law violator. [HUSBP]

Due to the volume of work, three secretaries were assigned to the parole board in addition to the administrative clerk. Two reporters were also employed to transcribe the board's hearings. [HUSBP]

Legislation was enacted providing for parole for the purposes of deportation. During this year, 133 such paroles were granted. [HUSBP]

1932

Two significant amendments were made to the parole law. First, it was provided that a parolee shall continue on parole until the expiration of the maximum terms specified in his sentence without deduction for such allowance for good conduct. Previously, in the case of a person who was released on parole, good conduct deductions earned in prison operated to shorten the period of parole. Second, it was provided that any person to whom parole is not granted, but who is released before the expiration of the maximum term because of good-conduct deductions, shall upon release be treated as if released on parole and shall be subject to all provisions of law relating to the parole of United States prisoners until the maximum term or terms specified in his sentence. [AGSRP]

Legislation creating a separate parole board for the District of Columbia removed from the federal parole board jurisdiction over prisoners confined in institutions of the District of Columbia. [HUSBP]

The National Prohibition Act was repealed, and there was a dramatic reduction in the number of this type of law violator in federal prisons. The proportion of parole grants to denial also declined. [HUSBP]

1936

Reports written during this year show that there was an emphasis by the board to ensure that parolees were returned to their bona fide residences at the time of their release. The board attempted to "diminish the assaults and larcenies committed against prisoners en route to their homes" by mailing most of the prisoners' money to them at their city of residence. [HUSBP]

1937

Myrl Alexander became the parole executive. Two years later he left the board and returned to his administrative duties at the Bureau of Prisons. Mr. Alexander later became the third director of the Bureau of Prisons. [HUSBP]

1938

The Federal Juvenile Delinquency Act was approved on June 16, 1938. This act provided that juveniles could be paroled by the Board of Parole at any time after commitment (i.e., that there was no minimum term of imprisonment required before the juvenile was eligible for parole consideration). [HUSBP]

1939

The board appointed its first hearing examiner on May 21, 1939. Three were eventually appointed. Initially, they held hearings in cases of prisoners serving terms of 1 year and 1 day. [HUSBP]

Attorney General Murphy called a National Parole Conference, which was held in Washington, DC. The conference followed a long-term fact-finding project financed largely by Works Project Administration (WPA) funds. The project was directed by Wayne L. Morse, who later became a U.S. senator, and resulted in the five-volume *Attorney General's Survey of Release Procedures*. As a result of this conference, "A Declaration of the Principles of Parole" was adopted. The conference proceedings were published as *Proceedings—National Parole Conference, Washington, DC, April 17–18, 1939.* [HUSBP]

In contrast to the liberal trend of granting reparole, which was extended by the board 5 or 6 years before, the board in 1939 granted no reparoles at all and rereleased only five conditional releasees. [HUSBP]

Parole Procedures (circa 1939)

Application for Parole. A short while before a federal prisoner becomes eligible for parole, he is furnished with an application form. This is a very brief form on which the applicant is to enter certain information about himself, his plans, the nature of his crime, his prospective employer, and the person he desires as his parole advisor. If a prisoner does not desire to apply for parole, he is directed to sign a waiver of his right to apply for parole on a form that will be furnished to him. [AGSRP]

Information About the Prisoner. When a federal offender is committed to a penitentiary or other institution, the judge and district attorney of the committing court file reports and recommendations concerning him. In some instances, a presentence report is made by a probation officer, and in such cases the probation officer's report is also forwarded to the institution to which the offender is committed. Each prisoner is studied closely in connection with the institutional classification procedure. Reports are filed concerning his progress by the various institutional officers from time to time. Immediately after his admission to the institution, the parole officers begin to study the family and the social and economic conditions with which he will be faced when he is released on parole. An

attempt is made to effect desirable community and home adjustments and to prepare the community to which the offender will go for his reception. [AGSRP]

Hearings. Parole hearings are held at each of the federal penal and reformatory institutions four times each year, or once every 3 months. The hearings are usually conducted by one member of the board. They are ordinarily attended only by the member, the institutional parole officer, the applicant, and a stenographic assistant. The warden and other institutional officers ordinarily do not attend the hearings. No attorney, relative, or other person may appear for or against the applicant. However, such persons may write to or interview members of the board. [AGSRP]

Disposition. After the return to Washington of the board member who held the hearing, a final determination is made by the whole board. [AGSRP]

Conditions of Parole. Before an offender is released on parole, he must agree to the conditions of his parole, and an adviser is secured for him. An effort is made to arrange suitable employment for him. Also upon release he is given the usual gratuities that are allowed to federal offenders upon their discharge from an institution. [AGSRP]

Supervision. Each person released on parole is required to file with the parole executive an arrival report and subsequent written reports at intervals of not more than 1 month. In some cases the parolee is required to report every few days while in other cases the parolee is required to report monthly. Each report must be countersigned by the parolee's adviser. Each parolee is under the supervision of a probation officer.

In some cases, the officer makes frequent visits to the parolee. In other cases, where the parolee has a strong adviser and his case is not a hazardous one, the probation officers may visit him infrequently. [AGSRP]

Each parolee has an adviser. In many cases, the person chosen is the person suggested by the parolee himself. In other cases, the parole executive finds it necessary to select some other person. In every case, an attempt is made to secure as adviser the person in the community in which the parolee will live who will be most able to direct him toward rehabilitation through the normal community agencies of social control. [AGSRP]

Violations of Parole. Sole authority to issue a warrant for the arrest of a parole violator rests with the Board of Parole or any member thereof. Such a warrant may be issued at any time before the expiration of the sentence if the board or any member thereof has reliable information that the offender has violated his parole. The violation of parole interrupts the running of the sentence in the manner of an escape. The warrant may be executed by any officer of the prison from which the parolee was released or by any federal officer authorized to serve criminal process within the United States. Upon return to a federal institution, the violator is given an opportunity to appear before the board at its next meeting. The board may then or at any time in its discretion revoke the order and terminate such parole or modify the terms and conditions thereof. When parole is revoked, the parolee shall serve the remainder of the sentence originally imposed, and the time that the prisoner was out on parole shall not be taken into account to diminish the time for which he was sentenced. [AGSRP]

A federal parole violator may be reparoled at any time by the Board of Parole. [AGSRP]

Final Discharge. Upon the expiration of the parolee's sentence, the parole executive sends him a letter stating that he has apparently completed his parole period satisfactorily. No formal certificate of discharge is issued to him. [AGSRP]

1940

On July 1, 1940, the Federal Probation Service was transferred from the Bureau of Prisons to the Administrative Office of the United States Courts. Responsibilities of probation officers with respect to parolees continued as before. [HUSBP]

During the 10 years the Probation System was under the supervision of the Bureau of Prisons, it expanded from one with eight officers in eight judicial districts to a nationwide program employing 238 officers in 83 U.S. courts [FP(4/2), statement by James V. Bennett, Director, U.S. Bureau of Prisons].

1941

In *The Pardoning Power of the President,* W. H. Humbert reported that "parole authorities have handled a considerable number of federal offenders since 1910. Though release on parole does not banish prospects for a pardon, the conclusion is inescapable that such release tends to keep down the number of requests."

1942

World War II radically changed the character of the federal prison population. Substantial numbers of selective service violators and conscientious objectors were incarcerated. In 1942, the President issued Executive Order 8641, making it possible for the Attorney General to grant special paroles to prisoners who might be useful in the war effort. Extensive use was made of this authority, with the parole board playing an unofficial role for the Attorney General. [HUSBP]

1943

Congress conducted hearings on legislation providing for a broader form of federal indeterminate sentence. The proposed legislation, entitled the "Federal Corrections Act," would have established a 10-member parole board with an adult division, a youth division, and a policy division. No legislation was enacted. [HUSBP]

1945

On August 28, 1945, the Attorney General ordered the parole board to report directly to him for administrative purposes. Staff formerly employed by the Bureau of Prisons and assigned to the board were transferred officially to the board on February 15, 1946. [HUSBP]

During the year, the character of the federal prison population changed in that the number of persons who had been court-martialed by military authorities and transferred to federal prisons increased. These offenders generally had longer sentences than those imposed by civilian courts. [HUSBP]

1946

With the end of gas rationing, there was a dramatic use of automobiles over the nation. Military prisoners decreased, and the number of violators of the National Motor Vehicle Theft Act rose sharply. [HUSBP]

1948

The Board of Parole was increased from three to five members by legislation enacted June 25, 1948. This increase was needed primarily because of an increase in prison population. Before the increase in the size of the board, the two examiners on staff conducted approximately one-third of the hearings. [HUSBP]

1950

On September 30, 1950, the Youth Corrections Act was passed by Congress. Under this legislation, federal offenders less than 22 years of age at the time of conviction could be sentenced to indeterminate sentences with no minimum period of parole ineligibility. The maximum period of imprisonment was fixed by statute at 6 years, but longer maximum terms were permitted in the case of very serious offenses. This act contained three other significant features. First, it stated that all youth offenders must be initially released on supervision at least 2 years before the expiration of the maximum sentence. Thus, each offender would be initially released with a period of supervision of at least 2 years. Second, it authorized a court to commit an offender for a period of observation and study before sentencing. Third, it provided that the parole board could grant an early discharge from parole supervision, an action that "set the conviction aside" and granted relief from various legal disabilities imposed by the conviction. The Youth Corrections Act was to become effective only upon the certification of the Attorney General that facilities to house such offenders were available. [HUSBP]

The Youth Corrections Act also changed the structure of the parole board. First, it created a three-member Youth Division within the parole board. Second, it increased the number of parole board members from five to eight. Third, it provided that all parole board members would be appointed by the President, with the advice and consent of the Senate, for 6-year, staggered terms. [HUSBP]

The Youth Corrections Act also provided for an Advisory Corrections Council to be composed of federal judges and federal correctional officials to study and advise on correctional practices. [HUSBP]

1950

Until this year, secretaries traveled with the board members to report institutional hearings. After 6 months of experimentation with recording devices, the board adopted a system of hiring local shorthand reporters on a contract basis. [HUSBP]

1951

Until 1951, prisoners released by expiration of sentence less good time were under supervision until the expiration of their maximum sentence. Legislation approved June 29, 1951, provided that such prisoners were to be released from supervision 180 days before the expiration of the maximum sentence. With the implementation of this act, the number of mandatory releasees under supervision dropped sharply. In general, prisoners with sentences of 18 months or less who were released by expiration of sentence

less good time would no longer be released to supervision. [HUSBP]

Legislation approved July 31, 1951, made two changes in parole eligibility. Up to this time, adult prisoners serving sentences of more than 1 year were eligible for parole after service of one-third of their sentences, except for prisoners serving life sentences who were eligible after the service of 15 years. Under the revised legislation, adult prisoners serving sentences of 180 days to 1 year were also eligible for parole after service of one-third of their sentences. In addition, prisoners serving terms of more than 45 years were eligible for parole after 15 years in the same manner as prisoners serving life sentences. [HUSBP]

1953

The first Presidential appointments were made to the parole board in 1953. [HUSBP]

Scovel Richardson became the first African American appointed to the parole board. [HUSBP]

By order of the Attorney General dated October 15, 1953, juveniles committed by the District of Columbia Juvenile Court to the National Training School for Boys came under the parole jurisdiction of the federal parole board. Before this time, the District of Columbia Visiting Committee had acted as the paroling authority for such juveniles. [HUSBP]

The board hired its first staff director. [HUSBP]

1954

On January 15, 1954, the Youth Corrections Act was made available to the federal courts east of the Mississippi River. [HUSBP]

1955

During 1955, the parole board began paroling prisoners to outstanding local detainers if they were otherwise considered to be suitable for parole. Previously, an outstanding detainer had acted as a bar to parole. [HUSBP]

1956

The Attorney General called the second National Conference on Parole, which was held in Washington, DC, on April 9–11, 1956. The Conference was sponsored by the federal parole board and the National Probation and Parole Association. Approximately 500 delegates attended. Out of this conference came *Parole in Principle and Practice: A Manual and Report*. One of the recommendations of this conference was that release from prison by expiration of sentence less good time be termed "mandatory release" rather than "conditional release." The U.S. Board of Parole implemented this recommendation. [HUSBP]

Congress enacted the Uniform Narcotic Control Act. This act provided for mandatory minimum terms of imprisonment for certain drug offenders. In addition, such offenders were made ineligible for parole consideration. [HUSBP]

On October 4, 1956, the Youth Corrections Act was made available to the federal courts west of the Mississippi River. [HUSBP]

1958

On August 25, 1958, Congress approved legislation that allowed courts to impose an adult sentence on which the prisoner would be eligible for parole consideration after serving less than one-third of the maximum sentence. That is, in addition to the traditional sentencing procedure under which the prisoner had to serve one-third of the maximum sentence before being eligible for parole, the court could now impose (1) a sentence with a period of parole ineligibility that was less than one-third of the maximum sentence or (2) a sentence with no period of parole ineligibility. In addition, this legislation authorized a court to commit an adult offender for a period of observation and study before sentencing, a provision that earlier had been available only for youthful offenders. Furthermore, this legislation provided for the judicial sentencing institutes for federal judges. Finally, this legislation authorized the parole board to terminate releasees from active supervision before the expiration of their maximum sentences. [HUSBP]

The legislative history of the 1958 act made clear that a key purpose was to reduce unwarranted sentencing disparity (1) by giving the parole board more authority as to the actual time to be served by the offender before release and (2) by the authorization of judicial sentencing institutes.

In addition, legislation passed in 1958 authorized the courts to use the provisions of the Youth Corrections Act in certain cases for persons who were less than 26 years of age at the time of conviction. [HUSBP]

1959

The first federal judicial sentencing institute was held at Boulder, Colorado. A primary topic was the issue of unwarranted sentencing disparity. [HUSBP]

Congress passed the Labor-Management Reporting and Disclosure Act. This legislation barred certain individuals with criminal records from serving in certain labor or labor-management positions. The federal parole board was given the authority to conduct a hearing for any person who applied for relief from the disabilities imposed by this legislation and to grant exemptions from these disabilities in deserving cases. [HUSBP]

The *Annual Report of the U.S. Board of Parole* describes the second phase of a research study on offenders sentenced under the Youth Corrections Act (pertaining to prison programming). [ARUSBP (1959)]

The *Annual Report of the U.S. Board of Parole* also notes that the parole board's evaluation of recidivism statistics indicates that (1) maturation appears to be a significant factor in rehabilitation in that adult offenders have lower recidivism rates than youth offenders, and (2) most parole violations occur within the first or second year after parole, and the number of warrants issued in the fifth year after parole is "practically nonexistent." [ARUSBP (1959)]

1961

In accordance with an opinion handed down by the Court of Appeals for the District of Columbia, the parole board adopted procedures allowing alleged parole/mandatory release violators to have an attorney and/or voluntary witnesses present at a revocation hearing conducted upon return to a federal institution. [HUSBP]

1962

The parole board began making use of a new program initiated by the Bureau of Prisons, involving the establishment of pre-release guidance centers in the community to which the prisoner was to be released. Centers were first opened in New York City, Chicago, and Los Angeles. The parole board could parole an individual with the understanding that the individual would reside in a pre-release center from 2 to 4 months before parole. Subsequently, additional pre-release centers were opened in other cities. Eventually, state and privately operated centers were used on a contract basis. [HUSBP]

1963

In accordance with an opinion handed down by the Court of Appeals for the District of Columbia, the parole board adopted procedures providing for preliminary interviews for alleged parole/mandatory violators in the community in which the alleged violation occurred. In addition, "local" revocation hearings, revocation hearings in the community in which the alleged violation occurred, were authorized to facilitate the appearance of voluntary witnesses. [HUSBP]

1966

The board cooperated with the Bureau of Prisons in the Bureau's development of work-release programs. Selected prisoners were permitted to leave the institution or a pre-release center to work in private industry or, in some cases, to attend a trade school or college. Such placements generally were made within 6 months of a projected release date. [HUSBP]

1967

Congress passed the Narcotic Addict Rehabilitation Act, which had provisions for civil commitment of narcotic addicts as well as special provisions for those convicted of criminal offenses. Under this act, the maximum period of imprisonment on a criminal commitment was fixed by the court with parole eligibility after 6 months in treatment. A certificate of release readiness from the Surgeon General was a prerequisite for parole. [HUSBP]

Congress also passed legislation transferring responsibility for DC youth offenders confined in the DC Youth Center from the federal parole board to the District of Columbia government. Supervision of such cases also was transferred from U.S. probation officers to the District of Columbia government. [HUSBP]

1968

The parole board adopted a procedure for a "dispositional review" where a parolee or mandatory releasee was serving a subsequent sentence and a violator warrant was lodged as a detainer. Such a review could include a hearing at the place of confinement if the parole board determined such a hearing was indicated. [HUSBP]

The National Training School for Boys was closed, and juveniles committed by the District of Columbia Juvenile Court were placed in DC institutions. Accordingly, the federal parole board had no further jurisdiction over DC juvenile offenders. [HUSBP]

1969

The parole board requested and received a grant from the Law Enforcement Assistance Administration for a large-scale, 3-year study of parole decision-making. This study, under the co-directorship of Don M. Gottfredson, director of the National Council on Crime and

Delinquency Research Center, and Leslie T. Wilkins, a professor at the School of Criminal Justice, State University of New York at Albany, led to a major revision in parole board practice. [HUSBP]

1970

The parole board hired its first legal counsel. [HUSBP]

1971

The parole board increased its complement of hearing examiners to eight. A schedule was adopted under which parole board members conducted about one-third of the hearings and hearing examiners conducted about two-thirds of the hearings. This allowed parole board members more time for voting on cases. In general, decisions were made by a concurrence of two parole board members. If the hearing was conducted by a parole board member, the parole board member hearing the case cast the first vote. The case file was then circulated among other parole board members at the parole board's office in Washington, DC, until a concurrence of two votes was obtained. If the hearing was conducted by a hearing examiner, the examiner made a recommendation but did not vote. The case file was then circulated among the parole board members at the parole board's office in Washington, DC, until a concurrence of two votes was obtained. [HUSBP]

Congress passed legislation authorizing the parole board to impose a special condition that a parolee or mandatory releasee reside in and/or participate in a program of a community treatment center (formerly called a pre-release guidance center) as a special condition of parole. This special condition could be used,

in some cases, as an alternative to parole revocation. [HUSBP]

Congress amended the Criminal Justice Act to provide for court-appointed counsel for alleged parole and mandatory release violators who could not afford to hire their own attorney. [HUSBP]

Congress also enacted legislation authorizing hearing examiners to conduct initial and revocation hearings for youth offenders. [HUSBP]

1972

The parole board began a pilot project that included the following goals: (1) the development of explicit paroling policy guidelines to provide greater consistency and equity in parole decision-making; (2) the provision of well-reasoned, written decisions; (3) more timely decisions; (4) the development of procedures to provide the opportunity for representatives to appear at parole hearings; (5) the development of a two-level appellate process to provide greater due process; and (6) increased liaison between the board and related agencies. Key features of this project were the decentralization of the parole board into five regions (each headed by a board member) with the Chairman and two other members forming a National Appeals Board in Washington, DC; the use of explicit guidelines for parole decision-making; hearings conducted by panels of two hearing examiners with review by the regional parole board member on the record; and the provision of written reasons for parole decisions. [EUSBPR]

The first hearings under this reorganization project were conducted at the Kennedy Youth Center in Morgantown, West

Virginia, in October 1972. [EUSBPR]

The pilot project comprised five federal institutions in the northeast region of the country. They were the Penitentiary, Lewisburg, Pennsylvania; the Kennedy Youth Center, Morgantown, West Virginia; the Reformatory for Women, Alderson, West Virginia; the Reformatory, Petersburg, Virginia; and the Correctional Institution, Danbury, Connecticut. [ARUSBP (1972–73)]

The parole board established a research unit and hired its first research director. [ARUSBP (1970: 72)]

The parole board implemented the procedures for due process in the revocation of parole set forth in *Morrissey vs. Brewer,* 408 U.S. 471, 92 S. Ct. 2593. [ARUSBP (1972–73)]

References

[ARUSBP] *Annual Report of the United States Board of Parole* (various years). Washington, DC: U.S. Board of Parole.

[AGSRP] *Attorney General's Survey of Release Practices,* Volumes I (*Digest of Federal and State Laws on Release Procedures*) and IV (*Parole*). (1939).

Washington, DC: U.S. Department of Justice.

[EUSBPR] *An Evaluation of the U.S. Board of Parole Reorganization.* (1975) Management Programs and Budget Staff, Office of Management and Finance. Washington, DC: U.S. Department of Justice.

[FP] *Federal Probation.* The volume and number are shown in parentheses.

[HUSBP] *History of the United States Board of Parole.* (undated, circa 1976). Washington, DC: U.S. Board of Parole. [A mimeographed document prepared by James C. Neagles, Staff Director of the U.S. Board of Parole.]

 Article Review Form at end of book.

Describe the major historical developments of the federal parole system from 1973 to 1997.

History of the Federal Parole System

Part 2 (1973–1997)

Peter B. Hoffman, Ph.D.

Staff Director (Retired), United States Parole Commission

Introduction

A solid grounding in history can be extremely useful to the legislator, correctional administrator, or practitioner involved in making or responding to change. Or, as George Santayana (1863–1952) stated somewhat more bluntly, "[t]hose who do not remember the past are condemned to repeat it." There have been substantial changes in the federal sentencing structure in recent years, including the abolition of parole release and the phasing down of the U.S. Parole Commission, the creation of the U.S. Sentencing Commission and the implementation of sentencing guidelines, a substantial reduction in authorized good-time credits, and the reappearance of long, mandatory minimum sentences. Given the recent passage of the Parole Commission Phaseout Act of 1996, it appears a particularly appropriate time to review the his-

tory of the federal parole system, as well as related sentencing and good-time provisions.

Chronological History

Significant events are shown corresponding to the date above each entry. At the end of the entry, an abbreviation for the source material used is shown in brackets; the full citation is given in the references at the end of the article. The few entries without a bracketed citation are based either on the source described in the entry itself or on the personal knowledge of the author.

1973

In May 1973, Maurice Sigler, Chairman of the U.S. Board of Parole, submitted a proposal for a reorganization of the parole board and revision of the parole board's procedures to the Department of Justice. Key features of this proposal were the use of explicit guidelines for parole decision-making; the decentralization of the parole board into five regions (each headed

by a board member) with the Chairman and two other members forming a National Appeals Board in Washington, DC; hearings conducted by panels of two hearing examiners with review by the regional parole board member on the record; the provision of written reasons for parole decisions; the opportunity for prisoners to have representatives at parole hearings; and an administrative appeal process. In July 1973, this proposal was approved by Attorney General Elliot Richardson. [EUSBPR]

The explicit paroling policy guidelines adopted by the parole board were published in the *Federal Register*. These guidelines were developed in cooperation with a project funded by the Law Enforcement Assistance Administration and conducted by the National Council on Crime and Delinquency. The guidelines were in the form of a two-dimensional grid. The seriousness of the prisoner's current offense (offense severity) was considered on the vertical axis with six categories (later increased to seven

Reprinted with permission from *Federal Probation*, December 1997, pp. 49–57.

and then eight categories). The prisoner's likelihood of recidivism (parole prognosis) was considered on the horizontal axis with four categories. The dimension of parole prognosis was determined by the use of a "salient factor score," an empirically derived parole prediction instrument. The intersections of the vertical and horizontal axes formed a grid containing time ranges (such as 12–18 months). The time range set forth the parole board's policy on the customary time to be served before release for a prisoner having that offense seriousness and parole prognosis, assuming good institutional conduct. Decisions outside the guidelines may be made for good cause and upon the provision of case-specific written reasons. For example, misconduct in the institution might warrant a decision above the applicable guideline range, and exceptionally good participation in institutional programs might warrant a decision below the applicable guideline range. [PDMR]

The Research Center of the National Council on Crime and Delinquency published a 14-volume set of reports on the Federal Parole Decision-Making Project. [PDMR]

1974

Regional offices were established in Philadelphia, Pennsylvania; Atlanta, Georgia; Dallas, Texas; Kansas City, Missouri; and Burlingame, California. Each regional office included a parole board member, five hearing examiners, two case analysts, and clerical staff. [EUSBPR]

The parole board's budget for fiscal year 1974 was $2,025,000, up from $1,391,000 in fiscal year 1973 and from approxi-

mately $500,000 in 1965. The increase from fiscal year 1973 to fiscal year 1974 included the cost of implementing the reorganization. Personnel increased from 48 positions in fiscal year 1965 to 125 positions in fiscal year 1974. [EUSBPR]

1975

Each regional office has approximately 20 employees. A typical regional office is staffed with a board member acting as the regional director, an administrative hearing examiner and four hearing examiners, a pre-release analyst, a post-release analyst, and administrative and clerical support personnel. [EUSBPR]

Hearing examiner panels, each consisting of two persons, conduct parole interviews at each institution within the region. At the conclusion of each interview, the examiners inform the prisoner of the recommended (tentative) parole decision. If the recommendations of the examiners differ, the prisoner is informed of both recommendations. All panel decisions are reviewed in the regional office by an administrative hearing examiner and the regional board member. It is the regional board member who makes the final decision, subject to certain limitations (if the regional board member wishes to alter a panel recommendation by more than 6 months, the case must be sent to the national board members for review). After a decision is made, a Notice of Action is mailed to the prisoner within 15 working days of the hearing. If the prisoner is not granted parole at that time, the reasons are given as part of the Notice of Action. If the prisoner is dissatisfied with the decision, he or she has available a two-step administrative appeal process. [EUSBPR]

According to a report of field visits by Department of Justice Management Programs and Budget staff, the average hearing lasted 30 minutes. Revocation hearings took anywhere from 45 to 90 minutes. The hearing began with a review of the inmate's file by one hearing examiner while the other examiner dictated the results of the last hearing. The review usually took 10 to 15 minutes. The offender's prior criminal history was closely examined during the file review. After the file was reviewed by one examiner, that examiner provided a brief summary of the file to the other examiner, who had completed dictating the results of the previous hearing.

Before the interview with the inmate, the hearing panel discussed the inmate's progress with the institutional case manager. At the beginning of the interview with the inmate, the hearing examiner carefully explained the board's procedures to the inmate and the inmate's right to appeal the decision. The principal discussion points initiated by the hearing examiners were: the validation of the salient factor score, the inmate's offense and the surrounding circumstances of the crime, and the inmate's institutional behavior and program participation.

The inmate's remarks usually began with a description of the mitigating circumstances of the offense and past criminal behavior. This most often was followed by the inmate's statements regarding his participation in institutional programs and his motivation to become a better citizen. The inmate usually made some reference to his parole release plan. The period of time for the discussion with the inmate ranged from 5 to 15 minutes.

When an inmate's representative was present, the discussion period required as much as one-half hour.

Following the inmate's discussion, he was asked if he had any questions he would like to ask the panel. If not, he left the room and the hearing examiners discussed the case. In most instances, the decision-making process, which takes from 2 to 5 minutes, was a straightforward application of the guidelines and salient factors to the individual case.

The inmate returned to the hearing room and was advised of the panel's tentative decision. When parole was approved, the discussion continued on the completion and validation of the release plan. When parole was denied, the examiners advised the inmate of the reasons and the right to appeal the decision. The process of advising the inmate of the decision required approximately 5 minutes.

Most representatives who were observed by the evaluation teams were institutional staff; however, relatives, prospective employers, and educators have appeared at a number of hearings. Generally, hearing examiners and Bureau of Prisons institutional staff agree that the inmate representative does not have a major effect on parole decisions; however, the representatives can have a positive effect on the inmate's attitude. Cases have occurred in which Bureau of Prisons institutional staff members serving as inmates' representatives have directly contradicted the observations and recommendations of the inmate's caseworker. In these instances, the examiner stated that the representative can have a major impact on the decision. [EUSBPR]

1976

The Parole Commission and Reorganization Act (Public Law 94-233) became effective on May 14, 1976. A major revision of the statutes pertaining to parole, this act retitled the agency as the United States Parole Commission. The primary provisions of this act are listed below.

- The U.S. Parole Commission is created with a membership of nine Commissioners. The Youth Correction Division was eliminated and its duties absorbed within the new Commission.

- No fewer than five regions are mandated; a Regional Commissioner is placed in charge of each. Three Commissioners are assigned to a National Appeals Board. Authority and responsibilities of the Commission, the Chairman, and the Regional Commissioners are set forth.

- Eligibility for parole for prisoners with long sentences, including life terms, is reduced to 10 years from the previous 15 years.

- Explicit Guidelines for Decision-Making are mandated.

- Reasons for denial of parole must be provided to the prisoner in writing. Decisions outside the guidelines must be for "good cause" and must contain specific written reasons for such departure.

- Parole applicants have a right to examine their own case file (with limited exceptions) before the hearing.

- Parole applicants may be accompanied at their hearings by a representative of their choice, who may make a statement on the applicant's behalf.

- If a prisoner's sentence is less than 7 years, he must be reviewed no later than at 18-month intervals after the initial hearing. If this sentence is 7 years or more, he must be reviewed no later than at 24-month intervals following the initial hearing.

- Prisoners with terms of 5 years or more and satisfactory institutional conduct must be paroled after service of two-thirds of the term, unless the Commission finds that there is a "reasonable probability" of further crime.

- A two-level appeal system is mandated.

- Regular and special conditions of release set by the Commission may be modified only after an opportunity has been offered to the releasee to comment on the proposed modifications. Such modifications also are appealable.

- The Commission must review a parolee's progress under supervision after 2 years and at least annually thereafter and may terminate supervision before completion of the sentenced term. Termination of supervision ends the jurisdiction of the Commission over the releasee.

- After 5 years of supervision in the community, the Commission must terminate jurisdiction unless it finds, after a hearing, that there is a likelihood of further crime. Such decision is appealable.

- At the discretion of the Commission, alleged violators may be summoned to a hearing in lieu of being arrested on a warrant and may be released under supervision pending a revocation hearing.

- Reviews of parole violation warrants placed as a detainer, while a prisoner is serving a subsequent sentence, must be reviewed within 180 days and a decision made with regard to disposition of the warrant.

- Alleged parole violators have the right to confront "adverse" witnesses at a preliminary interview and any revocation hearing held in the local community. At such interview or at any revocation hearing, the prisoner may be represented by an attorney (either retained or appointed). Voluntary witnesses also may be present.

- A preliminary interview is not necessary if the releasee has been convicted of a crime while under supervision.

- The Commission may subpoena witnesses in revocation proceedings.

- Following revocation, the parolee receives credit for time under supervision in the community unless he has been convicted of a crime committed while under supervision. If he absconded from supervision, he is credited with the time from the date of release to supervision to the date of such absconding.

- Attorney representation, privately retained or court appointed, is permitted in any revocation proceeding and at any termination hearing scheduled after 5 years on parole [ARUSPC (1976–78)]

1977

The Parole Commission modified the permissible grounds for a prisoner's appeal to make them more specific. The modified grounds for appeal are:

- That the guidelines were incorrectly applied.

- That a decision outside the guidelines was not supported by the reasons of facts as stated.

- That especially mitigating circumstances justify a different decision.

- That a decision was based on erroneous information and the actual facts justify a different decision.

- That the Commission did not follow correct procedure in deciding the case, and a different decision would have resulted if the error had not occurred.

- There was significant information in existence but not known at the time of the hearing.

- There are compelling reasons why a more lenient decision should be rendered on grounds of compassion. [ARUSPC (1976–78)]

Mexico and the United States signed a treaty for the mutual exchange of prisoners incarcerated for crimes while transient aliens within each nation's jurisdiction. The Commission's legal staff participated with the State Department and other units of the Department of Justice in the development of prisoner transfer treaties and implementing legislation. In December 1977, 154 U.S. citizens convicted of crimes in Mexico were transferred to the United States. A special docket was set up to provide prompt parole hearings to these cases. Shortly thereafter, Canada and Bolivia followed this precedent by establishing similar treaties with the United States. [ARUSCP (1976–78)]

After a pilot test of the concept in the Parole Commission's Western Region, the Commission implemented a new procedure that has come to be called "presumptive parole." The purpose of the presumptive parole procedure is to provide the prisoner at the beginning of his sentence a date on which it is presumed that release will take place, provided the prisoner maintains a good institutional adjustment and has developed adequate release plans. This procedure is designed to remove much of the dysfunctional uncertainty and anxiety surrounding the parole process while retaining the flexibility to deal with substantial changes in circumstances. Presumptive parole procedures went into effect in September 1977. All prisoners with 7 years or less (regardless of sentence procedure) and all prisoners with no minimum sentences are heard within 120 days of commitment or as soon thereafter as practicable. A presumptive release date may be set up to 4 years from the date of the initial hearing (previously, parole dates were set up to 6 months from the date of the hearing). If a presumptive release date is not set within 4 years from the date of the initial hearing, the prisoner will be continued to a reconsideration hearing 4 years from the date of the initial hearing (a "four-year reconsideration hearing"). In addition, interim hearings are conducted as required by statute to consider whether there are any substantial positive or negative changes in circumstances (e.g., outstanding institutional program achievement, disciplinary infractions) that may warrant modifying the presumptive release date originally set. In addition, a prerelease record review is conducted to ensure that the conditions of the presumptive release date (good institutional conduct and a suitable release plan) have been satisfied. Failure to satisfy these conditions may result in retardation of the release date or the scheduling of a rescission hearing. [ARUSPC (1976–78)]

1978

The Parole Commission published *Federal Parole Decision Making: Selected Reprints,* Volume I. [PDMSR (1)]

In October 1978, the Commission began a periodic review of its paroling policy guidelines at 28 C.F.R. 2.20 and 2.21. In addition to usual publishing and posting of the proposal, copies were sent to over 1,000 interested persons. Public hearings were held in Atlanta, Denver, and Washington, DC, and at the Atlanta and Englewood facilities of the Bureau of Prisons. Testimony was received from 69 witnesses, generating over 3,000 pages of transcript. Those giving their views included representatives from the judiciary, defense and prosecution attorneys, federal prisoners, enforcement agencies, the Bureau of Prisons, the probation system, state correctional systems, and scholars. As a result of this effort, certain listed offense behaviors were defined more specifically, certain previously unlisted offense behaviors were added to the guidelines, and certain offense behaviors were moved from one category to another or subdivided. The revised paroling policy guidelines became effective June 4, 1979. [ARUSPC (1978–80)]

1979

Decision guidelines were established for decisions to retard or rescind a parole on account of institutional misconduct. These guidelines are set forth at 28 C.F.R. 2.36. [ARUSPC (1978–80)]

Decision guidelines were established to reward sustained superior program achievement by a reduction from a previously established presumptive release date. The advancement for superior program achievement under these guidelines was deliberately kept modest. It is the intent of the Commission to encourage voluntary program participation, not superficial attendance in programs merely in an attempt to impress the parole decision-makers. These guidelines are set forth at 28 C.F.R. 2.60. [ARUSPC (1978–80)]

1980

The Parole Commission's presumptive release date procedures were expanded. Under the revised procedures, presumptive release dates are set up to 10 years from the date of the initial hearing. A defendant who does not receive a presumptive release date will be scheduled for a 10-year reconsideration hearing. Procedures for interim hearings, as required by statute, to review the case for any significant changes in circumstances are unchanged. [ARUSPC (1978–80)]

From April 9–11, 1980, the Parole Commission, in joint sponsorship with the National Institute of Corrections, conducted the Third National Parole Symposium. The conference was held at the University of Maryland at College Park. United States District Judge Frank A. Kaufman, Governor Brendan T. Byrne of New Jersey, and Charles Silberman, author of *Criminal Violence, Criminal Justice,* were featured ·speakers. Approximately 250 persons attended. The proceedings of the conference were published as *Parole in the 1980s: Proceedings of the National Parole Symposium.* [ARUSPC (1978–80)]

The Parole Commission published *Federal Parole Decision Making: Selected Reprints,* Volume II. [PDMSR (2)]

1981

The Parole Commission published *Federal Parole Decision Making: Selected Reprints,* Volume III. [PDMSR (3)]

Effective August 31, 1981, the Parole Commission, as a result of a research study, revised its Salient Factor Score, an actuarial device used in determining risk of recidivism. The new Salient Factor Score (SFS 81) includes six items which, when added together, produce a score with a range from zero to 10 points. The higher the score, the higher is the likelihood of favorable outcome. SFS 81 demonstrates predictive validity and stability equivalent to that of the seven-item predictive device previously used by the Commission. Of prime importance, the revised device holds promise for greater scoring reliability and ease of scoring. [ARUSPC (1980–83)]

1982

The Parole Commission published the first *Rules and Procedures Manual,* which consolidated the Parole Commission's rules (28 C.F.R. 2.1 *et seq.*) with the accompanying procedures. Previously, these had been published separately.

The Parole Commission published *Federal Parole Decision Making: Selected Reprints,* Volume IV. [PDMSR (4)]

1983

Effective January 31, 1983, the Parole Commission revised its offense severity scale. The revision, which used the format of the proposed revision of the federal criminal code, was designed to make the severity scale more comprehensive, to improve its clarity and organization, and to reflect changes in Commission policy for particular offenses. [ARUSPC (1980–83)]

1984

The Comprehensive Crime Control Act of 1984 (Public Law 98–473, October 12, 1984) was passed. This legislation provided for the creation of a United States Sentencing Commission to promulgate explicit decision guidelines (by May 1, 1986) to be used by federal judges in making sentencing decisions. The Chairman of the Parole Commission serves as an *ex officio,* non-voting member of the Sentencing Commission. The Parole Commission was to be abolished 5 years from the date the sentencing guidelines took effect. During the 5-year transition period, the Parole Commission was to continue in existence to handle cases of parole-eligible defendants convicted of offenses committed before November 1, 1987. Cases sentenced under the new law would serve determinate sentences with limited reduction for good time (about 15 percent). For such cases, post-release supervision would be called supervised release rather than parole, and decisions regarding the conditions of supervised release and revocation would be made by the courts rather than by the Parole Commission. This legislation also abolished the Youth Corrections Act. [ARUSPC (1985–86)]

The Comprehensive Crime Control Act of 1984 also eliminated the Parole Commission's intermediate administrative appeal (regional appeal), providing a one-step rather than a two-step administrative appeal. [ARUSPC (1986–87)]

The Parole Commission published *Federal Parole Decision Making: Selected Reprints,* Volume V. [PDMSR (5)]

1985

Due to a delay in the appointment of the first members of the Sentencing Commission, legislation was enacted that extended the date for the first sentencing guidelines by 1 year (until May 1, 1987).

1986

The Parole Commission sought various legislative initiatives to facilitate the transition between the current and new systems. Legislation was enacted (Public Law 99–646, November 10, 1986) containing two provisions that afforded the Parole Commission flexibility to facilitate its phase out. First, the legislation eliminated the requirement for no less than five regions. Second, the legislation authorized the use of single hearing examiners to conduct hearings (with the requirement of a panel of two hearing examiners met by a review on the record by the second examiner). [ARUSPC (1985–86)]

The Parole Commission also provided assistance to the newly created Sentencing Commission. As the move toward the establishment of federal sentencing guidelines was based, in large part, on the successful development and use of federal parole guidelines, much of the research conducted and experience gained in the parole context was directly relevant to the sentencing guidelines effort. The Parole Commission provided a number of databases for the Sentencing Commission's use, and staffs of both agencies met regularly to examine the data, review the documentation, and discuss the

empirical findings. [ARUSPC (1985–86)]

The Parole Commission published *Federal Parole Decision Making: Selected Reprints,* Volume VI. [PDMSR (6)]

In March 1986, the Parole Commission implemented an experimental program, called special Curfew Parole, to provide a substitute for Community Treatment Center residence for the 60-day period preceding the otherwise scheduled parole release date. This program, a joint effort of the Parole Commission, the U.S. Bureau of Prisons, and the U.S. Probation System, was designed for prisoners who were transferred to Community Treatment Centers for a 30- to 120-day period before parole, but who no longer required the support services provided there. Under this program, a qualified prisoner could have his release date advanced by up to 60 days on the condition that he remain at his place of residence between the hours of 9 p.m. and 6 a.m. each night unless given permission in advance by his probation officer. The probation system provided high-activity supervision of the parolee during this period (at least weekly in-person contact, as well as monitoring compliance with the curfew by random telephone calls). Failure to comply with this special condition could result in imposition of Community Treatment Center residence as a condition of parole or revocation of parole and return to prison. Implemented as a cost-reduction procedure through which the Bureau of Prisons could reduce the number and expense of inmates confined in Community Treatment Centers, this project saved over $1 million in its first 18 months of operation. [ARUSPC (1985–86)]

In collaboration with the Bureau of Prisons and the National Institute of Justice, the Parole Commission initiated an experimental program in which selected prisoners would have their parole dates advanced if they volunteered to complete 400 hours of "reparative work." Reparative work is defined as unpaid volunteer work for public or nonprofit private agencies (such as the Volunteers of America, the Salvation Army, or Goodwill Industries). The purpose of the project was to develop an alternative form of punishment that returned something of value to the community and, at the same time, saved prison bed space. During the first phase of the project, 100 prisoners in selected cities each completed the 400 hours of reparative work while residing in halfway houses. These prisoners logged 38,481 hours of unpaid service, work which would have cost the participating agencies over $168,000 for paid employees to perform. In return, release dates were advanced by 5,538 days, providing a substantial savings in prison bed space. Upon release, some parolees were offered full-time paid positions with the agencies they had worked for in the program. A second phase of the program was begun at the Federal Correctional Institution at Forth Worth. In this phase, a limited number of prisoners performed reparative work in the community while still residing at the institution. [ARUSPC (1985–86)]

The Anti-Drug Abuse Act of 1986 enacted long, mandatory minimum sentences for many drug offenders.

1987

On April 14, 1987, the U.S. Sentencing Commission transmitted its initial sentencing guidelines to Congress. These guidelines took effect, as scheduled, on November 1, 1987, and applied to all defendants whose offenses were committed on or after that date.

The Bureau of Prisons reported that the cumulative savings from the Special Curfew Parole Project exceeded $2 million and requested that the program be extended indefinitely. [ARUSPC (1986–87)]

The Parole Commission initiated a "Community Control Project," a joint effort with the Bureau of Prisons and U.S. probation system, using electronic monitoring to ensure compliance with a curfew. Because of population pressures, the Bureau of Prisons was placing offenders in halfway houses up to 6 months before release even if there was no treatment need for such placement. Under this experimental program, selected low-treatment-need offenders were released to the community up to 180 days before their normally scheduled parole date with a curfew, electronic monitoring, and intensive supervision substituted for Community Treatment Center placement. Two districts (Southern District of Florida and Central District of California) were selected for this project. [ARUSPC (1986–87)]

The Reparative Work Project was terminated. During the two phases, 132 offenders each performed 400 hours of reparative work and had their parole dates advanced by up to 60 days. A total of 51,281 hours of unpaid community service work was completed and participants had their parole dates advanced by a total of 7,458 days. The value of the work done was estimated to be over $225,000 (for paid employees to have done the same

work), and the project was well received by the nonprofit agencies involved. Despite these positive findings, the project was terminated because the Bureau of Prisons did not believe that the staff time needed to monitor the project could be spared given the level of overcrowding. [ARUSPC (1986–87)]

1988

The cumulative number of offenders participating in the Special Curfew Parole Project reached 3,000. Very few problems were reported; the revocation rate for violations on curfew parole was less than 3 percent. [ARUSPC (1987–88)]

The Community Control Project was expanded to four additional districts. To date, 120 offenders have participated in this project. [ARUSPC (1987–88)]

The Anti-Drug Abuse Act of 1988 broadened the scope of the mandatory minimum sentences for drug offenders enacted by the Anti-Drug Abuse Act of 1986.

The Anti-Drug Abuse Act of 1988 gave the Parole Commission jurisdiction over new-law transfer treaty cases (transfer treaty cases in which the offense was committed on or after November 1, 1987). In such cases, the Parole Commission is to determine the release date by applying the sentencing guidelines promulgated by the U.S. Sentencing Commission. [ARUSPC (1987–88)]

The Anti-Drug Abuse Act of 1988 also gave the Parole Commission continuing responsibility over all state defendants who are accepted into the U.S. Marshals Service Witness Protection Program. Once a state defendant is accepted into this program, the Parole Commission assumes jurisdiction over the case.

Fifty percent of the initial hearings conducted in fiscal year 1988 involved offenders with drug-related convictions, 26 percent involved property crimes, and another 11 percent involved crimes of violence (murder, kidnapping, arson, robbery, and assault). [ARUSPC (1987–88)]

1989

The Parole Commission began an Intensive Supervision Project with the U.S. Probation Office for the District of Maryland for high risk cases. [ARUSPC (1988–89)]

The number of hearings conducted by the Parole Commission began to decline as the sentencing guidelines took effect for defendants who committed offenses on or after November 1, 1987. In fiscal years 1987 and 1988, the Commission conducted 19,796 and 20,465 hearings, respectively. In fiscal year 1989, the number of hearings declined to 16,619. [ARUSPC (1988–89)]

1990

The Judicial Improvements Act of 1990 extended the life of the Parole Commission by an additional 5 years until November 1, 1997, because the Comprehensive Crime Control Act of 1984 had failed to make adequate provision for handling old-law cases. Retrospective abolition of parole consideration (for defendants who had already committed their offenses) would raise a serious constitutional issue under the *ex post facto* clause. [ARUSPC (1989–90)]

The Parole Commission has jurisdiction over the following cases: (1) "Old Law" Cases (persons sentenced to prison terms of more than 1 year for offenses committed before November 1, 1987, unless sentenced under a statute expressly prohibiting parole eligibility); (2) Transfer Treaty Cases (persons transferred to the United States from foreign countries to complete service of a foreign sentence, regardless of the date of the offense); (3) State Witness Protection Cases (probationers and parolees serving state sentences who are transferred to federal jurisdiction because of participation in the Federal Witness Protection Program, regardless of the date of the offense); (4) D.C. Code Cases in Federal Institutions (persons sentenced under the District of Columbia Code who are confined in correctional facilities of the U.S. Bureau of Prisons, regardless of the date of the offense); and (5) Military Prisoners in Federal Institutions (persons convicted of military offenses who are confined in correctional facilities of the U.S. Bureau of Prisons, regardless of the date of the offense).

The number of Parole Commission hearings continued to decline. There were 13,568 hearings conducted in fiscal year 1990, including 903 hearings for D.C. Code offenders housed in federal institutions. [ARUSPC (1989–90)]

1991

In August 1991, as part of its phase-down effort, the Parole Commission closed its Philadelphia and Atlanta Regional Offices and consolidated these operations in a new Eastern Regional Office co-housed with the Headquarters Office in Chevy Chase, Maryland. [ARUSPC (1990–91)]

The Special Curfew Parole Project, which had started in 1986, reached a cumulative total of 3,500 cases. As electronic monitoring (started under the Community Control Project) became available in each judicial district, it replaced the curfew parole project. [ARUSPC (1990–91)]

1992

The Parole Commission, in cooperation with the U.S. probation system, developed an experimental project to place technical parole violators in "sanction centers," rather than return them to prison. In 1992, two sanction centers were opened, one in the Baltimore, Maryland, area and one in the Washington, DC, area. [ARUSPC (1991–92)]

The Parole Commission's Intensive Supervision Project in Hyattsville and Baltimore, Maryland, which had started in 1988, was terminated due to the downsizing of the Commission. An evaluation of the Hyattsville project, prepared by the National Center on Institutions and Alternatives, concluded that the early intervention and increased surveillance of the project provided a tool for preventing escalating criminal behavior. [ARUSPC (1991–92)]

1993

The number of hearings conducted in fiscal year 1993 was 6,769, down from 10,720 hearings in fiscal year 1991 and 9,307 hearings in fiscal year 1992, and slightly less than one-half of the 13,568 hearings conducted in fiscal year 1990. [ARUSPC (1992–93)]

1994

As part of its phase-down effort, the Commission closed its Dallas Regional Office and consolidated that operation in its Eastern Regional Office co-housed with the Headquarters Office in Chevy

Chase, Maryland. This closing resulted in a savings of more than $1 million in operating funds and reduced the number of Commission personnel by 22 positions. The Commission also eliminated a number of mid-management positions. [ARUSPC (1993–94)]

Given the requirement for the downsizing of the Commission, the Commission began using single hearing examiners to conduct parole hearings. From 1974 to 1994, hearings had been conducted by two-person panels of hearing examiners. Under the revised procedure, a second examiner would review the case record and hearing summary at the Commission's office. [ARUSPC (1993–94)]

1995

The Parole Commission modified the Salient Factor Score by adding an additional item for older offenders (offenders at least 41 years of age on the date of the current offense). The revised Salient Factor Score is designated as SFS 95.

The Parole Commission published a 16-chapter *Desk Book on Training and Reference Materials* as part of a program of staff training.

1996

The Parole Commission closed its Kansas City Regional Office and consolidated that operation in its Eastern Regional Office co-housed with the Headquarters Office in Chevy Chase, Maryland. This action resulted in a savings of more than $1 million in operating funds and reduced the number of Commission personnel by 22 positions. With the closing of this office, all Commission functions will be conducted from its Chevy Chase, Maryland, office.

Congress passed the Parole Commission Phaseout Act of 1996. This act extended the life of the Parole Commission by an additional 5 years (until November 1, 2002). In addition, it reinstated the 12-year limitation on total service as a Parole Commissioner and provided for the reduction in the number of Parole Commissioners to two Commissioners on December 31, 1999, and to one Commissioner on December 31, 2001. Furthermore, it required the Attorney General to report to the Congress annually, beginning in May 1998, as to whether it is more cost effective for the Parole Commission to remain a separate agency or whether its functions should be transferred elsewhere. If the Attorney General recommends incorporating the Commission's functions in another component of the Department of Justice, the Attorney General's plan shall take effect in November of the year in which it is submitted unless Congress, by law, provides otherwise. If the Commission's functions are transferred to another component within the Department of Justice, all laws remaining to these functions remain in effect notwithstanding the November 1, 2002, termination date for the Commission set forth elsewhere in the legislation.

The Parole Commission, with the assistance of a grant from the Office for Victims of Crime, established two victim/witness coordinator positions and developed a program to enhance the Commission's responsiveness to victims and witnesses at revocation hearings.

The Parole Commission had 48 positions at the end of 1996, a substantial reduction from 145 positions in 1992. At the beginning of 1996, there were six Parole Commissioners. By the end of 1996, this number was reduced to three due to resignations and the provisions of the Parole Commission Phaseout Act of 1996.

1997

The Parole Commission began an experimental project in which parole hearings are conducted using video-conferencing equipment. In February 1997, the first hearings in this project were conducted for prisoners at the Federal Correctional Institution in Oakdale, Louisiana.

References

[ARUSBP] *Annual Report of the United States Board of Parole* (various years.). Washington, DC: U.S. Board of Parole.

[ARUSPC] *Annual Report of the United States Parole Commission* (various years). Washington, DC [Chevy Chase, MD, beginning in 1981]: U.S. Parole Commission.

[EUSBPR] *An Evaluation of the U.S. Board of Parole Reorganization*. (1975). Management Programs and Budget Staff, Office of Management and Finance. Washington, DC: U.S. Department of Justice.

[HUSBP] *History of the United States Board of Parole*. (undated, circa 1976). Washington, DC: U.S. Board of Parole. [A mimeographed document prepared by James C. Neagles, Staff Director of the U.S. Board of Parole.]

[PDMR] *Parole Decision-Making Reports*. (1973) Davis, CA: Research Center of the National Council on Crime and Delinquency. [A set of 14 reports describing the Parole Decision-Making Project.]

[PDMSR] *Parole Decision Making: Selected Reprints*, Volume I (1978), II (1980), III (1981), IV (1982), V (1984), VI (1986). Washington, DC [Chevy Chase, MD, beginning in 1981]: U.S. Parole Commission. [The volume number is shown in parentheses.]

 Article Review Form at end of book.

What are the consequences associated with the implementation of the "get-tough" sentences?

Three Strikes and You're Out!

The political sentencing game

Peter J. Benekos and Alida V. Merlo

Dr. Benekos is professor, Administration of Justice, Mercyhurst College. Dr. Merlo is professor, Department of Criminal Justice, Westfield State College.

The "war on crime" has added another weapon to the arsenal of getting tough on crime: "three strikes and you're out." From the slogans of "just say no" to "if you can't do the time, don't do the crime," it is ironic that the latest metaphor for crime policy parallels the baseball players' strike of 1994. The recent initiatives to mandate life sentences for three-time convicted felons are responses to the public's fear of crime and frustration with the criminal justice system and indicate the continuation of politicized crime policy.

In the 30 states that have introduced "three-strikes" legislation and in the 10 that have passed tougher sentencing for repeat offenders (*Criminal Justice Newsletter*, 1994c, p. 1), politicians have demonstrated quick-fix responses to the complex and diffi-cult issues of crime, violence, and public anxiety over the disorder and decline in America. The United States Congress also finally overcame differences to legislate a new get-tough crime bill that not only includes a provision of life imprisonment for a third felony conviction but also authorizes the death penalty "for dozens of existing or newly created federal crimes" (Idelson, 1994, p. 2138).

Notwithstanding the critics of these sentencing policies (Currie, 1994; Gangi, 1994; Gladwell, 1994; Kramer, 1994; Lewis, 1994; Raspberry, 1993) politicians have rushed to embrace the "get *even* tougher" sentencing proposals because they have learned that "politically, it still works" (Schneider, 1993, p. 24). "Crime used to be the Republicans' issue, just as the economy was the Democrats'. No more" (Schneider, 1993, p. 24). In his commentary on how the "misbegotten" three-strikes piece of legislation became part of the crime bill, Lewis writes that "the answer is simple: politics. Democrats wanted to take the crime issue away from Republicans. Republicans responded by sounding 'tougher' " . . . and "President Clinton wanted something—anything—labeled 'crime bill' " (Lewis, 1994, p. A13).

This article reviews the ideological and political context of these sentencing reforms, examines get-tough legislation in three states and on the Federal level, and considers the consequences of increasing sentencing severity. The review suggests that baseball sentencing will further distort the distribution of punishments and will contribute to an escalation of political posturing on crime policies.

Politicalization of Crime

In a sense, this is what baseball sentencing is about: using the fear factor as a political issue; relying on what Broder calls "bumper sticker simplicity" to formulate crime policy (1994b, p. 6), and taking a tough stance on sentencing criminals as symbolic of

Reprinted with permission from *Federation Probation*, March 1995, Vol. 59, No.1, pp. 3-9.

doing something about crime. The politicizing of crime as a national issue can be traced to the 1964 Presidential election when Barry Goldwater promoted the theme of "law and order" and challenged Lyndon Johnson's "war on poverty" as a soft-headed response to crime and disorder (Cronin, Cronin, & Milakovich, 1981).

Thirty years ago the voters chose "social reform, civil rights, and increased education and employment opportunities" over a "get-tough response to crime that included expanding police powers and legislating tougher laws" (Merlo & Benekos, 1992a, p. x). Today's election results reflect a reversal of policy and the expansion of the Federal role in crime control (*Congressional Digest*, 1994).

Even though Johnson won the 1964 election, the "nationalization" of the crime issue was established and the Federal Government began "a new era of involvement in crime control" (*Congressional Digest*, 1994, p. 162): "the law and order issue just wouldn't go away" (Cronin et al., 1981, p. 22) and it became embedded in the public's mind and on the national agenda (Merlo and Benekos, 1992a, p. x).

In his 1965 address to Congress, President Johnson "called for the establishment of a blue ribbon panel to probe 'fully and deeply into the problems of crime in our Nation'" (*Congressional Digest*, 1994, p. 162). This led to the Law Enforcement Assistance Act of 1965, the Omnibus Crime Control and Safe Streets Act of 1968, and more recently to the Comprehensive Crime Control Act of 1984, the Anti-Drug Abuse Act of 1986, the Anti- Drug Abuse Act of 1988, the Crime Control Act of 1990,

and finally, the Violent Crime Control and Law Enforcement Act of 1994 (*Congressional Digest*, 1994, pp. 163, 192), which was signed by President Clinton on September 13, 1994. Since 1965 to 1992, the Federal spending for the "administration of justice" has "risen from $535 million to an estimated $11.7 billion" (*Congressional Digest*, 1994, p. 162).

From Horton to Davis and McFadden

The lessons of crime and politics were learned again in the Presidential election of 1988 when the then Vice President George Bush invoked the get-tough issue when he challenged Massachusetts Governor Michael Dukakis on his state's correctional policies that allowed a convicted murderer serving a life sentence to participate in the furlough program (Merlo & Benekos, 1992a, p. x).

Willie Horton became the poster child of Republicans and reminded Democrats (as well as doubting Republicans) that appearing to be soft on crime (and criminals) was politically incorrect. The Willie Horton incident "effectively crystallized a complex problem by presenting it as a dramatic case history of one individual" (The Sentencing Project, 1989, p. 3). Ironically, even without the Willie Horton incident, the 1980's were a period of conservative crime policy in which get-tough sentencing reforms were implemented throughout the country (Merlo & Benekos, 1992b). As part of these get-tough, get-fair, just deserts, determinate sentencing reforms, penalties were increased, mandatory sentences were legislated, and prisons became overcrowded (Shover & Einstadter, 1988, p. 51).

Similar to the Willie Horton situation, in 1993 another tragic case also became a "condensation symbol" for the public's perception that crime was increasing, that violent criminals were getting away with murder, that sentences were too lenient, and that offenders were getting out of prison after serving only small portions of their sentences. The California case which outraged the public was the October 1, 1993, abduction and murder of 12-year-old Polly Klaas by a parolee who had been released after serving 8 years of a 16-year sentence for a 1984 kidnapping (*New York Times*, 1993, p. A22).

Richard Allen Davis, who was arrested November 30, 1993, had convictions for two kidnappings, assault, and robbery and had spent "a good part of his adult life in jail" (*New York Times*, 1993, p. A22). At the time of his arrest, he was in violation of a pass from the halfway house that he was released to and therefore was also charged as a parole violator.

This type of crime fuels public fear and outrage and becomes fodder for politicians who respond by calling for tougher sentences to curb the perceived increases in crime and violence. Coincidentally to Davis' arrest, the FBI released its semiannual tabulation of crime which "showed that the rate of crime as a whole declined 5 percent in the first six months of 1993 from the same period the year before and that the rate of violent crime dropped 3 percent" (Lewis, 1993, p. B6).

These data, however, are not comforting to a public which sees the Klaas incident as evidence of the horrific and violent crimes which grip the Nation in fear. "The public doesn't rely on statistics to generate their perception of the level of crime. People's perceptions are based on what they see and hear going on around them" (Michael Rand of the Justice Department, cited in Lewis, 1993, p. B6). In reviewing 1994 state political campaigns, Kurtz observed that "although other traditional hot-button issues—welfare, taxes, immigration, personal ethics—also are prominent, crime remains the 30-second weapon of choice, and the charge most often is that an incumbent is responsible for turning dangerous inmates loose" (1994, p. 12).

Recent "Baseball Sentencing" Legislation

In order to provide a clearer picture of the legislation that is designed to impose mandatory life sentences (without possibility of parole or early release), we examined the recently enacted Violent Crime Control and Law Enforcement Act of 1994 and similar statutes in the states of Washington, California, and Georgia. The Violent Crime Control and Law Enforcement Act of 1994, signed by President Clinton on September 13, 1994, authorizes mandatory life imprisonment for persons convicted on two previous separate occasions of two serious violent felonies or one or more serious violent felonies and one or more serious drug offenses. According to the new Federal code, a "serious violent felony" includes offenses ranging from murder and aggravated sexual abuse to arson, aircraft piracy, car-jacking, and extortion (U.S. Government Printing Office, 1994, pp. 194–195).

In the State of Washington, the "Persistent Offender Accountability Law" was approved by the

voters in November 1993 by a 3 to 1 victory and became effective in December 1993 (*Corrections Digest*, 1994a). Under the revised statute, an offender who is categorized as a "persistent offender" must be sentenced to life imprisonment without any hope of parole if he or she has been convicted of a "most serious offense" and has two prior separate convictions for crimes that meet the "most serious offense" definition (*Washington Laws*, 1994, p. 1). Included in the definition of "most serious offense" are crimes ranging from "manslaughter in the second degree" to "promoting prostitution in the first degree" or any felony defined under any law as a Class A felony or criminal solicitation of or criminal conspiracy to commit a Class A felony (*Washington Laws,* 1994, p. 13).

In March 1994, Governor Pete Wilson signed California Assembly Bill 971 into law. Its most publicized provision is the requirement that judges impose ". . . an indeterminate sentence of a minimum of 25 years to life, or triple the normal sentence, whichever is greater, on offenders convicted of certain serious or violent felonies if they have two previous convictions for any felony" (Tucker, 1994, p. 7). The offenses included in the category of serious or violent felony range from murder and rape to burglary, any felony using a firearm, and selling or giving drugs such as heroin, cocaine, and PCP to a minor (California Penal Code, s1192.7).

In Georgia the voters approved "The Sentence Reform Act of 1994" which authorizes life imprisonment without possibility of parole, pardon, early release, leave, or any other measure designed to reduce the sentence for any person convicted of a sec-

ond "serious violent felony." Under Georgia law, a serious violent felony is defined as ". . . murder or felony murder, armed robbery, kidnapping, rape, aggravated child molestation, aggravated sodomy and aggravated sexual battery" (Georgia Statutes, 17-10-6.1).

Despite the fact that this law became effective January 1, 1995, any felony committed before that date in Georgia or in another jurisdiction, which meets the Georgia definition of a "serious violent felony," would count as one of the "strikes." The Federal code and the Washington and California laws contain similar language. The offender's criminal record in the state where the most recent conviction occurs as well as his or her record in other states or on the Federal level determine the number of "strikes." In short, an offender may already have the requisite number of convictions even as the mandatory sentencing provisions first become effective.

When the Federal criminal code and the three strikes laws are compared, it appears that the Georgia law is the most restrictive. Unlike the others, it contains a "two strikes" versus a "three strikes" provision. However, upon closer inspection, Georgia's law is the only one of the four reviewed here that requires mandatory life imprisonment for crimes that can be strictly identified as violent. By contrast, the Federal law and the Washington and California laws include a variety of nonviolent crimes such as burglary, prostitution, and drug trafficking that can result in a mandatory life sentence in prison. In California, for example, a criminal twice convicted of the property crime of burglary may be sentenced to life in prison for a third burglary conviction.

In order to clarify the intent of the legislation—that these offenders serve lengthy prison sentences—some states such as Washington stipulate that the Governor is "urged to refrain from pardoning or granting clemency" to offenders sentenced until the offender has reached the age of 60 (*Final Legislative Report*, 1994, p. 1). In order to discourage the Governor's use of pardons as a way to minimize the effects of the legislation, Washington law mandates that the Governor provide reports twice each year on the status of these "persistent offenders" he or she has released during his or her term of office and that the reports continue to be made for as long as the offender lives or at least 10 years after his or her release from prison (*Final Legislative Report*, 1994, p. 1).

Effects of Baseball Legislation

Thermodynamic Effects of Baseball Punishment

While the get-tough rhetoric continues to capture the public's support, the consequences of increased sentencing penalties are having an unintended but not unanticipated impact on the criminal justice system. In California where the mandatory statute "makes no distinction between 'violent' and 'serious' felonies . . . a superior court judge, Lawrence Antolini, declared the three-strikes law unconstitutional" because it "metes out 'cruel and unusual' jail terms" for nonviolent criminals and "robs justices of the power to evaluate the nuances of individual cases" (Peyser, 1994, p. 53). In an article about the tough California sentencing law, a *New York Times* re-

port indicated that "judges in many California jurisdictions have been indicating their reluctance to follow the new law . . . by changing some felony charges to misdemeanors" (1994c, p. A9). In addition, Supreme Court Justice Anthony Kennedy has also criticized the "increasing use of mandatory minimum sentences, saying the practice was unwise and often unfair" (*New York Times*, 1994a, p. A14).

And, as some judges find fault with the harsher sentencing laws, prosecutors are also raising doubts about the ability of the courts to handle the number of cases which fall under the baseball sentencing provisions. In California, where the District Attorneys' Association opposed the three-strikes law, Los Angeles County District Attorney Gil Garcetti voiced concerns that the broad nature of California's sentencing law would expand the number of felons subject to life in prison (*Criminal Justice Newsletter*, 1994a, p. 6). In an interview with National Public Radio, Garcetti stated that Los Angeles County alone would need 40 more prosecutors to handle the increase in the number of cases (National Public Radio, 1994).

What Garcetti was referring to is the potential increase in the number of accused offenders who refuse to plea-bargain and would rather take their chances on a trial (Peyser, 1994, p. 53). For example, a convicted murderer in California, Henry Diaz, originally entered guilty pleas to three counts of child molestation. When he learned that "one of the incidents occurred after the 'three-strikes' law went into effect on March 7 (1994), making (him) eligible for sentencing under the new law," he withdrew his guilty plea and requested a trial (*New*

York Times, 1994d, p. A19). Responses such as this give the California Judicial Council reason to "estimate that the new law will require an additional $250 million per year to try more felony cases" (*Criminal Justice Newsletter*, 1994a, p. 7).

These types of judicial responses illustrate a hydraulic, thermodynamic effect where getting tough may in fact result in being softer. For example, "the law allows prosecutors to move to dismiss criminals' prior convictions 'in the furtherance of justice'—namely, if they believe the law mandates an elephantine sentence for a puny offense" (Peyser, 1994, p. 53). Another avenue to circumvent the law is a "wiggle" factor where district attorneys can "classify certain crimes that straddle the felony-misdemeanor line as misdemeanors" (Peyser, 1994, p. 53).

In addition, some district attorneys have reported "instances in which crime victims had told prosecutors they would not testify if a conviction meant the defendant would fall under the requirements of the new law" (*New York Times*, 1994c, p. A9). As Griset observed in her study of determinate sentence reforms, legislators fail to "recognize the inevitability of the exercise of discretion at all points in the criminal justice system" and as a result develop policies which are incongruent and inconsistent with the reality of the criminal justice system (1991, p. 181). The above examples illustrate her conclusions and also suggest an inverse relationship between the severity of sanctions and the likelihood that those sanctions will be applied (Black, 1976).

Police officers are also experiencing the effects of these baseball "swings" at offenders:

"suspects who are more prone to use violence when cornered" (Egan, 1994, p. A11). In one case in Seattle, a suspect threatened to shoot police after he was cornered. "After the suspect was taken into custody, the police were told by his acquaintances that he thought he was facing a three-strikes charge. Rather than face life in prison, he decided to confront officers" (Egan, 1994, p. A11).

Prisons and Prisoners: Economic and Social Impact

With crime uppermost in voters' minds, the new Federal crime bill was frequently featured in the 1994 election campaigns. Incumbent members of Congress informed their constituents of the immediate effects of the legislation on their home state. For example, New Jersey has been promised $77 million for new prisons and 3,800 police officers. Pennsylvania is slated for $110 million for prisons and 4,200 new police officers (*The Vindicator*, 1994, p. A5). These tangible results of the crime bill are intended to provide voters with a sense of security and satisfaction. However, the public has not yet focused on the long-term costs of these new initiatives.

There is little doubt that an immediate effect of the legislation will be to increase the already enormous prison population in the United States. According to The Sentencing Project research, there are currently 1.3 million Americans incarcerated (Mauer, 1994a, p. 1). The incarceration rate is 519 per 100,000, making the United States' rate second only to Russia's (Mauer, 1994a, p. 1). In the United States, the incarceration rate of African-Americans (1,947 per 100,000) as compared

to the incarceration rate of whites (306 per 100,000) is even more striking: Mauer's analysis illustrates that there are currently more African-American males in prisons and jails in the United States than enrolled in institutions of higher education (Mauer, 1994a, pp. 1–2). In terms of future projections, the National Council on Crime and Delinquency (NCCD) contends that if the remainder of the states follow in the footsteps of the Federal Government and of those states such as Washington and California, the inmate population in American prisons will rise to a minimum of 2.26 million within the next 10 years (*Corrections Digest*, 1994b, p. 1).

An increase of over a million inmates will mandate an increase in the level of funding necessary to accommodate such a large population. According to NCCD estimates, the Federal Government and the states will need an additional $351 billion during the next 10 years (*Corrections Digest*, 1994b, p. 1). In California, the effects of the three strikes provision are estimated to increase the costs of operating the state prisons by $75 million for fiscal year 1994–1995 (Tucker, 1994, p. 7). The requisite prison construction that will be necessary to fulfill the legislative provisions is estimated to cost California residents $21 billion (Mauer, 1994a, p. 22). The Federal grants that the states are hoping to receive from the Federal Government will fall far short of these costs.

In addition, there are also the costs associated with providing health care and security for inmates over the age of 50. Based upon demographic data obtained from the California Department of Corrections, NCCD projects that the number of inmates who

are 50 years of age or older will increase by 15,300 from 1994 to 1999. Although these older inmates comprised only 4 percent of California's prison population in 1994, it is estimated that they will represent 12 percent of the prison population in 2005 (NCCD, 1994, p. 3). State officials in California expect that the full impact of this legislation will be realized in the year 2020 at which time over 125,000 inmates or 20 percent of the prison population will be 50 years of age or older (NCCD, 1994, p. 3).

The New Jersey Department of Corrections has estimated that a new baseball sentencing bill would have a substantial financial impact on prison costs. In a financial impact statement, the Office of Legislative Services reported that "for every inmate who is not paroled as a result of this bill, an additional $80,000 in construction costs and $1 million in operating costs would be incurred over the lifetime of that inmate . . . that accounting breaks down to $25,000 per year per inmate for operating costs or an additional $3.75 million each year for 30 years, or $1.7 billion" (Gray, 1994, p. B9). In other words, Todd Clear estimates it would cost "$1 million to lock up a 30-year criminal for life" (Clear cited in Levinson, 1994, p. B2).

In his review of the costs of crime and punishment, Thomas not only finds that "the fastest growing segment of state budgets in fiscal 1994 is corrections" but he considers that as more funds are put into public safety and crime control, there are fewer funds for other public and social programs (Thomas, 1994, p. 31). For example, Geiger reports that "seventy percent of all the prison space in use today was built since 1985. Only 11 percent of our nation's classrooms were built during the 1980s" (1994, p. 22).

In an assessment of the consequences of baseball sentencing laws on prison costs, The Sentencing Project cautioned that "the most significant impact of these proposals, though, will begin to take place 10–20 years after their implementation, since the prisoners affected by these proposals would generally be locked up for at least that period of time under current practices" (1994, p. 2).

Confronted with the fact that an older inmate population will have a higher incidence of circulatory, respiratory, dietary, and ambulatory difficulties than younger inmates, prison officials need to anticipate and plan for geriatric services and programs now. Another realization is that these inmates pose the least risk in terms of criminal behavior. As a group, they are not a threat to society since crime is primarily an activity of young males. As a result, while the United States will be spending millions of dollars on the incarceration of these older prisoners, this is unlikely to reduce the incidence of crime.

Mauer (1994a) contends that these sentencing policies will have several lasting effects. First, the money spent to build new prisons will represent a commitment to maintain them for at least 50 years. Once the public has invested the requisite capital for construction, the courts will continue to fill the beds. Second, the funds that will be allocated to the increased costs of corrections will not be able to be used for other crime prevention measures. There will be little money available to improve the effectiveness of other components of the system such as juvenile justice, and diversion or early intervention programs will receive only limited funding and support. Third, the incarceration rate of African-American males will continue to increase. As a result, there is little reason to believe that the status of young African-American males will improve when their representation in American prisons and jails exceeds their representation in college classrooms. Fourth, there will be little opportunity to fully examine and discuss crime in the political arena because prevailing policies will be so dependent upon a limited range of sentencing initiatives (Mauer, 1994a, p. 23). Once the "quick fix" mentality to crime has been adopted, it is less likely to expect a divergence from the "punitive-reactive" response to crime.

Assessing the Effectiveness of Baseball Sentences

While some legislatures and policy wonks would disagree, "there is no reason to believe that continuing to increase the severity of penalties will have any significant impact on crime" (The Sentencing Project, 1994, p. 2). In their critique of incarceration trends, Irwin and Austin observed that political rhetoric has distorted rational sentencing policies and resulted in large increases in the number of prisoners, many of whom are nonviolent, without any corresponding reductions in crime (1994).

In a study of California's get-tough-on-crime strategy, "which quadrupled the prison population between 1980 and 1992," Joan Petersilia concluded "that the much higher imprisonment rates in California had no appreciable effect on violent crime and only slight effects on property crime" (Petersilia, cited in Broder, 1994a, p. 4). Despite such findings that these measures may be ineffective in reducing crime, and notwithstanding the spiraling costs of baseball sentencing, the punishment model continues to prevail.

In her review of retributive justice and determinate sentencing reforms, Griset (1991, p. 186) concludes that:

the determinate ideal arose as a reaction, a backlash against the perceived evil of the reigning paradigm. While the theoretical underpinnings of determinacy attracted a large following, in practice the determinate ideal has not lived up to the dreams or the promises of its creators.

With a similar argument, Robert Gangi, executive director of the Correctional Association of New York, writes that "three strikes and you're out represents extension of a policy that has proven a failure" (1994, p. A14).

With a strong momentum toward tougher sentences and the success of get-tough political posturing on crime issues, it is unlikely that baseball metaphors will fall into disuse. For example, a proposal in Oregon would offer voters a "grand slam" package for crime. This package would require prisoners to work or study, prohibit sentence reductions without a two-thirds legislative vote, make sentencing alternatives to prison more difficult, and impose mandatory minimum sentences for all violent offenders older than 15 (Rohter, 1994, p. A12).

Conclusion

In this review of the recently enacted Federal crime bill and the Washington, California, and Georgia statutes, and in the assessment of the anticipated consequences of recent sentencing statutes, baseball punishment is characterized as the latest episode in the search for the "quick fix" to a complicated and disturbing social problem. These attempts to prevent crime, however, are misguided and will prove to be far more costly and ineffective than their proponents and the public could have anticipated. In the rush to enact "three strikes legislation," elected officials and the electorate appear to have given little thought to the long-term effects of these provisions.

In terms of additional systemic costs, these laws will have a considerable effect on an already over-burdened court system. The process of justice relies extensively on an offender entering into a plea agreement. Once these laws become enacted, there will be little incentive for an offender to plead guilty to any charges which could result in longer periods of incarceration. If offenders know that pleading guilty will constitute a first or second strike let alone a third, there is a greater likelihood that they will demand a trial. As a result, such legislation will necessitate additional funding for more prosecutors, judges, and court administrative and support staff.

One of the distressing aspects of these sentencing proposals is that they seem to have far-reaching effects on other offender populations. Included in the newly enacted Federal code is a provision to try as adults those juveniles who are 13 years of age and charged with certain violent crimes. It will be possible for the first strike to have been committed at age 13. This tendency to treat juvenile offenders more harshly is but one manifestation of a trend in juvenile justice mandating waiver into the adult court and sentencing younger juveniles to prison. Efforts to confront the crime problem would be more effective if society addressed the tough issues of gun availability, family violence, and drug prevention (Mauer, 1994c).

The "three strikes" legislation has also raised public expectations far beyond the likelihood of success. A *Wall Street Journal*/NBC News poll found that 75 percent of Americans interviewed believed that enacting such legislation would make a "major difference" in the crime rate (*Criminal Justice Newsletter*, 1994d, p. 1). Apparently, elected officials and the media have succeeded in pandering to the American penchant for oversimplifying the causes of crime.

Despite legislative sentencing changes, the *crime* problem has not been addressed. Absent a commitment to do more than get tough on criminals, the "three strikes" legislation is just one more costly slogan which will have no appreciable benefit for society. Research and commentary on the consequences of baseball punishment suggest that prison populations will continue to grow, corrections expenditures will consume larger percentages of government budgets, and sentence severity will have "no discernible effect on the crime rate" (Currie, 1994, p. 120). As the rhetoric pushes punitive policies to the margin, baseball metaphors and politicalization of sentencing will continue to divert attention from addressing the antecedents and correlates of crime. It is not surprising that the emotionalizing of policy results in "feel-good bromides, like 'three-strikes' . . . that create the illusion of problem solving" (Kramer, 1994, p. 29).

References

Allen, Harry (1994) Personal Communication. (September 17).

Balz, Dan (1994) "Pete Wilson: Practicing the Politics of Survival." *The Washington Post National Weekly Edition.* (August 29–September 4): 14.

Black, Donald (1976) *The Behavior of Law.* New York, NY: Academic Press.

Booth, William (1994) "Florida Turns Up the Heat on Crime." *The Washington Post National Weekly Edition.* (February 21–27): 37.

Broder, David (1994a) "Population Explosion." *The Washington Post National Weekly Edition.* (April 25–May 1): 4.

——— (1994b) "When Tough Isn't Smart." *The Criminologist.* (July/August) 19:4; 6.

California Legislative Service (1994) Chapter 12 (A.B. No. 971) (West) 1994 Portion of 1993–94 Regular Session "An Act to Amend Section 667 of the Penal Code."

California Penal Code Section 1192.7

Congressional Digest (1994) "The Federal Role in Crime Control." Washington, DC (June-July).

Corrections Digest (1994a) "Experts Doubt '3 Strikes You're Out' Laws Will Effectively Curb Crime." (February 9): 7–9.

——— (1994b) "Senate Crime Bill Will More Than Double American Prison Population by Year 2005." (March 9): 1–4.

Crime Control Digest (1994) "Three-Time Loser' Bill to Be Introduced in House." (January 24): 5–6.

Criminal Justice Newsletter (1994a) "California Passes a Tough Three-Strikes-You're-Out Law." (April 4): 6–7.

——— (1994b) "Texas Comptroller Warns of 'Prison-Industrial Complex.' " (May 2): 2–3.

——— (1994c) "State Legislators Moving Toward Tougher Sentencing." (June 15): 1–2.

——— (1994d) "State Chief Justices Oppose Senate Crime Bill Provisions." (February 15); 1–3.

Cronin, Thomas, Tania Cronin, and Michael Milakovich (1981) *U.S. v. Crime in the Streets.* Bloomington, IN: Indiana University Press.

Currie, Elliot (1994) "What's Wrong with the Crime Bill." *The Nation.* (January 31) 258:4; 118–121.

Egan, Timothy (1994) "A 3-Strike Penal Law Shows It's Not as Simple as It Seems." *New York Times.* (February 15): A1; A11.

Final Legislative Report (1994) Fifty-Third Washington State Legislature. 1994 Regular Session and First Special Session.

Gangi, Robert (1994) "Where Three-Strikes Plan Takes Us in 20 Years." *New York Times.* (February 7): A14.

Geiger, Keith (1994) "Upgrading School Buildings." *The Washington Post National Weekly Edition.* (September 26–October 2): 22.

Georgia Statues 17-10-6.1 Code of Georgia, Title 17. Criminal Procedure, Chapter 10 Sentence and Punishment, Article 1. Procedure for Sentencing and Imposition of Punishment.

Gladwell, Malcolm (1994) "The Crime Bill May Not Be the Cure." *The Washington Post National Weekly Edition.* (June 6–12): 33.

Gleason, Bucky (1994) "Anti-Crime Packages Don't Work." *Erie Times News.* (October 9): A1; A12.

Gray, Jerry (1994) "New Jersey Senate Approves Bill to Jail 3-Time Criminals for Life." *New York Times.* (May 13): A1; B9.

Griset, Pamala (1991) *Determinate Sentencing: The Promise and the Reality of Retributive Justice.* Albany, NY: State University of New York Press.

Idelson, Holly (1994) "Crime Bill's Final Version." *Congressional Quarterly.* (July 30) 52: 30; 2138.

Irwin, John and James Austin (1994) *It's About Time: America's Imprisonment Binge.* Belmont, CA: Wadsworth Publishing Co.

Kramer, Michael (1994) "Tough. But Smart?" *Time.* (February 7): 29.

Kurtz, Howard (1994) "The Campaign Weapon of Choice." *The Washington Post National Weekly Edition.* (September 19–25): 12.

Levinson, Arlene (1994) "Three Strikes and You're Out." *Erie Morning News.* (January 25): B2.

Lewis, Anthony (1994) "Crime and Politics." *New York Times.* (September 16): A13.

Lewis, Neil (1993) "Crime Rates Decline; Outrage Hasn't." *New York Times.* (December 3): B6.

Mauer, Marc (1994a) "Americans Behind Bars: The International Use of Incarceration, 1992–1993." The Sentencing Project. Washington DC.

——— (1994b) "An Assessment of Sentencing Issues and the Death Penalty in the 1990s." The Sentencing Project. Washington DC.

——— (1994c) "Testimony of Marc Mauer before the House Judiciary Committee, Subcommittee on Crime and Criminal Justice on "Three Strikes and You're Out." (March 1): 1–13.

Merlo, Alida and Peter Benekos (1992a) "Introduction: The Politics of Corrections" in Peter Benekos and Alida Merlo (eds.) *Corrections: Dilemmas and Directions.* Cincinnati, OH: Anderson Publishing Co.

——— (1992b) Adapting Conservative Correctional Policies to the Economic Realities of the 1990s." *Criminal Justice Policy Review.* (March) 6:1, 1–16.

National Council on Crime and Delinquency (1994) "The Aging of California's Prison Population: An Assessment of Three Strikes Legislation." 1–6.

National Public Radio (1994) Broadcast of "All Things Considered" (September 30).

Neri, Albert (1994a) "With Candidates in Dead Heat, Ridge Uses Casey in Ad." *Erie Morning News.* (October 6): A14.

——— (1994b) "Singel Faces Up to His Worst Nightmare." *Erie Times News.* (October 9): B3.

New York Times (1993) "Hunt for Kidnapped Girl, 12, Is Narrowed to Small Woods." (December 3): A22.

——— (1994a) "Mandatory Sentencing is Criticized by Justice." (March 10): A14.

——— (1994b) "Georgia Voters to Consider '2-Strikes' Law." (March 16): A10.

——— (1994c) "California Judge Refuses to Apply a Tough New Sentencing Law." (September 20): A9.

——— (1994d) "Killer Withdraws Plea in a '3 Strikes' Case." (September 28): A19.

Peyser, Marc (1994) "Strike Three and You're Not Out." *Newsweek.* (August 29): 53.

Raspberry, William (1993) "Digging In Deeper." *The Washington Post National Weekly Edition.* (November 1–7): 29.

Reno, Janet (1994) "Memorandum from the Attorney General: The Violent Crime Control and Law Enforcement Act of 1994." (September 15): 1–5.

Rohter, Larry (1994) "States Embracing Tougher Measures for Fighting Crime." *New York Times.* (May 10): A1; A12.

Schneider, William (1993) "Crime and Politics: Incumbents Got Mugged by Fear in Our Streets." *The Washington Post National Weekly Edition.* (November 15–21): 24.

Shover, Neal and Werner Einstadter (1988) *Analyzing American Corrections.* Belmont, CA: Wadsworth Publishing Co.

The Sentencing Project (1989) "The Lessons of Willie Horton." Washington, DC.

———(1994) "Why '3 Strikes and You're Out' Won't Reduce Crime." Washington, DC.

The Vindicator (1994) "Law Will Star in Fall Campaigns." (August 28): A5.

Thomas, Pierre (1994) "Getting to the Bottom Line on Crime." *The Washington Post National Weekly Edition.* (July 18–24): 31.

Tucker, Beverly (1994) "Can California Afford 3 Strikes?" California Teachers Association *Action* (May): 7; 17.

U.S. Government Printing Office (1994) "The Violent Crime Control and Law Enforcement Act of 1994." Conference Report. Washington, DC.

Walker, Samuel (1994) *Sense and Nonsense About Crime and Drugs: A Policy Guide,* Third Edition. Belmont, CA: Wadsworth Publishing Co.

Washington Laws (1994) *1994 Pamphlet Edition Session Laws* Fifty-Third Legislature 1994 Regular Session. Chapter 1 "Persistent Offenders-Life Sentence on Third Conviction." (Statute Law Committee) Olympia, WA.

 Article Review Form at end of book.

Provide a current overview of supermax prisons.

Assessing Supermax Operations

Richard H. Franklin

Richard Franklin is a correctional program specialist with the NIC Prisons Division in Washington, D.C. For more information on technical assistance or training on this topic, contact Dick Franklin at 1-800-995-6423, ext. 145. For the complete results of Supermax housing: A survey of current practice, contact the NIC Information Center at 1-800-877-1461.

Legislators, policy-makers and the public have expressed a need to "get tough on crime" and often view the creation of harsher prison environments as an appropriate response. Many feel that institutions should attempt to control inmate behavior by emphasizing the use of restrictions and sanctions—reduced rehabilitation activity and high-level incapacitation—while decreasing the use of incentives. Super-maximum security (or "supermax") prisons are an outgrowth of this shift in emphasis. Increasingly, some elected officials embrace supermax as a preferred construction alternative when confronted with the need for more prison cells.

As a result, supermax prisons are proliferating and, as their numbers grow, their operations are being examined and discussed by correctional leaders, courts, human rights groups, the media and others. A broad range of opinion has emerged concerning the legitimacy, constitutionality and propriety of this degree of incapacitation. These facilities also raise a number of compelling questions for the field of corrections. For instance, what defines a supermax prison and which offenders comprise its population? What, if any, are appropriate programs for inmates and how are they delivered? How is the facility staffed and what is the impact on those working in a supermax prison?

Recognizing the supermax phenomenon as an issue of importance to many jurisdictions and the corrections field as a whole, the National Institute of Corrections (NIC) Advisory Board urged NIC staff to focus on the issue. In December 1996, the NIC Prisons Division and the NIC Information Center conducted a nationwide survey of supermax policies and practices. Survey responses were received from correctional systems in all 50 states and the District of Columbia; the Federal Bureau of Prisons; Correctional Services of Canada; New York City; and Cook County, Ill.

The survey offered a working definition of supermax as a facility or unit within a facility which provides management and control of inmates who have exhibited violent or seriously disruptive behavior while incarcerated. The survey results, however, showed that a common definition of supermax does not exist. What is considered "supermax" in one jurisdiction may not be "supermax" in another. Jurisdictions varied widely on such issues as housing and resources available, the forces precipitating supermax development, the inmate population and classification strategies.

The survey provided a current overview of the supermax phenomenon.

- Thirty-four prison systems are either operating or soon will open supermax facilities/units. Four others are considering the need for supermax facilities or are actively pursuing construction funds.

Reprinted with permission from *Corrections Today*, July 1998, Vol. 60, No. 4, pp. 126–127.

- Thirty-six prison systems cited the need to better manage violent and seriously disruptive inmates as a major factor in their jurisdictions' development of supermax housing; 17 of these systems include gang members as appropriate candidates for supermax housing.

- Jurisdictions vary greatly in the length of time inmates are confined in supermax facilities and the criteria for admission and release. Approval authority for admission and release of inmates varies from the warden or superintendent to the director/commissioner of the prison system.

- Programs in supermax facilities range from "none available" to "cell-front only," television/ video programming or limited group programming.

- Jurisdictions differ in whether mentally ill and/or developmentally disabled inmates are placed in supermax housing.

- Transitional programming is available only in some jurisdictions.

For several years, NIC has offered technical assistance to jurisdictions considering or operating supermax housing and will do so again in 1999. In addition, a seminar will be offered in fiscal year 1999 (between Oct. 1, 1998, and Sept. 31, 1999) for correctional administrators and wardens/superintendents responsible for prison planning or operations. The seminar focuses on planning, program and operational issues specific to supermax facilities.

To assist corrections managers and decision-makers as they assess current supermax operations, plan high-custody facilities or enter discussions about the nature of and need for such facilities, the NIC Prisons Division is developing a monograph on supermax prisons. It will cover the history of supermax, issues of definition, operational considerations, staffing and legal issues, and critical design issues. A checklist that suggests guidelines or considerations for supermax planning, design and operations will be included.

 Article Review Form at end of book.

Why do legislators misread the opinions of their constituents regarding capital punishment?

The Misperception of Public Opinion toward Capital Punishment

Examining the spuriousness explanation of death penalty support

Edmund F. McGarrell
Marla Sandys
Indiana University

In the United States, one of the key legal issues surrounding the death penalty is whether its imposition violates the Eighth Amendment's prohibition against cruel and unusual punishment. Complicating this issue is the understanding that the meaning of the cruel and unusual punishment clause is dynamic and "must draw its meaning from the evolving standards of decency that mark the progress of a ma-

turing society" (*Trop v. Dulles*, 1958, p. 101). Two mechanisms for determining "evolving standards of decency" are to examine public opinion and to analyze trends in legislative decisions at the state level.

The U.S. Supreme Court has often cited attitudes toward capital punishment in their opinions on the constitutionality of the death penalty. For instance, in a 1968 decision prohibiting the practice of summarily banning death penalty opponents from capital juries, the court cited public opinion polls and noted that such a prohibition would elimi-

nate too large a segment of the populace (*Witherspoon v. Illinois*, 1968). In the 1976 *Gregg v. Georgia* decision that approved the constitutionality of the death penalty,[1] the court again noted public opinion polls that indicated a majority of the public favored the death penalty. In the same decision, Justice Stewart also argued that the passage of death penalty legislation by 35 separate states indicated that capital punishment did not violate "evolving standards of decency."

As recently as February of 1994, Justice Blackmun referred to public support for capital punishment in his dissent from the denial of certiorari in the case of *Callins v. Collins* (1994):

Although *most of the public seems to desire* [italics added], and the Constitution appears to permit, the penalty of death, it surely is beyond dispute that if the death penalty cannot be administered consistently and rationally, it may not be administered at all. (p. 1131)

Finally, the recently passed federal crime bill provides further evidence of political support for capital punishment. Although there was debate over the inclusion of the Racial Justice Act provision, in the end the bill excluded the provision thus signaling the strength of the presumption of popular support for the death penalty as approximately 60 capital offenses were created (Federal Death Penalty Act of 1994).

The commonly held belief that the American public strongly endorses capital punishment is derived from public opinion polls that find that over 70% of the public favor capital punishment when asked the question "Do you favor or oppose the death penalty for persons convicted of murder" (Bohm, 1991). Bohm's (1991) review of Gallup Poll data shows that after reaching a low point in the mid 1960s, support has increased to current levels of around 75% (see also Death Penalty Information Center, 1993; Flanagan & Maguire, 1992; Fox, Radelet, & Bonsteel, 1990–1991). Although there are some demographic differences in level of support, majorities of all major demographic groups state that they generally favor the death penalty. Given such findings, state legislators enacting death penalty statutes and Justices interpreting the Eighth Amendment appear to be on solid ground in assuming popular support for the death penalty. Some research, however, questions this assumption.

At a general level, political scientists have noted that elites such as state legislators are often misinformed about public opinion on given issues (Uslaner & Weber, 1979). Studies of public and elite opinion on criminal justice issues suggest that such misperceptions are common on crime policy. For example, Riley and Rose (1980), building on Berk and Rossi's (1977) study of correctional elites, found the public in Washington state to be much less punitive than estimated by correctional elites.[2] Similarly, Gottfredson and Taylor (1984) compared correctional policy makers with the general citizenry and found the public to be more reform oriented than believed by the policy makers (see also Johnson & Huff, 1987).

More specifically, some researchers (Bohm, 1991; Bowers, 1993) have questioned whether evaluations of public support for capital punishment are accurate. Much of the knowledge nonacademics have on crime comes from the mass media (Graber, 1980). Sensationalism sells and thus the most heinous crimes are likely to receive the most media attention. Not surprisingly, some capital cases embody the desired fodder for the evening news reports. As such, people have a distorted view of the typical capital case, and they generalize from the atypical case in forming an attitude toward the death penalty (e.g., Hamill, Wilson, & Nisbett, 1980).[3]

The most important research that questions the assumed public support for capital punishment comes from surveys that ask respondents not only whether they generally favor the death penalty but also whether they would favor alternatives to capital punishment. Most commonly, respondents are asked whether they would favor life without the possibility of parole (LWOP) or life without parole coupled with a requirement that the offender work in prison and make restitution to the victim's family (LWOP plus work).

As early as 1986, a study in the state of Florida revealed that although general support for capital punishment was at 84%, only 24% of the 900 registered voters who were surveyed said that they would *not* support a sentence of LWOP plus work (Cambridge Survey Research, 1986). Similar findings were obtained by Haney and Hurtado (1989) for the state of California. In particular, 79% of their respondents indicated that they were at least somewhat in favor of capital punishment. However, only 26% of the respondents maintained their preference for a sentence of death when provided with the alternative of LWOP plus work.

More recently, Bowers and Vandiver (1991a, 1991b) also have found general support for capital punishment among citizens in New York and Nebraska (71% and 80%, respectively), yet a preference for LWOP plus work (73% and 64% favor LWOP plus work, 19% and 26% favor death penalty, respectively).[4] Thus although general support is high, it drops substantially when citizens are provided with the LWOP plus work alternative.

These findings have led Bowers (1993; see also Williams, Longmire, & Gulick, 1988) to argue that rather than reflect a deep commitment to the death penalty, the traditional question of whether one generally favors capital punishment merely demonstrates that in the absence of a harsh, meaningful, alternative punishment, the public will endorse death. This is, he argues, a spurious indication of the public's endorsement of the death penalty. Bowers's (1993, pp. 163–167) spuriousness explanation rests on three hypotheses:

1. "People will abandon the death penalty when presented with a harsh but meaningful alternative."

2. "People see fundamental shortcomings in the death penalty as a punishment."

3. "People accept the death penalty because they believe currently available alternatives are insufficiently harsh or meaningful."

The present study provides an opportunity to examine Bowers's (1993) thesis. The survey of Indiana residents included items on general support for capital punishment, support for LWOP and LWOP plus work, the perceived arbitrariness of the death penalty, estimates of time served for murder, and related items. Thus we can test whether Bowers's findings are replicated in another state. In addition, by conducting the legislator survey we can directly examine Bowers's implication that lawmakers misperceive citizens' attitudes toward capital punishment.

Method

Citizens Survey

The surveys conducted for this study most closely followed the legislative survey conducted by Flanagan, Brennan, and Cohen (1991) in New York State as well as surveys conducted by others in recent years in a number of states (e.g., California, Florida, Georgia, and Nebraska; see Bowers, 1993).

The survey was pretested through administration by Indiana University students during the fall and winter of 1991–1992. The citizen survey was administered in June 1993 by the Indiana University Public Opinion Laboratory in Indianapolis. The interviews were conducted by professional interviewers specially trained for this project.

The sample was obtained by using a proportionally representative sample based upon gender and age groupings for each of the 92 counties in Indiana. A computer program was used to randomly generate telephone numbers for all exchanges in Indiana. The resulting sample is representative of the over 18 years of age population of the state. A total of 514 interviews were completed. The characteristics of the sample are presented in Table 1.

Legislative Survey

The legislative survey was conducted by five graduate students as part of a seminar taught by the second author on capital punishment. The students were trained specifically for this project.

The graduate students began attempting to contact the legisla-

| Table I | Characteristics of Citizen Sample |

	Percentage		Percentage
Gender		**Income**	
Female	54.5	Under $10,000	7.8
Male	45.5	$10,001–20,000	14.6
Age		$20,001–30,000	19.6
18–34	35.2	$30,001–40,000	16.1
35–54	36.0	$40,001–50,000	14.6
55+	28.8	$50,001–75,000	8.0
Race/Ethnicity		Over $75,000	6.4
White	90.3	Refused	12.8
Black	6.4	**Home ownership**	
Other	2.0	Own	73.7
Refused	1.4	Rent	22.2
Education		Refused	4.1
Grade school	2.7	**Political orientation**	
Some high school	10.1	Very liberal	3.1
High school graduate	45.5	Liberal	17.3
Technical/vocational	3.3	Middle of the road	37.4
Some college	16.7	Conservative	30.0
College graduate	16.0	Very conservative	7.2
Graduate/professional degree	4.9	Refused	5.1
Don't know/not applicable	0.8	**Political party affiliation**	
Marital status		Republican	36.8
Married	59.1	Democrat	31.3
Remarried	5.4	Independent	17.5
Single, never married	19.5	Not registered	2.7
Divorced/separated	8.4	Other	11.7
Widowed	7.2		
Refused	0.4		

Note: N = 514.

tors by telephone on November 15, 1991 and continued through the first week of December.[5] The second phase of telephone calls began in the middle of January and continued through April (1992). A copy of the instrument was mailed to legislators who wanted to participate in the study but preferred to complete it on their own. In addition, copies of the instrument were mailed to all legislators who could never be reached by telephone.

Most of the data were collected during the first phase of interviewing (n = 78, 69%). Of these 78 completed questionnaires, 66 were based on telephone interviews and 12 were completed by mail. An additional 35 completed questionnaires were obtained during the second phase of interviewing, 17 of which were conducted over the phone. Thus our data are based on 83 telephone interviews and 30 mail questionnaires. Of 150 state legislators in Indiana, 113 participated in this study for a response rate of 75%.[6]

Findings

Citizens of Indiana, consistent with findings from other states and from nationwide polls (Bohm, 1991; Bowers, 1993; Death Penalty Information Center, 1993; Flanagan & Maguire, 1992; Fox et al., 1990–1991), voiced strong support for the death penalty when asked whether they generally favor or oppose the death penalty for persons convicted of first degree murder. As the column marginal in Table 2 indicates, over three quarters expressed general support for capital punishment. Only 14% voiced opposition to the death penalty. These, of course, are the type of findings that lead to the commonly accepted wisdom that American citizens strongly favor capital punishment.

Support for the death penalty dropped considerably, however, when Indiana residents were asked whether they would prefer life in prison with absolutely no chance of being released on parole (LWOP). Indeed, more of the respondents (45% compared to 40%) preferred the LWOP alternative to

Table 2 General Attitudes toward Death Penalty by Preference for LWOP and LWOP Plus Work (percentages)

	Generally Favor or Oppose Capital Punishment[a]					
	Strongly Favor	Somewhat Favor	Somewhat Oppose	Strongly Oppose	Don't Know	Total
Prefer LWOP[b]						
Yes	29	51	84	81	67	45
No	59	25	12	6	6	40
Not sure	9	21	2	13	15	12
No answer	3	3	2	0	12	4
Total	56	20	8	6	9	100
	(n = 287)	(n = 105)	(n = 43)	(n = 43)	(n = 48)	(N = 514)

χ^2 = 133.7, 12 df, Significance = .000.

Prefer LWOP plus work[c]						
Yes	50	77	81	84	73	62
No	39	12	7	10	6	26
Not sure	9	10	9	6	12	9
No answer	2	1	2	0	8	2
Total	56	20	8	6	9	100
	(n = 287)	(n = 105)	(n = 43)	(n = 43)	(n = 48)	(N = 514)

χ^2 = 69.3, 12 df, Significance = .000.

a. Do you generally favor or oppose capital punishment in cases where people are convicted of first degree murder?
b. If convicted first degree murderers in Indiana could be sentenced to life in prison with absolutely no chance of ever being released on parole, would you prefer this as an alternative to the death penalty?
c. If convicted first degree murderers in Indiana could be sentenced to life in prison without parole and also be required to work in prison industries for money that would go to the families of their victims, would you prefer this as an alternative to the death penalty?

capital punishment (see row marginal, Table 2).

The shift in support was even more dramatic when citizens were asked whether they would prefer LWOP if coupled with a requirement that the offender work in prison industries for money that would go to the families of the murder victim (LWOP plus work). When presented with this option, 62% preferred it over a sentence of death (see Table 2). Whereas 76% of Indiana citizens favored capital punishment when provided no alternative, preference for the penalty was reduced to 26% when respondents were given the option of choosing life in prison without parole coupled with work and restitution to the victim's family.

Table 2 also indicates that preference for the LWOP and LWOP plus work options varies among respondents who expressed different levels of support for capital punishment generally. As would be anticipated, opponents of capital punishment were more likely to favor LWOP than were supporters of capital punishment. Yet it is interesting to note that among those who stated they somewhat favor capital punishment, over half preferred LWOP. Only among those strongly in favor of capital punishment did respondents continue to prefer the death penalty.

When the focus shifts to the option of LWOP plus work, the movement away from capital punishment support was even more pronounced. Among those somewhat in favor of capital punishment, over three quarters stated a preference for LWOP plus work. Even among those most in favor of capital punishment (those claiming to strongly favor), one half preferred LWOP

plus work. Only 39% of this group rejected the LWOP plus work option.[7]

The results from the Indiana survey are consistent with findings from several other states and thus provide strong support for Bowers's (1993) hypothesis that people will abandon their support for capital punishment when provided with a harsh, meaningful, alternative sentence.

In an attempt to discern whether citizens held concerns about the unfairness of the death penalty's application, similar to the concerns given voice by the Supreme Court in the *Furman* decision (*Furman v. Georgia*, 1972), Bowers asked whether "the death penalty is too arbitrary because some people are executed and others are sent to prison for the very same crimes" (Bowers, 1993, p. 165). Over three quarters of the respondents in New York City, New York State, and Nebraska agreed with this statement. In our survey of Indiana residents, 79% of the respondents agreed that the death penalty is too arbitrary. Further evidence of perceived arbitrariness was observed in the finding that 96% agreed that laws are needed to guarantee against racial bias.

A third hypothesis is that the public may want the death penalty because it offers a sure incapacitative sentence. As a way of addressing this issue, Indiana respondents were asked to estimate the number of years actually served by someone sentenced to a life term. Over one quarter responded that persons given a life sentence would actually serve 10 years or less. Over 60% stated that life sentences meant less than 20 years in prison. Only 9% believed that a person sentenced to life would serve more than 30 years. Indiana residents then be-

lieve that one major alternative to the death penalty, a sentence of life imprisonment, does not mean that the person will be kept out of society for life.[8]

Perceptions of the length of time served under a life sentence also are related to general support for the death penalty. Respondents who believe that life sentences result in shorter sentences were more likely to favor the death penalty than were respondents who believe life sentences result in longer sentences ($\chi^2 = 17.49$, 3 *df*, significant $\leq .001$). Evidently, many respondents do not believe that *life* sentences actually provide for sufficient incapacitation of persons convicted of capital offenses. Hence one possible explanation for the strong support for LWOP evidenced in this study may be that such a sentence provides for the incapacitative benefits desired by the citizens of Indiana.[9]

Spuriousness among Lawmakers and Their Constituents

Do Indiana lawmakers accurately perceive their constituents' willingness to abandon the death penalty for alternative sentences? The parallel administration of a legislative survey allowed us to address this question. When Indiana legislators were asked whether their constituents would prefer capital punishment, LWOP, LWOP plus work, or LWOP plus work with the possibility of parole after 30 years, most believed their constituents would prefer the death penalty. All told, 50% believed their constituents would prefer capital punishment and 40% believed their constituents would prefer one of the three variations of LWOP (see Table 3). As noted earlier, however, 62% of

Table 3 Indiana Citizens' and Legislators' Perceptions of Their Counterparts' Preferences for Death Penalty Proposals

Citizens:

Which punishment do you suppose your representative to the state legislature would prefer?

	Percentage
Death penalty	15
LWOP	5
LWOP plus work for restitution	36
LWOP plus work for restitution with chance for parole after 30 years	32
Don't know/not applicable	11
N = 514	

Legislators:

Which punishment do you suppose your constituents would prefer?

	Percentage
Death penalty	50
LWOP	5
LWOP plus work for restitution	27
LWOP plus work for restitution with chance for parole after 30 years	8
Don't know/not applicable	9
N = 111	

the citizens preferred LWOP plus work and only 26% continued to support the death penalty.

In contrast, citizens overestimated lawmakers' support for LWOP alternatives. Only 15% of the public stated that their representative would favor the death penalty if given the various LWOP options. In reality, however, 38% of the lawmakers continued to support the death penalty (51% preferred LWOP plus work).

Thus it appears, in Indiana at least, that lawmakers underestimate the degree of public support for LWOP, particularly LWOP coupled with work for restitution. Further, citizens overestimate the support of their lawmakers for LWOP. In reality, there appears to be much more support for alternatives to the death penalty among the public than that assumed by legislators.

Conclusion

In the post-*Gregg* era, most state legislatures, operating under the assumption of overwhelming public support for the death penalty, have passed death penalty legislation.[10] The courts, in turn, have had to review this legislation and have attempted to apply the legal concept of "evolving standards of decency" in determining the constitutionality of death penalty statues. Bowers's (1993) spuriousness thesis of public support for capital punishment, supported by the present research in Indiana, suggests that legislators and judges have made such decisions under a mistaken impression of public sentiments. Indeed, 20 years of statutory provision and judicial decision making may be based on a "house of cards." Rather than a public clamoring for executions, this line of

research[11] suggests that what the public wants is for persons convicted of a capital offense to be handled in a way that prevents them from ever repeating the offense again. In the absence of serious sentences that can provide such assurance, the public expresses support for the death penalty. Given an option that provides the goal of incapacitation (LWOP) and that offers the benefit of addressing in some fashion the needs of murder victims' families, the public shows solid support for alternatives to the death penalty. This is true even for those who claim they strongly favor capital punishment.

Perceptions of Life without the Possibility of Parole

The findings of this study are clear-cut: People prefer alternatives to capital punishment. Yet the fact remains that there has been no shortage of people sentenced to death in recent years. One reason may be that, as revealed in this study, most people think that convicted murderers who are not sentenced to death serve relatively short prison terms. In reality, at the time of this study murderers in Indiana who were not given a death sentence had to serve 30 years (on the murder charge) before becoming *eligible* for parole.,[12] However, only 9% of the respondents believed that convicted murderers given a life sentence would *serve* 31 years or more in prison. The results of a recent national survey are similar: only 11% of the 1,000 registered voters questioned believed that a person sentenced to life without parole would never be released from prison (Death Penalty Information Center, 1993).

The crux of Bowers's (1993) thesis rests on the availability of *meaningful* alternative sentences.

In the current research (and Bowers's as well), the LWOP alternative was phrased as "life in prison with absolutely no chance of ever being released on parole." When presented with this explicit definition of LWOP, people prefer it as an alternative to capital punishment. Thus a major obstacle to a greater reliance on LWOP sentences appears to be people's (jurors in most death penalty states decide the sentence in capital cases) belief that a sentence of death is the only way to ensure that the defendant will never be released back into society.

The importance of an accurate understanding of the meaning of a life sentence was the issue in a recent U.S. Supreme Court case (*Simmons v. South Carolina*, 1994). During the original trial, the state alluded to the defendant's future dangerousness. The defense, however, was prohibited from informing the sentencing jury that the defendant was ineligible for parole. The jury even sent a note to the judge, during the sentencing deliberations, asking whether a life sentence included the possibility of parole. Theoretically, jurors are not to discuss or consider parole eligibility in arriving at their sentencing decisions. The judge informed the jury of this requirement, adding that the terms should be understood in their "plain and ordinary meaning." Twenty-five minutes later the jury returned with a sentence of death.

On appeal to the U.S. Supreme Court, Simmons argued that he had the right, under the Due Process Clause of the Fourteenth Amendment, to inform the sentencing jury that he was ineligible for parole. The Court concurred and thus reversed the judgment.

Justice Blackmun, writing for the majority, noted: "It can hardly be questioned that most juries lack accurate information about the precise meaning of 'life imprisonment' as defined by the States" (*Simmons v. South Carolina*, 1994, p. 8). This "lack of accurate information" was the determining factor in the Court's reversal. In this explicit fashion, the U.S. Supreme Court has acknowledged that capital jurors may indeed prefer a sentence of LWOP to death, *if* the jurors are informed that LWOP truly means LWOP.

Pluralistic Ignorance

The policy implications of this study are troubling. In a democracy, the ideal is that the majority view should prevail. However, that requires accurate knowledge of the majority view. The results of this study suggest that no such knowledge exists: Legislators underestimate the public's preference for LWOP alternatives, and citizens overestimate their representatives' support for LWOP alternatives. Thus there are reciprocal misperceptions (albeit in opposite directions) among lawmakers and their constituents concerning the death penalty. The result is that both lawmakers and citizens act (pass laws and vote, respectively) based on their (mis)*perceptions* of each other.

To the extent that legislators and their constituents continue to operate in the quagmire of reciprocal misperception, the situation can be best described as one of "pluralistic ignorance" (Krech & Crutchfield, 1948): (Hardly) no one prefers death to a sentence of LWOP, but everyone believes that everyone else prefers a sentence of death.

In sum, the state of pluralistic ignorance exists due to faulty communication practices. Again,

the media play a critical role by focusing on the atypical, most brutal crimes. No one who watches television or reads a newspaper is immune to daily crime reports. The most angered citizens are likely to make their views known to their representatives. The legislators, acting on a biased sample of the most vocal citizens, turn to an endorsement of capital punishment as a means to curb violence, thus overestimating the public's support for capital punishment. In contrast, citizens are bombarded with reports of violent crime, leading them to conclude that their representatives are not doing enough to combat crime. Moreover, the media is most likely to report exceptional sentences, such as a defendant who is eligible for a sentence of death yet who receives a lesser sentence and is released early. Consequently, citizens, who support capital punishment in general, are likely to believe that their representatives are too lenient (otherwise they would not have passed legislation that would allow for such sentences), thus underestimating lawmakers' support for capital punishment.

Further, it should be noted that Doob and Roberts (1984) have found that perceptions of leniency in sentencing are eliminated when the facts of a case, based on court documents, are made known to people. As the authors conclude: "This suggests that policy makers should not interpret the public's apparent desire for harsher penalties at face value; they should understand this widespread perception of leniency is founded upon incomplete and frequently inaccurate news accounts" (p. 277). A prime example of this phenomenon is the Susan Smith case. Whereas public opinion polls indicated that over 60% of the public supported the death penalty in this case (Morganthau, Smith, O'Shea, & Carroll, 1995), the jury, confronted with the facts of the case, opted for a life sentence.

The implications of pluralistic ignorance are quite straightforward: "People will stay in line because their fellows do, yet, if they only knew that their comrades wanted to kick over the traces too, the institutional conformity of the group would quickly vanish" (Katz & Schanck, 1938, p. 174). Thus our current system of capital punishment is likely to remain intact until the preference that already exists for alternative penalties is deemed newsworthy.

Notes

1. *Gregg v. Georgia* approved "guided discretion" statutes governing the administration of capital punishment.
2. Members of the public were, however, much more likely to favor capital punishment than were correctional elites (Riley & Rose, 1980).
3. Previous research has found that a majority of people are willing to express an attitude toward the death penalty, yet they also simultaneously lack knowledge about its imposition and effects (Bohm, Clark, & Aveni, 1991; Sarat & Vidmar, 1976; Vidmar & Ellsworth, 1974).
4. Bowers (1993, p. 163) presents similar findings from California, Florida, and Georgia.
5. The initial contact with legislators came in the form of a letter from the directors of the Indiana Prosecuting Attorneys Council and the Public Defenders Council explaining the project and requesting participation.
6. Because of the possibility of bias introduced through the different methods of administration with the legislators, a number of analyses were conducted to verify the representativeness of the legislative sample. We compared responses obtained by telephone interviews to those completed as mail questionnaires on seven characteristics: (a) years as a member of the legislature, (b) education, (c) race, (d) gender, (e) political party, (f) legislative house, and (g) membership on a criminal justice committee. None of the comparisons was significant. In addition, we compared telephone and mail survey responses on the general attitude toward capital punishment item and we contrasted the responses obtained during the first versus the second phase of interviewing. Again, none of the comparisons was significant.

   Finally, we compared respondents and nonrespondents on the seven characteristics mentioned above. Only one of the seven chi-square analyses was significant: Legislators who participated in the study tended to have completed more years of formal education than those who did not participate. However, the results are not clear-cut. For example, 31% of the survey respondents have less than a college degree compared to 45% of the nonrespondents. Yet, 21% of the nonrespondents compared to 14% of the respondents hold law degrees.

   Due to the general lack of significant differences in the analyses, we are confident that our sample is representative of the legislature as a whole.
7. The differences in support for LWOP and for LWOP plus work among those somewhat in favor of capital punishment compared to those strongly in favor of capital punishment were statistically significant (for LWOP, $\chi^2 = 29.5, 1$ *df*, significance $\leq .000$; for LWOP plus work, $\chi^2 = 27.7, 1$ *df*, significance $\leq .000$).
8. In reality, at the time this survey was conducted, 60 years in prison with parole eligibility after 30 years was the alternative to a death sentence.
9. There was, however, no statistically significant relationship between estimated years served by persons sentenced to life imprisonment and either of the LWOP proposals.
10. This is not meant to suggest that lawmakers' support for capital punishment merely reflects responsiveness to constituents' demands. Clearly, there is symbolic value in support for the death penalty.
11. Clearly this is not the final word and more research is warranted. The consistency between the present research and Bowers's (1993, p. 164) findings in states as diverse as California, Florida, Georgia, Nebraska, and New York, however, is striking.
12. In a more recent legislative session (February of 1994), the Indiana legislature passed a law that now provides for LWOP as a sentencing option in capital cases. It remains to be seen whether the new law will be accompanied by a decrease in the number of death sentences. However, we are somewhat skeptical of such a result because Indiana is a judge-override state. It may be that capital juries in Indiana become more likely to recommend LWOP sentences, but it will probably take many such occurrences for judges to realize a shift in juries' recommendations.

References

Berk, R. A., & Rossi, P. H. (1977). *Prison reform and state elites.* Cambridge, MA: Ballinger.

Bohm, R. M. (1991). American death penalty opinion, 1936–1986: A critical examination of the gallup polls. In R. M. Bohm (Ed.), *The death penalty in America: Current research* (pp. 113–145). Cincinnati, OH: Anderson.

Bohm, R. M., Clark, L. J., & Aveni, A. F. (1991). Knowledge and death penalty opinion: A test of the Marshall hypothesis. *Journal of Research in Crime and Delinquency, 28,* 360–387.

Bowers, W. J. (1993). Capital punishment and contemporary values: People's misgivings and the court's misperceptions. *Law and Society Review, 27,* 157–175.

Bowers, W. J., & Vandiver, M. (1991a). *New Yorkers want an alternative to the death penalty.* Boston: Northeastern University, Criminal Justice Research Center.

Bowers, W. J., & Vandiver, M. (1991b). *Nebraskans want an alternative to the death penalty.* Boston: Northeastern University, Criminal Justice Research Center.

Callins v. Collins, 114 S.Ct. 1127 (1994).

Cambridge Survey Research, Inc. (1986). *Attitudes in the state of Florida on the death penalty: Executive summary of a public opinion survey.* Washington, DC: Author.

Death Penalty Information Center. (1993). *Sentencing for life: Americans embrace alternatives to the death penalty.* Washington, DC: Author.

Doob, A. N., & Roberts, J. V. (1984). Social psychology, social attitudes, and attitudes toward sentencing. *Canadian Journal of Behavioural Science, 16,* 269–280.

Federal Death Penalty Act of 1994, Title 6, § 60001 *et seq.* of H.R. 3355 Violent Crime Control and Law Enforcement Act, 103d Cong., 2nd Sess. (1994).

Flanagan, T. J., Brennan, P. G., & Cohen, D. (1991). *Attitudes of New York legislators toward crime and criminal justice: A report of the state legislator survey—1991* (Hindelang Criminal Justice Research Center, School of Criminal Justice Working Paper). Albany: University of New York at Albany.

Flanagan, T. J., & Maguire, K. (1992). *Sourcebook of criminal justice statistics—1991* (U.S. Department of Justice, Bureau of Justice Statistics). Washington, DC: U.S. Government Printing Office.

Fox, J. A., Radelet, M. L., & Bonsteel, J. L. (1990–1991). Death penalty opinion in the post-*Furman* years. *New York University Review of Law and Social Change, 18,* 499–528.

Furman v. Georgia, 408 U.S. 238 (1972).

Gottfredson, S.D., & Taylor, R. B. (1984). Public policy and prison populations: Measuring opinions about reform. *Judicature, 68,* 190–201.

Graber, D. A. (1980). *Crime news and the public.* New York: Praeger.

Gregg v. Georgia, 428 U.S. 153 (1976).

Hamill, R., Wilson, T. D., & Nisbett, R. E. (1980). Insensitivity to sample bias: Generalizing from atypical cases. *Journal of Personality and Social Psychology, 39,* 578–589.

Haney, C., & Hurtado, A. (1989). *Californian's attitudes about the death penalty: Results of a statewide survey.* Santa Cruz: University of California Santa Cruz.

Johnson, B. A., & Huff, C. R. (1987). Public opinion and criminal justice policy formulation. *Criminal Justice Policy Review, 2,* 118–132.

Katz, D., & Schanck, R. L. (1938). *Social psychology.* New York: John Wiley.

Krech, D., & Crutchfield, R. S. (1948). *Theory and problems of social psychology.* New York: McGraw-Hill.

Morganthau, T., Smith, V. E., O'Shea, M., & Carroll, G. (1995, August 7). Condemned to life. *Newsweek,* pp. 18–23.

Riley, P. J., & Rose, V. M. (1980). Public vs. elite opinion on correctional reform: Implications for social policy. *Journal of Criminal Justice, 8,* 345–356.

Sarat, A., & Vidmar, N. (1976). Public Opinion, the death penalty, and the Eighth Amendment: Testing the Marshall hypothesis. *Wisconsin Law Review, 1976*(1), 171–206.

Simmons v. South Carolina, 1994 WL 263483 (U.S.S.C) (1994).

Trop v. Dulles, 356 U.S. 86 (1958).

Uslaner, E. M., & Weber, R. E. (1979). U.S. state legislators' opinions and perceptions of constituency attitudes. *Legislative Studies Quarterly, 4,* 563–585.

Vidmar, N., & Ellsworth, P. (1974). Public opinion and the death penalty. *Stanford Law Review, 26,* 1245–1270.

Williams F. P., Longmire, D. R., & Gulick, D. B. (1988). The public and the death penalty: Opinion as an artifact of question type. *Criminal Justice Research Bulletin, 3,* 1–5.

Witherspoon v. Illinois, 391 U.S. 510 (1968).

 Article Review Form at end of book.

What is the role of restorative justice in the criminal justice system?

Restorative Justice

Framework for the future of corrections

Greg D. Richardson

Greg D. Richardson is director of the Restorative Justice Institute in Washington, D.C., and a member of ACA's Restorative Justice Committee.

When I was very young, before I ever went to school, I learned a lot about criminal justice and corrections from the Lone Ranger and Perry Mason.

The Lone Ranger taught me that people in the community were not able to cope with their own problems. Each week, the community would pity the victims, but it was up to the criminal justice professional—objective, separate, behind a mask—to take care of the crime problems.

One effective practitioner, with one faithful Indian companion, always succeeded where the community always failed. The community's primary role in the criminal justice system was to get out of the way and let the professionals solve the problems.

Perry Mason showed me that people from the community could have a slightly more active role in the process; they could serve on the jury, testify as witnesses and admit guilt when their story was broken down through insightful, dramatic cross-examination by a defense attorney. The community still felt sorry for the victims of crime, but still could not solve its own problems. Again, this was the job of the professionals.

Many people have a basic perception of criminal justice and corrections that is based on the Lone Ranger and Perry Mason, or other similar television shows. For me, it was not until after I completed law school and began practicing as a criminal prosecutor that I really came to appreciate that criminal justice is much more than what I learned from watching television.

I began to see that crime is not just a violation of a state statute; crime causes real harm to real people. I heard crime victims who had serious questions about what had happened to them, and who did not feel that they had received any answers from our criminal justice system. Soon, I understood how crimes that I regarded as minor had a very significant impact on the community in which I lived.

I saw that people who had served time in prison and been released back into the community usually were the first to be suspected when new crimes were discovered. It seemed to me that, if the correctional system was doing its job, those people should be the last ones we suspected of committing new crimes, rather than the first.

Restorative justice is a comprehensive way of understanding and practicing corrections that encompasses this larger view. More than simply an approved menu of programs, an authentically restorative approach results in public policy and practices that grow out of basic values, reflect underlying principles and fit within a concise theoretical framework.

Rather than just some new ways to deal with property offenders, restorative justice applies to every aspect of how we think about and respond to crime; how we make criminal laws and policy; how we enforce our standards; how we determine guilt or innocence; how we sanction those who commit crimes; and how we prevent future crimes.

Reprinted with permission from *Corrections Today*, Dec. 1997, Vol. 59, No. 7, p. 20.

We must recognize that while the values and principles of restorative justice are drawn from ancient sources, contemporary models for putting restorative justice to work in meaningful ways still are being developed. Implementing an authentically restorative approach will take time and the willingness to risk making mistakes. Those who say, as I heard recently, "We tried restorative justice, and it didn't work," may have tinkered with a few program components, but they have not grasped their essential importance.

This is particularly important as we develop restorative methods for dealing with violent offenders. It is a challenge to develop and implement restorative approaches, and more difficult than continuing to do business as usual. Meeting this challenge will create significant benefits.

Correctional institutions will operate in ways that recognize the injuries caused by crime and seek to heal them. They will provide opportunities for crime victims, offenders and the community to be actively involved in their efforts. All those affected by crime will be able to meet their responsibilities and find ways to ensure that their needs are met.

It can be difficult for us to even think about an approach to corrections that helps heal the injuries caused by crime, an approach that leaves crime victims, offenders, the community and the government better off than they were before the crime took place. A truly restorative approach promises such results, and provides the framework and mechanisms that make such results possible. Restorative justice is more than a simple list of programs to try; instead, it may point the way toward the future of criminal justice.

 Article Review Form at end of book.

Critique the implementation and role of law-related education (LRE) programs.

Legal Education for Juveniles

Bebs Chorak

Bebs Chorak is deputy director of the National Institute for Citizen Education in the Law.

Do you remember when you were a student? What was it about the classroom you liked? What did you dislike? Let's visit two classrooms in a juvenile facility to see what takes place. First, picture a traditional classroom where the students are sitting at desks and reading from textbooks. The students range in age from 13 to 17 and function at various educational levels. The textbooks are selected by grade level from their home schools. After they finish reading, the students are given worksheets to complete individually. At the end of the day, they may have a test on what they read or what was covered on the worksheets. There is little discussion, but the teacher moves around the class to encourage and help individuals complete their assignments.

Now, imagine yourself in the day room of the local juvenile justice detention center. Though the setting is informal, the students are attentive and actively involved in presenting arguments in a mock city council meeting. Students are playing the roles of parents, police, business leaders and other community members as they testify before the council about a proposed city curfew law. Students make persuasive and informed arguments representing various interests. After the groups finish testifying, the "city council" discusses the most important issues that arise from these arguments and decides whether or not to implement a curfew law. At this point, the teacher asks the visiting city attorney, who is providing procedural assistance, to comment on the process and lead a discussion on the issues that a curfew law raises for local communities. The students are engaged completely by the attorney, who discusses with them issues concerning community and youth safety, the constitutional rights of minors, and the need for all citizens to be involved in lawmaking.

Both of these situations probably involve students who either have failed or had very negative school experiences. These young people have made a career of not letting the teacher know what they know or don't know. Is one setting more threat-ening than the other? Is one more conducive to learning? In the second classroom, the teacher is using interactive methods that allow the students to work at their own levels. Interaction promotes thinking and develops interpersonal skills. The teacher has enhanced the interaction with relevant content and the involvement of a community expert. It is a friendly, positive environment in which all students can participate and learn. The first classroom, as we know, easily can become a prescription for boredom and unproductive educational time.

Law-Related Education

Law-related education (LRE) is a program designed to teach non-lawyers about the law, the legal system and the basic principles and values underlying our constitutional democracy. LRE also shows promise for being able to reach students who have not been reached through traditional teaching. LRE demystifies the law and the community's systems by providing practical information about the legal system. LRE encourages youths to become effec-

Reprinted with permission from *Corrections Today*, April 1997, Vol. 59, No. 2, pp. 152–155.

tive, law-abiding citizens by promoting civic responsibility and community participation. Students learn substantive information about their rights and responsibilities, practice cooperative learning, experience positive interaction with adults and each other, and begin to appreciate rules. Perhaps this is why you can visit juvenile facilities across the country today and see enthusiastic students in interactive law-related education classes.

Law-related education's popularity with juvenile justice staff and students continues to grow. Staff like it because students respond to lessons with excitement. They also recognize that this information is useful to them and that students are practicing skills important to their success.

Jan Cowin, executive director of the Alabama Center for Law and Civic Education, reports that Department of Youth Services teachers attending LRE workshops say that LRE helps them better understand the complexities of the justice system. As a result, they are in better positions to help their students.

Administrators embrace LRE because it is flexible in its delivery, inexpensive to implement and adaptable to a variety of settings. Debra Williamson, LRE program manager at the Administrative Office of the Courts in Frankfort, Ky., says intake officers appreciate the 10 different LRE programs offered in her state because of their popularity among participants and the community.

Parents often thank an intake officer for the LRE program assignment for their children. The juvenile court there has found that insights developed through community participation in LRE classes improve understanding of court-referred youths.

Why LRE Works

Juvenile justice and other educational program developers recognize that young people need to be taught certain skills. This is best achieved by placing learning within real environments, rather than insisting that students first learn in the abstract and later be expected to apply it. The concept of teaching in context implies that the lesson will provide students with the opportunity to apply knowledge in real life situations or simulations. Specific activities can include problems or projects related to home, school and job situations. To internalize skills, students must practice them in the context of a discussion or simulation that has meaning for them.

Research on risk factors and delinquency theories has contributed significantly to our understanding of prevention and intervention. According to Richard Catalano and David Hawkins of Development Research and Programs Inc. in Seattle, there are identifiable risk factors that make young people more susceptible to behavioral problems, such as substance abuse and delinquency. They include alienation or lack of bonding, family conflict, early and frequent antisocial behavior, high-risk family behaviors, poor family management practices, poverty, school failure, community disorganization, association with delinquent peers and transitional problems.

However, this research does not explain why most youths—even those facing multiple risks—manage to avoid antisocial and self-destructive behavior. These young people appear to be resilient. Resiliency is the ability to overcome the effects of a high-risk environment and to develop social competence and problem-solving skills. According to Bonnie Bernard, of Far West Laboratory Educational Research and Development, resilient children have the following characteristics and skills:

1. Social competence

- responsiveness to others
- conceptual and intellectual flexibility
- caring for others
- good communication skills
- sense of humor

2. Problem-solving skills

- abstract thinking (understanding rules and laws)
- reflective thought
- critical reasoning skills
- ability to develop alternative solutions in frustrating situations (calculate consequences of actions, cause and effect)

3. Sense of autonomy

- positive sense of independence
- emerging feelings of efficacy
- high self-esteem
- impulse control
- planning and goal setting
- belief in the future

A properly implemented law-related education class emphasizes the development of social competence and problem-solving skills that can foster success. While factors related to developing a sense of autonomy cannot be taught directly, they can be fostered in LRE classrooms. For example, a student feels good about his role in a mock trial (efficacy), is proud that his teacher and/or classmates thought his opinion was worth hearing (self-esteem), waits on his classmates before giving his input (impulse control), learns about his rights and responsibilities in the community and, most important, learns where he fits in (belief in the future).

Properly taught, LRE offers many ingredients for building resiliency. For example, community resource professionals can be integrated into lessons to clarify community information, demystify legal roles, provide positive interaction with an adult, and show that youths are valued by the community. Youths who learn to interact with community resource officers begin to perceive the community as positive and supportive. A 16-year-old male at the Cedar City, Utah, detention facility said, "Yesterday we got to talk to a real police officer. I always thought they were all mean, but he was pretty cool. You see how hard their job is. If they're mean, it's nothing personal."

EdWynn Weaver, program coordinator at the Cedar City Detention Center, says the students look forward to this positive interaction and always ask, "Who are you going to bring in today?" Eleven community leaders (small claims court judges, police, lawyers and others) have continued to participate in lessons at this center for more than five years because of the positive interaction between adults and youths.

LRE lessons are inherently high in student interest. Relevant content is a powerful motivator, but beyond the acquisition of useful information, the way in which LRE is taught provides a unique opportunity to positively impact skills related to resiliency. For this reason, just as educators and justice system volunteers work together to add LRE to the K-12 curriculum in schools across the country, juvenile justice professionals eagerly are integrating LRE into their programs.

 Article Review Form at end of book.

Explain some of the elements taken into consideration before community corrections was defined.

Defining Community Corrections

Donald G. Evans

Donald G. Evans is president of Donald G. Evans & Associates and chair of ACA's Community Corrections Committee.

At the commencement of her term in office, Bobbie Huskey provided a challenging charge to the Community Corrections Committee. She requested that the committee prepare a statement describing the community corrections purpose and mission and prepare an initial set of principles that would drive the development of community corrections.

After reviewing President Huskey's charge at the ACA Winter Conference in Dallas in January 1995, the committee initiated a very useful, as well as difficult, dialogue on the definition of community corrections. Committee members decided that it would be necessary to develop a definition of community corrections before embarking on the creation of a mission statement and supporting principles.

Attempts to define community corrections usually have met a series of problems. Most practitioners are aware of the usual method of defining community corrections; namely, describing what it is not. "Community cor-rections is not incarceration," has been the main beginning point, but, as we are aware, there are many programs providing more structured residential services that are more like traditional incarceration.

David Duffee, co-author of *Community Corrections: A Community Field Approach,* notes that "while it may be difficult to derive an authoritative definition of community corrections, it is important to understand that simple definitions are becoming increasingly more difficult to sustain."

The committee debates bear out Duffee's conclusion regarding simple definitions—especially since the growth of intermediate sanctions also has fostered a certain element of confusion when attempting to define community corrections.

Again, Duffee notes that "changes in sentencing practice, prison policy, and probation and parole supervision have blurred considerably what once may have been a clear line between community and non-community corrections."

It is clear that the use of probation detention centers, restitution centers and boot camps has contributed to the widening of the concept of community corrections. Also, the changing role of jails and their development of programs that resemble traditional community corrections has added to the confusion.

With the help of ACA and the National Institute of Corrections (NIC), the committee continued to work on the challenge of defining community corrections. At an all-day meeting at ACA headquarters in Lanham, Md. on May 10, 1996, members attempted to bring closure to their discussions.

The committee found that defining community corrections was a difficult task. Members had struggled during the past two years with all the nuances, contradictions and paradoxes surrounding the current debate on community corrections. The committee did not want to fall into the trap of defining community corrections in terms of what it was not, and every effort was made to seek positive and accurate descriptors of what is involved in a community corrections endeavor. The result of their deliberations may not be perfect but, it still is a line in the sand, and like any line in the sand, it is

Reprinted with permission from *Corrections Today,* Oct. 1996, Vol. 58, No. 6, pp. 124–125.

subject to some movement as the climate changes. However, the committee is confident that it has made a significant gain in efforts to set boundaries around the concept of community corrections.

In arriving at a proposed definition, the committee noted that there were some elements of a definition of community corrections that needed to be taken for granted. These elements included the following:

- Community corrections is part of the justice system, which involves both adults and juveniles and also includes a broader context containing elements of social justice.

- Community corrections agencies are involved in administering sanctions and providing services. Services are provided to victims, defendants and offenders.

- Community corrections agencies acknowledge that they exist to enhance public safety.

- Community corrections is effective and efficient when it works in partnership with local communities and other agencies interested in safer communities and justice.

Considering these taken-for-granted statements, the committee offers the following as a definition of what community corrections involves:

"Community corrections is that part of the justice system providing sanctions and services to enhance public safety and maintain offenders/defendants within the community. These goals are accomplished by selecting appropriate participants, holding offenders accountable, repairing the harm done to victims and the community, supervising and treating offenders/defendants, involving citizens, and maintaining positive ties between the community and the offender."

For me, the acknowledgment that community corrections is a part of the broader justice system is a key element in the definition. It provides for the growing interest in what is being referred to as community justice (Barajas Jr., 1996 and Reeves, 1992) and is inclusive of adult and juvenile systems and human service systems that are important in tackling crime.

The second part of the definition stresses the two key tasks of community corrections—the administration of the court's sentence and the provision of services that will enhance public safety. This twinning of sanctions and services is in keeping with recent research that underscores the value of providing appropriate interventions with sanctions in order to reduce reoffending. But, the services also are linked to notions of restorative justice that involve victims and communities in solutions to the problems created by offending behavior.

Finally, the definition stresses that the work of community corrections is accomplished by maintaining offenders within the community. The definition explains how community corrections can accomplish its goal of enhanced public safety by listing six important tasks:

- assessment of offenders for community placement;

- responsibility of offenders for their behavior;

- emphasis on reparative strategies for victims and communities;

- provision of supervision and treatment interventions geared to reduce reoffending;

- the encouragement of citizens to join in the challenge of creating safer communities; and

- recognition of the importance of positive relationships between the community and the offender.

These tasks support the definition of community corrections and help corrections practitioners decide when a program can be classified as community corrections.

The committee still has one more meeting to fulfill President Huskey's charge. Members finalized a definition and proposed a mission statement with supporting principles at the 126th Congress of Correction in Nashville.

Whether or not you agree with the committee's efforts, please recognize the work they've done as a starting point for your own rethinking of what defines community corrections.

As the committee's mandate draws to a close, members hope they have left a beacon to guide the next committee's work. Committee work is cumulative, and one needs to build on the efforts of those who have gone before.

References

Barajas Jr., Eduardo. 1996. Moving toward community justice. Perspectives. (Spring).

Duffee, David and Edmund F. McGarrell. 1990. Community corrections: A community field approach. Cincinnati: Anderson Publishing Co.

Reeves, Rhonda. 1992. Community justice. State government news. (November).

 Article Review Form at end of book.

Describe the results of the Bureau of Justice Statistics (BJS) study regarding convicted sex offenders.

Fewer Sex Offenders on Community Release Programs Than Other Criminals

Kelly McMurry

While the prospect of sexual predators on conditional release in the community is unnerving to many, the results of a recent Bureau of Justice Statistics (BJS) report may allay some fears. The study—which is based on 1994 data, the most recent year for which information is available—showed that convicted sex offenders are less likely than other convicts to be placed in community release programs.

On average for all offenders, the ratio of offenders on probation or parole to those incarcerated in jail or prison is nearly 3 to 1. For those convicted of rape or other sexual assault, however, the ratio of those on conditional release to those incarcerated is much lower: 1.4 to 1.

Sex offenders represent 4.7 percent of the almost 5 million convicted offenders serving time in federal or state prisons, or in jails or on probation or parole, according to the study's statistician, Lawrence Greenfeld. They comprise 1 percent of the federal prison population, 3.4 percent of the nation's jail inmates, 3.6 percent of the offenders on probation, and 4 percent of the offenders on parole (Bureau of Justice Statistics, U.S. Department of Justice, Sex Offenses and Offenders, NCJ-163391 (Dec. 1996).)

Prior BJS follow-up studies of sex offenders discharged from prison or sentenced to probation showed that sex offenders have a generally lower rate of re-arrest than other violent offenders but are substantially more likely than other violent offenders to be rear-rested for a new violent sex offense. For example, about 8 percent of 2,214 rapists released from prisons in 11 states in 1983 were arrested for a new rape within three years, while only about 1 percent of released prisoners who served time for robbery or assault were re-arrested for violent sex offenses.

The figures showing that sex offenders have a lower rate of re-arrest than other violent criminals do not surprise Fred Berlin, founder of the Johns Hopkins School of Medicine's sexual disorders clinic in Baltimore. "The study's findings go against the commonly held notion that most sex offenders are recidivists." Berlin said. "For example, out of 2,214 rapists surveyed, 92 percent did not commit other rapes—only 8 percent did.

"I'm pleased to see these results because they put into perspective what we at the clinic already know to be true—that most sex offenders do not reoffend," said Berlin.

However, released rapists were found to be 10.5 times as likely as non-rapists to be rearrested for rape. Offenders who served time for other sexual assaults were 7.5 times as likely to be arrested for a second sexual assault as those convicted of other crimes.

Berlin was not surprised by these results, either. 'You have to understand that career sex offenders are like most other career criminals in that if sex offenders reoffend, it's likely to be a sex offense." he said. "But the same is true for most career burglars. If they re-offend, they burgle."

According to BJS, the survey is the first national estimate of the size of the convicted sex offender population under the jurisdiction of federal, state, and local correctional authorities.

 Article Review Form at end of book.

How does technology influence probation?

Probation

My profession, my lifetime employment, my passion

Sylvia J. Johnson

Sylvia J. Johnson: Chief Probation Officer for the Alameda County Probation Department in Oakland, California.

I was invited to contribute an article for the special NCCD 90th birthday edition of *Crime and Delinquency,* and I accepted without realizing the memory lane walk I would experience. I have respected, read, and appreciated the publication, research, service, and impact of the NCCD on my profession for more than a third of those 90 years. Happy birthday, NCCD, and may we share another "few" years. My special acknowledgment and thanks to Dr. Barry Krisberg, your president, and a major influence to all members of the probation family, staff, clients, volunteers, and children who avoided this probation system because of his vision.

My article is a very "up close" and personal summary of my probation experiences from 1960, when I entered the field, to the present and my vision for the year 2000 and beyond. No statistics, no footnotes, no research or validation, just my account from a memory full of friendships, love, pain, and hope for children wounded and hardened by poverty and racial isolation. A memory of the mothers of the 1960s (very few fathers), mostly Black or Hispanic, who worked hard though on welfare, loved their children, and yet did not know how to be parents and in control of their day-to-day lives.

During the 1960s and when I began my career, the racial conflicts involved primarily White, Black, and Hispanic. This was prior to the Miranda warning, and the nature of the juvenile court was a more informal atmosphere. The faces and complexity of the issues have dramatically changed over the years, and today the issues of diversity include many more ethnic groups, as well as advocacy from the special rights' groups (e.g., handicapped, gay employee organizations and unions, etc.). Today's "new poor" are better informed regarding the justice system, are represented by counsel, and are informed regarding their children's rights, yet the issues continue to be the consequences of poverty and racism, as evidenced by the minority overrepresentation in the juvenile probation system.

Advanced technology has also been a factor in the recent years of my career in that we have entered the age of technology, including electronic voice mail, electronic monitoring of clients, telephone probation reporting, and computerized management of caseloads. During the time that I began my career, there was a people-to-people response, and my experience with the introduction of technology in probation is a system that has depersonalized client contact. Clients are discussed in the context of data, in the abstract, rather than a more personalized discussion. I believe this had been further complicated by a mixed response of staff in regard to the use of technology. These concepts were introduced at a time when staff resources were diminishing and caseloads were increasing in numbers. In spite of the advanced technology, the question remains, Are our clients better served?

The representation by lawyers and the formality of the proceedings in the court have resulted in a legal process of evidencing confusion. Attorneys often express a need for a case manager to assist in their clients' needs assessment and dispositional plans, yet the design of the system does not typically involve this dialogue between a probation officer and attorney. The issue of overwhelming caseload size provides a minimum of time for adequate representation.

I recall in the 1960s that the issues most frequently discussed in probation planning meetings and case management reviews were the following:

• Planning for riot aftermath/violence prevention

• Cultural sensitivity to program delivery;

• High levels of commitments to California Youth Authority of children in the ghettos

• The need for drug abuse treatment programs

• Subsidy dollars to fund the Reduction of Delinquency through the Expansion of Opportunity (RODEO) program. RODEO was a community-based intensive supervision program targeting ghetto youth with a team approach involving probation officers teamed with community residents (including welfare recipients) hired into the program.

• New career opportunities for clients in probation agencies recognizing employment as one solution to gang violence

• Increasing the opportunities for promotion and leadership positions for minorities working in probation

Today in the 1990s, as I make notes for this article, I am interrupted by the TV news report of President Clinton's speech suggesting that Americans bridge their racial differences and engage in a new national dialogue on racial reconciliation. He continues to talk about employment for youthful offenders as a solution to gang problems. I look back at my list of issues in the 1960s and here I sit 30 years later—same primary issues.

The issues of poverty have resulted in several subsystems—the first being the young Black male who is poorly educated, poor, and unprepared for job performance, becoming involved in the sales of drugs as a "quick fix" to poverty and creating an economic subsystem. The justice system and probation have a subsystem that includes drug courts, drug testing, drug treatment, drug detoxification beds, drug laboratories, drug education, and specialized drug caseloads. I am not sure if either of these subsystems addresses the primary factors involved in the use and abuse of drugs, nor has there been a significant change in the incidence of use. These subsystems have not addressed the true factors that contribute to the cycle of poverty and racism and hence the cycle of violence.

When I began as a probation professional in the 1960s, I experienced a great deal of pride and honor in the profession. People in the community recognized a probation officer as a respected professional, and I was proud and confident in my role. Today, the public, the courts, and legislature define probation with ambivalence, confusion, and unrealistic expectations. We are expected to totally correct the clients' behavior without adequate resources. The battle cry is zero tolerance for alcohol, tobacco, truancy, violence, curfew violation, and so forth. We are at war with our teenage children. The public attitude in the 1990s does not recognize the clients (the children and adults on probation) as members of the community or understand the impact of high caseloads and the need for investment in the resources necessary to provide meaningful intervention and services. We have not clearly defined when a child is a child, a youthful offender, or an adult offender and are discussing execution or prison for children as young as 13 years of age. This public policy debate is very confusing to me when we continually express the cliché, "Our children are our future."

In the 1960s, my role in probation was that of service provider. In subsequent years as a manager, the expectations have changed considerably. The management today involves the "alphabet soup" of compliance regulations, including the following: EEOC, MOU (labor contracts), ADA, FLSA, FMLA, and OSHA. Each of these guidelines comes with a separate set of expectations and mandates, many times in conflict with one another and certainly not considering the mission and goals of probation. Legislation and bureaucracy's response to the issues continue to involve quick-fix solutions and rarely consider the research that clearly defines program models that have been successful. The probation agencies are confronted with a real management challenge in that the number of clients that they are expected to serve has certainly increased at a far greater pace than revenues available, as well as the agency being a large-scale bureaucracy that does not readily adjust to change. For example, agency work hours are typically 8:00 a.m. to 5:00 p.m., whereas our clients and our youth are expected to be at work and in school during those hours, and the "alphabet soup" compliance agencies, previously mentioned, frequently offer the employees who are unwilling to change working hours an "out."

Given this opportunity of reflection, I have shared the initial phase of my career in the 1960s, when the youth movement expressed a distrust for adults and authority. The youth from that period of my career are the parents today, and I represent the leadership of today planning for 2000 and beyond. Should we be trusted? Only if:

- Research-based data are the information source to problem solve, and programs are designed with the understanding that there is no "one way" or "right way."

- Give consideration to creative thinking of all people and DREAM.

- A continuum of care is absolutely necessary, offering choices to meet the needs of all families and children at risk.

- The first choice on the continuum is the empowerment of the family, including an expanded definition of family—defined by the client and the care providers.

- Accept and guarantee that the youthful offender is a powerful part of planning for the future of probation services.

- The war on poverty and racism must begin again and start with a focus on "me and you."

No government program can make our children as healthy as you and I can.

In conclusion, I still have hope and love for my profession,

probation. I owe a lifetime debt to the countless numbers of judges, referees, probation staff, foster parents, community-based organizations, and volunteers who have both supported me and taught me new ways of providing services. In particular, I owe a great deal of gratitude to Ruth L. Rushen, a retired probation and corrections administrator, who has challenged me every step of the way as my mentor and friend. Our society must not forget or abandon all children and families in need, and through public policy and a private sector call to action, we can and must improve their quality of life.

 Article Review Form at end of book.

WiseGuide Wrap-Up

- The implementation of "get-tough" sentencing legislation has led to grave consequences.

- There is no consensus regarding the definition of a supermax prison.

- Public support for the death penalty vanishes when citizens are given the option of life in prison without the possibility of parole coupled with a requirement of work and restitution.

- Restorative justice attempts to heal the injuries that result from crime through the participation of correctional institutions, victims, and offenders.

- Convicted sex offenders are less likely than other convicts to be placed in community release programs.

R.E.A.L Sites

This list provides a print preview of typical **coursewise** R.E.A.L. sites. (There are over 100 such sites at the **courselinks**™ site.) The danger in printing URLs is that Web sites can change overnight. As we went to press, these sites were functional using the URLs provided. If you come across one that isn't, please let us know via email to: webmaster@coursewise.com. Use your Passport to access the most current list of R.E.A.L. sites at the **courselinks**™ site.

Site name: National Criminal Justice Reference Center

URL: http://www.ncjrs.org/corrhome.htm

Why is it R.E.A.L.? This site contains online documents on corrections. The topics range from alternative sanctions in Germany to an evaluation of boot camps in the United States. In addition to these documents, this site contains numerous links where you could obtain additional information regarding various correctional issues. In this site, you can also find links to several correctional listservs.

Try this: What do recent statistics suggest about the present usage of the death penalty? What are the main similarities and differences between state and federal prison inmates?

Key topics: batterer programs, boot camps, capital punishment, state and federal correctional facilities, comparison of state and federal prison inmates, Prison Industry Enhancement Certification Program

Site name: Federal Bureau of Prisons

URL: http://www.bop.gov/

Why is it R.E.A.L.? This site is maintained by the federal agency that oversees all of the federal prison activities. The information contained in this site can be of much use to you if you are interested in the latest federal prison trends or if you are curious about the types of jobs available at the Federal Bureau of Prisons. The site also contains online documentation regarding various interesting topics, such as the history of Alcatraz and the execution of federal prisoners since 1927.

Try this: Describe the history of Alcatraz. What are some of the characteristics of federal inmates?

Key topics: inmate information, drug treatment evaluation, Facts and Statistics Weekly Population Report, *Federal Prison Journal*

Site name: American Jail Association

URL: http://www.corrections.com/aja/

Why is it R.E.A.L.? This page provides online jail-related publications, information on becoming an AJA member, and an opportunity to subscribe to the *American Jails* magazine.

Try this: Compare and contrast jails and prisons.

Key topics: *American Jails* magazine, Jail Operations Bulletin, Jail Managers Bulletin

section 4

Learning Objectives

After studying this section, you will know

- that discrimination takes place in the system of justice.

- that the United States Supreme Court has recently reviewed a case dealing with the notion that federal officials unfairly select minorities to prosecute.

- that African Americans are less likely than whites to endorse police illegal use of deadly force.

- that recent highly publicized cases have renewed questions of bias in the criminal justice system.

- that African American jury members have a tendency not to convict African American defendants.

- that African Americans feel that, in order to properly address the crime problem and improve race relations, government intervention is needed, while whites regard these problems as evidence of a decline in values.

- that family problems, including abandonment, are the primary causes of crime.

- that Hispanics, much in the same way as the Irish, are joining the criminal justice workforce as part of an effort to improve their standing in U.S. society.

Race and Crime

WiseGuide Intro

Criminologists have reacted in different ways to the notion that race has a direct impact on crime. Some argue that this impact has been negative. In other words, their position is that the presence and activities of certain minority groups prompt the crime rate to increase. In order to validate their argument, most supporters of this view cite statistics that suggest the presence of criminal activity in areas of a city that are highly populated by members of minority groups. However, critics of this view argue that the reason minority members appear to have greater participation in criminal acts than whites may be that minorities live in areas that are the most frequently patrolled and, therefore, where most arrests take place. Other critics argue that statistics are biased and do not address the possible causes of this minority overrepresentation in the criminal justice system. Regardless of which of these perspectives you follow, the facts are that minorities are constantly being processed in the criminal justice system and that this merits further examination.

As we begin the process of learning about the relationship between members of a particular minority group and their alleged aggressive criminal participation, it is important that we recognize the fact that each social control agency of the criminal justice system—police, courts, and corrections—comes in contact with minorities and minority-related issues on a daily basis. In the United States, police agencies responsible for training their officers are concerned that their staff receive adequate minority sensitivity training. In part, this may be due to the fact that several highly publicized cases, which have demonstrated to the public the abuses minorities endure from some law enforcement officers, have given rise to public demands that police officers act in a more responsible way toward members of these groups. In addition, due to the growing Hispanic population, law enforcement agencies are adjusting to the new needs their departments are experiencing by encouraging their officers to learn Spanish.

In addition to law enforcement agencies, courts are also concerned with the handling of minority offenders. In large cities, it is not uncommon to find court translators assisting offenders of different races and ethnic groups who do not speak English. Recently, courts have been facing criticism regarding the implementation of more severe sentences for drug-related offenses committed mostly by minority members (i.e., possession of crack cocaine), as opposed to drug offenses committed more frequently by whites (i.e., possession of powder cocaine). These laws are being modified, thanks in part to the voices of critics who, in public forums, have made us all aware that these sentences are not only unfair but also unconstitutional.

In addition to the police and courts, the system of corrections is also constantly responding to minorities and their specific needs. Lately, there has been much debate regarding the existing prison population. Some argue that, if society were to address the major issues that affect minorities—poverty, unemployment, and education—we would enjoy a smaller prison representation of individuals who belong to these minority groups. Others, however, argue that we should continue to build more prisons, regardless of the growing minority prison population.

It is my hope that, after reading the articles selected for this section, you will have attained a more insightful understanding of some of the complex interactions between members of minority groups and the social control agencies of the criminal justice system.

Questions

Reading 24. Why are minorities overrepresented in the prison population?

Reading 25. Discuss the uniqueness and importance of *U.S. vs. Armstrong.*

Reading 26. Does race have an impact on the support for police use of deadly force on fleeing felons? How?

Reading 27. Why do many African Americans argue that the criminal justice system is inherently biased against them?

Reading 28. Why are African American jury members reluctant to convict African American defendants?

Reading 29. What is the opinion of African Americans regarding government intervention to help reduce the crime problem and improve race relations? How does this relate to the opinion of whites?

Reading 30. What are the causes of violent crime in the United States?

Reading 31. Describe the similarities that exist between Irish and Hispanics in relation to their role in the criminal justice system.

Why are minorities overrepresented in the prison population?

Race and the Criminal Justice System

Malaika Horne

An overwhelming sea of blackness recently engulfed the mall of the Washington Monument. It was a sea of faces, faces of African American men of peace, right conduct and love. The media image of black men, largely portrayed as menacing, threatening and dangerous, was a far cry from the image of the march of a million men strong. The now historic gathering portrayed a vivid picture of God fearing, law abiding, taxpaying black Americans. In fact, these merits contrasted sharply with the black men televised on that holy day of atonement.

While crime among juveniles in particular is growing by leaps and bounds throughout the nation, black communities are likewise experiencing an unparalleled crime epidemic. The epidemic has community leaders in a dilemma and an intensive debate has ensued. Essentially, many are beginning to struggle with the question of how to battle this torrential downpour of crime without sacrificing a whole generation of men and perhaps the next generation as well.

There is also a widespread belief that blacks are far more prone to violence than whites. Conservatives point to moral deficits while progressives say it is based on discrimination and poverty. While debates continue to be waged, increasingly conservative policies are resulting in millions of African Americans being committed to a harsher penal system.

Studies are showing that blacks and Hispanics are more likely to go to jail while whites are more likely to receive probation. African Americans are 10 times more likely than whites to have been shot at by police officers and 18 times more likely to be wounded. They are five times more likely to be killed.

It is true that crime is wreaking devastating social and economic havoc in black and Hispanic communities. Substance abuse, teen-age pregnancy and the dissolution of the family are usually linked to black violence. Black imprisonment for possession and trafficking of drugs as well as for non-drug offenses have prisons bursting at the seams. The building of jails is now big business. Civil rights ad-

vocates are crying foul, pointing to the "jail-industrial complex" and the frenzy to build more prisons as putting corporate profits before human suffering and misery.

The prison-population boom, confining increasing numbers of blacks and other people of color, has many pondering the issue of racism in the justice system. Criminologists have long noted that the higher arrest, conviction and incarceration rates for African Americans have been going on for at least a century. The soaring rates of imprisonment recently led the director of the American Civil Liberties Union, Laura Murphy, to call race bias in the system as "the new frontier" of civil rights.

The disparate treatment of African Americans involved in drug cases illustrates the point. There are increased penalties for possession and trafficking of crack cocaine, the drug of choice for many low-income African Americans. While users and small time dealers of smokeable cocaine are facing the heavier hand of the law, more lenient sentences are imposed on those convicted of trafficking in as opposed to possessing similar amounts of powder cocaine. The disparate

From *Crisis*, January 1996, Vol. 103, Issue 1, page 10. The author wishes to thank The Crisis Publishing Co., Inc., the publisher of the magazine of the National Association for the Advancement of Colored People, for authorizing the use of this work.

sentencing for crack cocaine versus powder cocaine, many say, has an obvious class imprint.

The low income crack user does the jail time while the more affluent powder cocaine user is allowed to remain on the streets.

For example, the mandatory minimum prison sentence for a person convicted of simple possession of five grams of crack cocaine (the weight of a nickel) with no intent to sell is five years in prison. It takes 500 grams of powder cocaine, well over a pound and 100 times the amount of crack cocaine to trigger the same penalty. Despite a report by the United States Sentencing Commission saying that crack sentences were too harsh when compared to those for similar crimes involving powder cocaine, Attorney General Janet Reno disagreed.

"I strongly oppose measures that fail to reflect the harsh and terrible impact of crack on communities across America," she said. Reno then requested the Congress to reject the plan that would reduce sentences for selling crack cocaine.

As a result, more African Americans than ever are being arrested, convicted and jailed. While African Americans make up 12 percent of the nation's population and constitute 13 percent of all monthly drug users, they represent 35 percent of arrests for drug possession. They comprise 55 percent of all convictions and 74 percent of all prison sentences. African Americans are approximately 38 percent of crack users but comprise a staggering 90 percent of crack defendants in federal court. By contrast, white Americans are 46 percent of crack users, but account for a mere 3.5 percent of convictions for federal crack offenses. This disparity has resulted in African Americans serving sentences that are 41 percent longer than whites.

Further, race may affect sentence severity indirectly through its effect on factors such as bail status, type of attorney or type of disposition. Because discrimination is difficult to detect, it does not mean it does not exist. Clearly, there are disparities but many experts are reluctant to say discrimination exists. Some say the disparities are more attributed to class than race. But race and class are so inextricably linked it seems to be a moot point since blacks are disproportionately poor.

The U.S. now has one of the highest incarceration rates in the world. More than 1 million Americans are in prison, surpassing both South Africa's rate and second to the Soviet Union. These higher U.S. incarcerations are costing taxpayers a whopping $16 billion a year and the cost is growing.

In addition to the more than 1 million in prisons another half million fill the nation's jails; 600,000 are on parole and 3 million are on probation. There are another 100,000 in juvenile facilities. Death row numbers are even more chilling. While blacks make up a small percentage of the total U.S. population, they comprise 40 percent of those on death row.

Professor of Criminology G. David Curry at the University of Missouri at St. Louis said while figures show greater rates of criminality for blacks than for whites—three to four times higher among men and four to five times higher among women—whether blacks offend more remains inconclusive. In fact, studies usually focus on sentencing data and not specifically on offenses and arrests. For example, there are many undocumented offenses that never come to the attention of the criminal justice system not to mention the innumerable unsolved crimes.

"There is a reaction to crime which also must be considered such as in Philadelphia which uncovered police corruption and planting of evidence," commented Dr. Curry who also asserted that one must "control for situational factors like the economy" if communities are serious about solving lawlessness.

"There are social factors that cause people to engage in criminal activities—poverty, discrimination, inadequate education. Plus, it's important to understand that Native Americans and Hispanics are also over represented in the criminal justice system."

Curry said the overreaction to crimes committed by blacks contributes to higher arrests, conviction and incarceration rates. A case in point is the beating of Rodney King which exposed police racism and crimes of violence perpetrated against blacks.

When a white is a victim of a black perpetrated crime, "there is more severe punishment." A University of Chicago trained criminologist said that while there may be more fear regarding whites as victims of black crime, "most crimes are intra-racial." In other words, the victim and the offender are of the same race.

By the same token, whites are greater victims of crime by white perpetrators or what is called white on white crime. Whites are three times more likely to be victims, according to the National Crime Survey. This should be unsurprising given the relative size of the black population to the white population. In actuality, the rate of black males who are victims of aggravated assault is virtually identical to white males. While there is virtually no differences in crimes in certain categories, this serious social problem continues to take a terrible toll on black communities. So whether black crime is more one of perception than reality is almost irrelevant. Because blacks are more visible and tend to be more vulnerable to social ills, high rates of crime have a more devastating impact on these communities.

"Crime is a serious issue for African Americans, for the victimized aspect alone," said Dr. Curry who served as the statistical expert for the NAACP Legal Defense Fund from 1977 to 1983. "They are also more likely to be victims of the response of crime. Victimization occurs both ways in the African American community."

At their wits' end, many are calling for "locking them up and throwing away the key," however, the system does not demonstrate that incarceration can deter, prevent nor rehabilitate. By the same token, research has not been able to ferret out race bias in the criminal justice system. Curry explained that there is a subtlety to racism. Modern day racism is less overt making it more difficult for researchers to "pin it down."

John Dovidio in his article, "The Subtlety of Racism," says: "Like a virus that has mutated, racism has evolved into a new form that is difficult to recognize and harder to combat."

Because of these continuous mutations, race bias remains ill-defined. Vague notions of bias likewise further contribute to the difficulty in the scientific method's attempt to expose it. Lack of consensus has also resulted in disagreement and controversy over the racism issue.

Hence, many say there is no conclusive answer whether blacks simply offend more or if there is racial bias in the system. And many experts are reluctant to conclude that African Americans are more crime-prone than whites.

As mentioned earlier, much of the research on race bias in the system has focused on the sentencing stage where data collection is apparently more abundant and its collection less problematic. Arrest data become more hazy due to law enforcement officials' discretion in making arrests. Prosecutors also have similar authority which has led to greater prosecutorial inequality. Prosecutors decide what charges to be filed in a particular case, what charge revisions to accept in exchange for a guilty plea and how those charges relate to laws limiting sentencing discretion in particular cases.

Because African American neighborhoods are more heavily patrolled by the police, blacks are more likely to be scrutinized and arrested, more likely to be convicted and, therefore, more likely to be repeat offenders. Not only are blacks more likely to come to the attention of authorities because of greater police presence, heavy handed police tactics make them more prone to be targeted for arrest. Studies are beginning to point out police over-arrest of blacks and Hispanics relative to the number of crimes they actually commit, suggesting discrimination against minorities.

Root causes of black crime remain a controversial issue. Some specialists in the field reject notions of situational or social factors. "We want no more excuses, that's history, we need to give it a decent burial," said

Leroy Warren who stridently objected to social factors such as discrimination and poverty as the primary reasons for the increase in black crime rates. "We are part of the problem and you can't blame the system. Be more responsible for yourself."

Warren is chairman of the National NAACP Criminal Justice Committee. It is undertaking an ambitious project this summer, surveying 50 states on race issues in the criminal justice system. "We will be dealing with the problem of who is in prison and why they are there. We will also be looking at why we are having so much trouble with these young people. We will be dealing with the whole system."

While Warren places more emphasis on the moral responsibility of the individual, he says the committee will explore bias in the criminal justice system which could be exacerbating the high rates of black incarceration.

Warren said the committee has already spotted the resistance to appoint black federal judges and is pressing the American Bar Association, which reviews candidates, to be more impartial. The survey will also examine if there is bias in the appointment of judges at every level.

"We will be looking at who is staffing the courts and the whole criminal justice system and who's managing the place. We will be looking at the percentage of women and the percentage of minorities on staffs." Warren said, "The treatment of African Americans in the criminal justice system is bad and getting worse. People are tired. The taxpayers are tired of taking care of prisoners. They want to make prisons a very cruel place to live. They want to take out exercise equipment, air conditioning and cable television."

Elected officials are reacting to public pressure to make prison a less comfortable place to live, he contends, because the public "is tired of the tax burden," adding that black voters are also alarmed because "blacks with money think a lot like other taxpayers."

Warren places almost the sole blame on the family for crime. "Kids are not receiving discipline from their parents. . . . Kids don't go to school and all the parents do is blame the man."

While crime rates are showing a steady decline over the last few years, juvenile offenses have continued to rise, leading experts to caution the public not to be too optimistic. As youthful offenders age, they will most likely be repeat adult offenders and crime is likely to rise steadily. Moreover, many of these juveniles are committing violent crimes with weapons. Alcohol and other drug use among youths is also on the rise.

Warren says he is a realist and while the system is unfair he says "black people should know by now that the system is going to be harder on them, so they should stop committing the crimes."

An engineer residing in Silver Springs, Maryland and a member of the NAACP for 40 years, Warren says he is more interested in "saving these kids" and so he is encouraging more activism, urging adults to empower themselves and organize to unify their neighborhoods.

"We are not well today. We need to rise up. We are asleep and are not willing to fight. When you go into a community where people are on top of things, there is respect."

Warren therefore would like to see more pressure placed on the parents. "We have sorry parents, sorry excuse-offering parents. In Maryland, we are making parents pay to go to parenting school. The juvenile is placed on probation and then the charges are dropped."

Disagreeing with the argument that poverty is a primary reason for criminal activity, he retorts: "I grew up with that (poverty). A lot of people did and they aren't criminals. . . . I don't accept that."

The problem, he says, is that "Parents are not taking the time with their children." Further, he notes that too many black parents have created a value system for their children that mainly focuses on materialism. Faced with tougher economic times, resulting from "corporate down sizing, right sizing and out sizing," he said families are not coping very well. "Kids were used to getting everything" now they have difficulties learning how to sacrifice.

"What's more important, for a kid to buy a pair of sneakers or save money for college?" he asked. "You can't pay for both. There is no value on education and too much value on consumerism."

Warren painted a pessimistic picture if parents fail to change. While he sees the problem falling more on the shoulders of the individual, he said the government also has not done much to help.

"It's the government and us; it's both. How many preachers are speaking out. We cannot get beyond race. We won't criticize the drug dealer because he is black." By failing to take a stand against crime, he says the black community is further doomed.

The justice system has seemingly targeted the soft underbelly

Criminal Injustice: A Study in Black and White

Young, Black, Male and Doing Time—	
Percent of men age 20 to 29 in state and federal prisons, jail, probation, parole on any given day	
Black	32%
White	7%

Blacks and Drugs—	
Blacks constitute 12% of the total population of the U.S., yet receive a disproportionate share of police and judicial attention.	
Users	13%
Arrests	35%
Convictions	55%
Sentences	74%

Crack: Who's Using and Who's Getting Busted—	
White use	48%
Black use	38%
White conviction	3.5%
Black conviction	90%

—the weakest part of the society, argues Noelle Hanrahan of Equal Justice USA. The system protects the privileged, she says, creating a double standard when it comes to white collar crime. For instance, white collar crime was not even recognized until the 1930s and many offenders continue to receive "only a slap on the wrist" in comparison to crimes against property. The attention given to organized crime and mob violence also fades in and out.

Equal Justice USA of Hyattsville, Maryland is waging a protracted struggle to free Mumia Abu-Jamal of Philadelphia, on death row in Pennsylvania despite evidence that points to his innocence. "We think the way Mumia does about these things," said Hanrahan. "In every single facet of the justice system there is systematic racism and that is what contributes to the high incarceration rates. The abandoning of inner cities, red-lining, unemployment and many other conservative policies must be looked at. How sentencing is handled plays an important role; for example, the way they adjudicate white collar crime and how they treat other crimes like crimes against property, leads to who is in prison."

Hanrahan, also director of the Prison Radio Project, said even lack of access to good lawyers contributes. Some death row cases are revealing that sentences were meted out merely because the lawyer fell down on the job. Not that they committed the worst crime; they were simply given the worst lawyer. In fact, people committed to death row usually have no political clout.

Those who have overworked public defenders or incompetent lawyers cannot afford to do any better and hence could pay the terrible price with their life.

"Racial, economic and political biases are imbedded in our criminal justice system," said Hanrahan. "There's no such thing as equal justice, only justice for the rich."

 Article Review Form at end of book.

Discuss the uniqueness and importance of *U.S. vs. Armstrong.*

One Crime, Two Sentences

Blacks see bias over cocaine

Lighter sentences for whites lead to criminal case at Supreme Court.

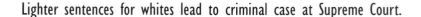

Robert Marquand,

Staff writer of The Christian Science Monitor

Dateline: WASHINGTON

When Christopher Lee Armstrong and four other young blacks were indicted by federal prosecutors on cocaine and firearms charges, their defense took an unusual tack; rather than a plea of innocence, they argued discrimination.

The men's lawyers told a Los Angeles district judge that all 24 federal cocaine prosecutions in L.A. the previous year were of blacks and said that the system was biased. The judge dismissed the case when prosecutors refused to reveal the basis for the charges.

This week the U.S. Supreme Court agreed to hear the case, *U.S. v. Armstrong,* the first of its kind in years to test if federal officials unfairly select minorities to prosecute.

A high-court hearing on race and bias in the criminal-justice system is of legal and social import in any year. But the Supreme Court's announcement this week is especially notable.

It came only hours before President Clinton joined with Capitol Hill's Republican majority to maintain heavy federal prison sentences for the possession and distribution of even small amounts of crack cocaine. The move was strongly opposed by the Congressional Black Caucus, which says it unfairly targets the black community, since penalties for powder cocaine—more commonly used by whites—are dramatically lighter.

Moreover, charges of unequal treatment and racism raised by the O.J. Simpson trial are still fresh, as are the concerns about black men highlighted by the Million Man March in Washington last month.

The White House decision on crack cocaine is a highly sensitive one, mixing race, crime, justice, and election-year politics.

For the first time since 1984, the president and members of Congress disregarded new guidelines by the nonpartisan U.S. Sentencing Commission.

The new sentencing rules, which judges and prosecutors follow in deciding prison terms, would have equalized the penalties for crack cocaine and powder cocaine. Crack, which is simply powder cocaine cut with baking soda and treated to make it cheap and smokable, is heavily used in the inner city and is associated with gang activity and violence. Powder cocaine is found more often in the suburbs.

Black Caucus members were enraged at the decision to ignore the new rules. They argued in a letter to Mr. Clinton that 96 percent of crack arrests are of minorities, and that between 1988 and

1994 in Los Angeles, the only persons prosecuted for crack-cocaine sales were blacks and Latinos.

Under current federal law, which toughened during the "war on drugs" in the 1980s, crack cocaine carries a mandatory minimum sentence 100 times longer than the penalty for a pure-cocaine arrest. Possession of 50 grams of crack cocaine results in a 10-year sentence, while it takes possession of some 5,000 grams of pure cocaine to land in prison for the same duration.

The commission argued prison terms for the two drugs should be changed from a "100 to 1" basis to a "1 to 1" basis. In order to provide the possibility of discretion to what is normally a very rigid federal sentencing system, however, it added penalties to crack-cocaine arrests based on the circumstances of the crime.

Late last month, prisoners rioted in federal facilities in Illinois and Alabama after hearing that Congress was preparing to reject the commission's guidelines. Twenty of 85 federal prisons are still on a state of alert.

"Everybody who really knows this issue here wants to change the law," says a senior staffer on the House Judiciary Committee. "But nobody wants to seem soft on crime. If [Sen. Bob] Dole says he favors a 5 to 1 ratio, what is [Sen.] Phil Gramm going to say?"

Attorney General Janet Reno supports the president's decision to reject the Sentencing Commission, arguing that the drug promotes street violence. But she has stated that the "100 to 1" ratio should be reexamined.

The Justice Department is using the Armstrong case to halt what it feels are a growing number of delays in "prompt and effective enforcement" of the law by defendants arguing discrimination. Defense lawyers will point to the vast disparity between the numbers of blacks and whites prosecuted in the federal system.

The federal-justice system does not offer the same flexibility as the state system. A five-year sentence for crack in a federal court is mandatory. In the state system, the sentence could be reduced to 10 months, or even probation.

With a mandatory five-year sentence for only five grams of crack, the federal prisons contain thousands of black males, many of whom feel their sentence is too heavy.

"At some point," says the judiciary source, "you're going to have a lot of angry people coming out of prison and onto the street."

 Article Review Form at end of book.

Does race have an impact on the support for police use of deadly force on fleeing felons? How?

"Stop or I'll Shoot"

Racial differences in support for police use of deadly force

Francis T. Cullen
University of Cincinnati

Liqun Cao
Eastern Michigan University

James Frank
Robert H. Langworthy
Sandra Lee Browning
Reneé Kopache
University of Cincinnati

Thomas J. Stevenson
Cincinnati, Ohio

Police use of deadly force is a relatively rare event: Despite making over 14 million arrests (Federal Bureau of Investigation, 1994) and having untold disputatious encounters with citizens, it is estimated that the half million police in the United States shoot about 3,600 people each year, with fatal results in as many as 1,000 of these incidents (Fyfe, 1988; Geller, 1988). Still, such deadly force warrants special scrutiny because it is, similar to capital punishment, the most extreme form of state power turned against its citizenry. Indeed, Sherman (1980, p. 71) terms killings by police as "execution without trial."

Police use of deadly force shares another characteristic with capital punishment: These forms of state power appear inextricably intertwined with the enduring issue of race. Hacker (1992) claims that America remains "two nations, Black and White, separate, hostile, unequal." State executions, with and without trial, seem to reflect this reality: African American males disproportionately populate death row (Keil & Vito, 1990; Mann, 1993) and disproportionately are killed by police (Fyffe, 1988; Geller, 1988; Sherman, 1980). Of course, commentators debate whether this exercise of force is produced by discriminatory decision making by criminal justice officials or simply is a response to higher levels of street crime among minority citizens (Fyffe, 1988; Mann, 1993; Tonry, 1995; Wilbanks, 1987). In either case, state use of deadly force raises the issue of racial injustice; police violence in inner-city areas holds the special risk of inciting spontaneous protest, if not insurgency.

Despite the salience of the issue, there is surprisingly little research on potential racial differences in attitudes toward police use of deadly force. Existing attitudinal studies suggest, however, that race may divide citizens in how they view criminal justice and, by implication, in the extent to which they would support law enforcement officials responding to crime with force.

First, although the studies are not uniform in their results and differences are often more a matter of degree rather than qualitative in nature (Miller, Rossi, & Simpson, 1986; Secret & Johnson, 1989), research has found that compared to Whites, Blacks are more likely to perceive the criminal justice system as unjust (Hagan & Albonetti, 1982; see also Browning, Cullen, Cao, Kopache, & Stevenson, 1994), to be liberal as opposed to conservative in their crime ideology

F. T. Cullen, L. Cao, J. Frank, R.H. Langworthy, S.L. Browning, R. Kopache, T.J. Stevenson. *American Behavioral Scientist*, Feb. 1996, Vol. 39, No. 4, pp. 449–460. Copyright © 1996 by Sage Publications, Inc. Reprinted by permission of Sage Publications Inc.

(Browning & Cao, 1992), to be less sanguine about punitive crime-control policies (Blumstein & Cohen, 1980; Maguire & Pastore, 1994), to be more in favor of rehabilitation programs (Maguire & Pastore, 1994), and to be less supportive of the death penalty (Bohm, 1991). Second, apart from a few exceptions (Brandl, Frank, Worden, & Bynum, 1994; Frank, Brandl, Cullen, & Stichman, 1993), previous research reports that African Americans hold less favorable attitudes toward the police than do whites (see, for example, Albrecht & Green, 1977; Bordua & Tifft, 1971; Cao, Frank, & Cullen, in press; Erez, 1984; Hindelang, 1974; Jacob, 1971; Parks, 1984; Peek, Lowe, & Alston, 1981; Percy, 1980; Scaglion & Condon, 1980; Smith & Hawkins, 1973).

Third and perhaps most instructive, there is some evidence that African Americans are less willing to endorse the use of force by police. For example, polls show a clear racial gap in reactions to the incident in which Rodney King was beaten by Los Angeles police. Thus 92% of Blacks versus 62% of Whites stated that they would have voted guilty if they had been on the jury in the trial of the police officers accused of using excessive force in arresting Rodney King (Church, 192); 82% of Blacks versus 44% of Whites responded that the verdict would have been different if "the police and the man they had beaten had all been White" (Lacayo, 1992, p. 32); and 92% of Blacks versus 72% of Whites said that the force used by police as shown in the Rodney King videotape "was excessive under any circumstance" (Lacayo, 1992, p. 32).

More broadly, a 1991 national poll found that Blacks were more likely than Whites (45% to 33%) to answer "yes" to the question, "Do you think there is any police brutality in your area, or not?" And a 1992 poll reported that Blacks were more likely than Whites (46% to 26%) to answer "only fair" or "poor" to the question, "How would you rate the police in your community on . . . not using excessive force?" (Maguire, Pastore, & Flanagan, 1993, pp. 172–173).

Similarly revealing are 1993 national poll data that are based on responses to the question, "Would you approve of a policeman striking a citizen who . . . ?" On two items, Black-White answers were similar: About 9 in 10 supported the use of force if the citizen "was attacking the policeman with his fists," whereas the same proportion opposed police force for a citizen "who had said vulgar and obscene things to the policeman." Blacks were more likely (12% versus 6%) to favor the use of force for a citizen "who was being questioned in a murder case." Most illuminating, however, was that Blacks were markedly less likely (59% to 75%) to favor an officer striking a citizen "who was attempting to escape from custody" (Maguire & Pastore, 1994, p. 170).

The issue of "escape from custody" is of special relevance, because it relates closely to the celebrated case of *Tennessee v. Garner* (1985), in which the U.S. Supreme Court delineated the limits of police discretion in the use of deadly force. In this case, Edward Garner, a 15-year-old unarmed burglar, was fatally wounded by a Memphis police officer when he failed to heed the officer's call to halt and tried to escape by climbing over a 6-foot fence. The Supreme Court ruled

that the use of deadly force in this instance was a violation of the Fourth Amendment's prohibition of unreasonable "seizure." More broadly, the Court indicated that deadly force was constitutional only when an offender posed an imminent danger or when an offender had demonstrated dangerousness by committing a crime that involved actual or threatened physical harm (Kappeler & Kaune, 1993; Skolnick & Fyfe, 1993). According to the Court:

Where the officer has probable cause to believe that the suspect poses a threat of serious physical harm, either to the officer or to others, it is not constitutionally unreasonable to prevent escape by deadly force. Thus, if the suspect threatens the officer with a weapon or there is probable cause to believe that he has committed a crime involving the infliction or threatened infliction of serious harm, deadly force may be used if necessary to prevent escape, and if, where feasible, some warning has been given (*Tennessee v. Garner*, 1985, pp. 11–12).

In light of the continuing salience of the issue of police force (Skolnick & Fyfe, 1993) and the corresponding lack of public opinion research, the current study attempts to explore the impact of race on support for police use of deadly force. More specifically, building on the *Tennessee v. Garner* (1985) decision, we explore how support might vary by whether the use of deadly force is legal or illegal according to the constitutional standards demarcated by the U.S. Supreme Court. Finally, the data set allows us to assess how a range of demographic, crime-related, neighborhood, and ideological factors both influence support for the use of deadly force and potentially account for differences in opinion that emerge by race.

Methods

Sample

Data for this study were obtained from telephone interviews in Cincinnati, Ohio in the fall of 1991. To ensure that interviews were conducted with a meaningful number of African Americans, the sample was stratified. The 1990 Census Profile of Neighborhoods was used to select nine neighborhoods: three predominantly composed of African Americans, three predominantly White, and three racially mixed. Seven of the neighborhoods included in this study were within the boundaries of the city of Cincinnati, while the other two neighborhoods were contiguous with the city.

Three hundred and nine telephone numbers were randomly selected from three area telephone directories that covered the nine neighborhoods. To ensure randomness of the respondents within each household, we conducted the interview with the household member over age 18 who celebrated his or her birthday closest to the date of our survey (Fowler, 1984). The response rate for the survey was 77.3% (N = 239), which included 103 African Americans and 136 Whites. The sociodemographic characteristics of the sample have been reported previously by Browning and Cao (1992) and by Browning et al. (1994).

Given the salience of the Rodney King trial, especially to African Americans (Church, 1992), it is possible that this case might have temporarily inflated Blacks' sensitivity to the use of force by law enforcement officials. Although this possibility cannot be discounted, the timing of our survey decreases the likelihood that the Rodney King affair substantially influenced re-

sponses on the survey. As mentioned, our survey was conducted in the fall of 1991, months after Rodney King's beating/arrest and the subsequent indictment of the officers involved in the incident (both of which occurred in March, 1991). Further, the trial of the officers and their initial acquittal, which prompted the Los Angeles riots and an intense national conversation regarding the excessive use of force by police, took place after our survey had been completed in February to April, 1992.

Measures

Dependent Variable

To measure support for police use of deadly force, the respondents were first told the following:

While on patrol, police officers may be in the position of seeing someone who has broken the law and is fleeing the scene of the crime. And they may have to decide whether they should use their gun to stop the suspected offender—that is, they may have to decide whether to shoot at the suspect to stop the person from getting away.

The respondents were then asked to indicate whether they "approved or disapproved of a police officer using his or her gun to stop" a person who was committing one of eight crimes: purse snatching, motor vehicle theft, larceny from a store, drunk driving, selling drugs, burglary, rape, and armed robbery. The wording of each offense-item is presented in Table 1.

Each of these items shares the feature of involving a "fleeing felon." Accordingly, caution must be exercised in attempting to generalize the findings of this study to other forms of deadly force. The items differ, however, in whether the offender has manifested evidence of past danger-

ousness, which according to *Tennessee v. Garner* (1985) would make police use of deadly force constitutionally permissible. Six of the items do not involve a display of past dangerousness. These items, which we term the "illegal deadly force scale," have a reliability coefficient of .86. The remaining two items, fleeing felons who have committed rape and armed robbery, seem to meet the constitutional standard of past dangerousness—that is, of having "committed a crime involving the use or threatened use of serious physical harm" (Kappeler & Kaune, 1993, p. 65). We term these items the "legal deadly force scale"; the Cronbach's alpha for this measure is .80.

Independent Variables

Race, the major independent variable, was coded 1 = African American and 0 = White. We also included four sociodemographic characteristics of the respondents. Age and education were coded in years. Gender was treated as a dummy variable: 1 = female and 0 = male. Income was coded 1 < $10,000 a year to 7 > $60,000 a year.

To explore a range of potential sources of attitudes toward police use of deadly force, we included three other sets of variables in the analysis. First, to measure experiences with the criminal justice system we included a two-item measure, *hassled by the police* (α = .78), which assessed whether the respondent either personally had been, or knew someone who had been, "stopped or watched closely by a police officer, even when you [they] had done nothing wrong." *Contact with the criminal justice system* (α = .67) was tapped with two items, which asked if in the

Table 1 Public Support for Police Use of Deadly Force by Race

	Percentage Approve		
Items	**Sample**	**Black**	**White**
I. Illegal Deadly force Scale			
1. A person who is seen snatching a purse and is fleeing to avoid arrest	16	14	18
2. A person who is seen stealing an automobile and is fleeing to avoid arrest	19	9	27
3. A person who is seen stealing jewelry from a store and is fleeing to avoid arrest	19	8	27
4. A person who is seen driving while drunk and is fleeing to avoid arrest	23	16	28
5. A person who is seen selling drugs and is fleeing to avoid arrest	40	35	45
6. A person who is seen burglarizing a house at night and is fleeing to avoid arrest	46	39	52
II. Legal Deadly Force Scale			
1. A person who is seen raping a woman and is fleeing to avoid arrest	84	89	81
2. A person who is seen using a gun to stick up a convenience store and is fleeing to avoid arrest	90	93	87

Alpha of Illegal Deadly Force Scale = .858. Alpha of Legal Deadly Force Scale = .798.

past 2 years the respondent had "visited someone you knew personally while they were in jail or in prison" and knew someone "personally who was arrested while committing a crime." On the contact and hassled measures, all items were answered either yes = 1 or no = 0, with a scale score thus ranging from 0 to 2.

A second set of variables measured experiences with crime. Following Skogan & Maxfield (1981), we included not only having been a *crime victim* (in the past 2 years) but also *vicarious victimization* ("In the past 2 years, did you personally know anyone who had been a victim of . . . burglary, robbery, an attack by a stranger, sexual assault, murder?"). The crime victim measure was coded yes = 1, no = 0; vicarious victimization was coded from 0 to 5 (α = .63). Further, past research has suggested the utility of

distinguishing between being afraid of crime and feeling sensitive or vulnerable to the consequences of a criminal victimization (Warr, 1995). Thus we incorporated a measure of *fear of crime*—"In your neighborhood, how afraid would you be that someone might commit a crime against you?"—with responses ranging from 1 = *not afraid* to 4 = *very afraid,* and we used a measure of *vulnerability to crime*—"If you were out walking and someone tried to mug you, do you believe that you would be able to defend yourself without getting hurt?"—with responses ranging from 1 = *I could defend myself* to 4 = *I could not defend myself.*

Third, we included two variables to assess the possible effects of neighborhood conditions on attitudes toward the use of force. To measure *incivility* or the outward manifestation of physical and so-

cial disorder (Lewis & Salem, 1986; Skogan, 1990), we employed the item: "My neighborhood often is too noisy and the streets have too much litter in them." To measure *social disorganization* or the extent of informal social control (Sampson & Groves, 1989), we incorporated: "In my neighborhood, people would call the police right away if they think a crime is being committed." The respondents rated the items with a 4-point agree/ disagree scale. One note of caution should be mentioned: Because these items assess people's perceptions of their community, the results could vary if more objective indicators of neighborhood conditions were used.

Fourth, the analysis incorporated three measures of ideology. General *political ideology* was measured by asking respondents to rate themselves on a 6-point continuum ranging from 1 = *very liberal* to 6 = *very conservative.* This measure has been used in previous research (Dunaway & Cullen, 1991). Drawing on the work of Cullen, Bynum, Garrett, and Greene (1985) and McGarrell and Flanagan (1987), we also included an 11-item *conservative crime ideology* scale (α = .87) and an 8-item *liberal crime ideology* scale (α = .82). In brief, the conservative crime ideology measure was composed of statements showing support for punitive policies and attributing crime to permissiveness, whereas the liberal crime ideology measure was composed of statements favorable to rehabilitation and attributing crime to social inequality (see Browning & Cao, 1992 for a list of these items). The respondents assessed these statements by using a 4-point agree/disagree scale, with a high score coded to mean support for the ideology.

Results and Discussion

Table 1 presents the percentage of the sample approving the use of deadly force to stop offenders fleeing from arrest for the eight crimes included in the survey. Across the whole sample, the public appears to endorse the distinction made by the U.S. Supreme Court in *Tennessee v. Garner* (1985) regarding when deadly force is permissible. Thus over four-fifths of the respondents favored the use of deadly force to stop offenders who had manifested past dangerousness (a rapist and an armed robber). In contrast, consistent with the Supreme Court's ruling in *Garner*, a majority of the sample disapproved of using force when felons had not committed a violent crime.

Some dissensus is apparent, however, for the items of drug selling and burglary, for which 40% and 46% of the sample approved using deadly force. This finding suggests that although citizens wish to restrain police power for property and motor vehicle offenses in which no physical harm is indicated, this opposition diminishes for a substantial minority of the public when an offense may involve a clearer threat. Thus selling drugs poses a potential threat to a person's physical well-being, while the burglary item involves the invasion of a home "at night" when residents are likely to be present.

A related interpretation is that citizens will be more supportive of using deadly force as the perceived seriousness of the offense increases. Consistent with this view, research reveals that the public rates drug selling as well as rape and armed robbery as serious offenses and, as our findings show, citizens also are more likely to approve use of force to stop offenders who commit these illegalities. However, this correspondence between seriousness and support for the use of deadly force is less apparent for burglary and drunk driving. Although burglary receives twice the percentage of approval for using deadly force than that accorded drunk driving, studies reveal that these offenses are perceived to have similar levels of seriousness (see Cullen, Link, & Polanzi, 1982; Rossi, Waite, Bose, & Berk, 1974). In any event, future investigations might profit from exploring the relationship of offense seriousness to support for the use of police force.

As Table 1 reports, although Blacks and Whites had similar patterns of responses, Blacks were slightly more likely to approve the use of legal deadly force and markedly less likely to approve the use of illegal deadly force. Across the six offense scenarios in the illegal deadly force scale, the mean percentage of approval was 12.6% higher for Whites (32.8%) than for Blacks (20.2%). Most noteworthy, a majority of Whites, as opposed to 39% of Blacks, approved the use of deadly force to stop a felon fleeing after a nighttime house burglary, a case that approximates the offense involved in *Tennessee v. Garner* (1985).

To assess the independent effects of race, we conducted multivariate analyses for the illegal and legal deadly force scales, controlling for sociodemographic characteristics, experiences with the criminal justice system, crime-related experiences, perceived neighborhood conditions, and political and crime ideology. For the legal deadly force scale, the equation as a whole was not statistically significant ($p = .435$) and explained a negligible amount of variance ($R^2 = .068$). Because the level of approval was not differentiated by any of the independent variables, these findings indicate that there was general consensus in the sample that legal deadly force is warranted.

In contrast, the independent variables explained 23.4% of the variance in the use of illegal deadly force (Table 2, Equation 5). The data suggest that this scale is not affected by sociodemographic factors or by experiences with the criminal justice system. Feelings of fear or vulnerability and having been a crime victim also were insignificant predictors, but vicarious victimization was significantly related to support for illegal deadly force. In short, personal crime experiences had less influence on attitudes than knowing other people who had been victimized. Further, those living in neighborhoods that are disorganized or lack informal social control were less supportive of illegal deadly force. It is possible that these neighborhoods are the site of more police surveillance and negative citizen-officer interactions, which may make the residents more suspicious of police power. Finally, although political ideology was not related to the dependent variable, support for illegal deadly force was lower for those who endorse a liberal crime ideology and higher for those who endorse a conservative crime ideology.

The main focal point of this research is whether racial differences exist in attitudes toward deadly force. We explore this issue in Table 2 through five separate equations. The first equation shows that being African American decreased approval for

Table 2 Sources of Public Support for Police Use of Illegal Deadly Force

	Equation 1		Equation 2		Equation 3		Equation 4		Equation 5	
	Beta	Sig.T	Beta	Sig.T	Beta	Sig.T	Beta	Sig.T.	Beta	Sig.T
Independent Variables										
Race (Black = 1)	−.164	.011*	−.172	.026*	−.185	.018*	−.154	.046*	−.053	.488
Sex (male = 1)	−.104	.099	−.101	.112	−.079	.261	−.068	.329	−.097	.154
Age	.202	.002*	.219	.003*	.189	.026*	.158	.062	.152	.064
Education	−.093	.195	−.098	.175	−.110	.129	−.098	.172	−.037	.598
Income	.110	.126	.128	.081	.149	.055	.097	.218	.068	.376
Hassled			−.077	.401	−.090	.335	−.089	.334	−.030	.738
Contacts			.112	.204	.086	.347	.084	.352	.090	.301
Fear of crime					.001	.995	−.018	.842	−.072	.409
Vulnerability					.043	.665	.065	.504	.042	.652
Crime victim					.095	.164	.081	.231	.041	.532
Vicarious victim					.150	.044*	.165	.025*	.173	.015*
Incivility							.148	.034*	.103	.130
Disorganization							−.217	.004*	−.186	.010*
Liberal crime ideology									−.170	.021*
Conservative crime ideology									.193	.014*
Political ideology									.050	.456
R^2	.097		.104		.126		.162		.234	
F	5.032		3.832		2.976		3.355		4.246	
Significance	.000		.001		.001		.000		.000	

*$p < .05$.

police use of illegal deadly force even with controls introduced for sociodemographic characteristics. In the subsequent four equations, we introduce four sets of variables to see if the race effects can be explained. As can be seen, race remains significant through Equation 4, even with controls for sociodemographic characteristics, criminal justice experiences, crime-related experiences, and neighborhood conditions.

Race loses statistical significance only in Equation 5, where it is accounted for by the crime ideology measures. This finding suggests that African Americans' more pronounced opposition to police use of deadly force is rooted in a broader view of crime and criminal justice (see Albrecht & Green, 1977). Previous analyses have shown that in our sample, African Americans hold more liberal and less conservative crime ideologies than Whites (Browning & Cao, 1992).

Conclusion

This research suggests three major conclusions. First, public approval of police use of deadly force largely coincides with the constitutional standards demarcated by the U.S. Supreme Court in *Tennessee v. Garner*. A notable exception to this finding, however, is the willingness of a majority of White respondents to support the use of deadly force to stop a fleeing house burglar. Second, although Blacks and Whites largely concur in their assessment of legal deadly force, African Americans are less supportive of illegal deadly force. Although more a matter of degree than qualitative (a majority of Whites also tend to oppose illegal deadly force), these attitudinal differences may be the basis of the racial cleavages that arise in specific cases—especially when the justification for using force is ambiguous and deadly force is directed by a White police officer to a Black offender. Third, African Americans' views toward deadly force should not be seen as a distinctive set of attitudes. Rather, they appear to be part of a more global liberal crime ideology that shapes views on a variety of specific policy issues.

References

Albrecht, S. L., & Green, M. (1977). Attitudes toward the police and the larger attitude complex: Implications for police-community relationships. *Criminology, 15,* 67–86.

Blumstein, A., & Cohen, J. (1980). Sentencing of convicted offenders: An analysis of the public's view. *Law and Society Review, 14,* 223–261.

Bohm, R. M. (1991). American death penalty opinion, 1936–1986: A critical examination of the Gallup Polls. In R. M. Bohm (Ed.), *The death penalty in America: Current research* (pp. 113–145). Cincinnati, OH: Anderson.

Bordua, D. J., & Tifft, L. L. (1971). Citizen interviews, organizational feedback, and police-community relations decisions. *Law and Society Review, 6,* 155–182.

Brandl, S. G., Frank J., Worden, R. E., & Bynum, T. S. (1994). Global and specific attitudes toward the police: Disentangling the relationship. *Justice Quarterly, 11,* 119–134.

Browning, S. L., & Cao, L. (1992). The impact of race on criminal justice ideology. *Justice Quarterly, 9,* 685–701.

Browning, S. L., Cullen, F. T., Cao, L., Kopache, R., & Stevenson, T. J. (1994). Race and getting hassled by the police: A research note. *Police Studies, 17,* 1–11.

Cao, L., Frank, J., & Cullen, F. T. (in press). Race, community context, and confidence in the police. *American Journal of Police.*

Church, G. J. (1992, May 11). The fire this time. *Time,* pp. 18–25.

Cullen, F. T., Bynum, T. S., Garrett, K. M., & Greene, J. R. (1985). Legislator ideology and criminal justice policy: Implications from Illinois. In E. S. Fairchild & V. J. Webb (Eds.), *The politics of crime and criminal justice* (pp. 57–76). Beverly Hills, CA: Sage.

Cullen, F. T., Link, B. G., & Polanzi, C. W. (1982). The seriousness of crime revisited: Have attitudes toward white-collar crime changed? *Criminology, 20,* 83–102.

Dunaway, R. G., & Cullen, F. T. (1991). Explaining crime ideology: An exploration of the parental socialization perspective. *Crime and Delinquency, 37,* 536–554.

Erez, E. (1984). Self-defined desert and citizens' assessment of the police. *Journal of Criminal Law and Criminology, 75,* 1276–1299.

Federal Bureau of Investigation. (1994). *Crime in the United States: Uniform crime reports.* Washington, DC: U.S. Government Printing Office.

Fowler, F. J. (1984). *Survey research methods.* Beverly Hills, CA: Sage.

Frank, J., Brandl, S. G., Cullen, F. T., & Stichman, A. (1993, September). *Reassessing the impact of race on citizens' attitudes toward the police.* Paper presented at the meeting of the Midwestern Criminal Justice Association, Chicago, IL.

Fyfe, J. J. (1988). Police use of deadly force: Research and reform. *Justice Quarterly, 5,* 165–205.

Geller, W. (1988). *Deadly force: Crime file study guide.* Washington, DC: National Institute of Justice.

Hacker, A. (1992). *Two nations: Black and White, separate, hostile, unequal.* New York: Scribner's.

Hagan, J., & Albonetti, C. (1982). Race, class, and the perception of criminal injustice in America. *American Journal of Sociology, 88,* 329–355.

Hindelang, M. J. (1974). Public opinion regarding crime, criminal justice, and related topics. *Journal of Research in Crime and Delinquency, 11,* 101–116.

Jacob, H. (1971). Black and White perceptions of justice in the city. *Law and Society Review, 5,* 69–89.

Kappeler, V. E., & Kaune, M. (1993). Civil liabilities for police use of excessive force. In V. E. Kappeler, *Critical issues in police civil liability* (pp. 57–71). Prospect Heights, IL: Waveland.

Keil, T. J., & Vito, G. F. (1990). Race and the death penalty in Kentucky murder trials: An analysis of post-Gregg outcomes. *Justice Quarterly, 7,* 189–207.

Lacayo, R. (1992, May 11). Anatomy of an acquittal. *Time,* pp. 30–32.

Lewis, D. A., & Salem, G. (1986). *Fear of crime: Incivility and the reduction of a social problem.* New Brunswick, NJ: Transaction Books.

Maguire, K., & Pastore, A. L. (1994). *Sourcebook of criminal justice statistics—1993.* Washington, DC: U.S. Government Printing Office.

Maguire, K., Pastore, A. L., & Flanagan, T. J. (1993). *Sourcebook of criminal justice statistics—1992.* Washington, DC: U.S. Government Printing Office.

Mann, C. R. (1993). *Unequal justice: A question of color.* Bloomington, IN: Indiana University Press.

McGarrell, E. F., & Flanagan, T. J. (1987). Measuring and explaining legislator crime control ideology. *Journal of Research in Crime and Delinquency, 24,* 102–118.

Miller, J. L., Rossi, P. H., & Simpson, J. E. (1986). Perceptions of justice: Race and gender differences in judgments of appropriate prison sentences. *Law and Society Review, 20,* 313–334.

Parks, R. B. (1984). Linking objective and subjective measures of performance. *Public Administration Review, 44,* 118–127.

Peek, C. W., Lowe, G. D., & Alston, J. P. (1981). Race and attitudes toward local police: Another look. *Journal of Black Studies, 11,* 361–374.

Percy, S. L. (1980). Response time and citizen evaluation of police. *Journal of Police Science and Administration, 8,* 75–86.

Rossi, P. H., Waite, E., Bose, C. E., & Berk, R. E. (1974). The seriousness of crimes: Normative structure and individual differences. *American Sociological Review, 39,* 224–237.

Sampson, R. J., & Groves, W. B. (1989). Community structure and crime: Testing social-disorganization theory. *American Journal of Sociology, 94,* 774–802.

Scaglion, R., & Condon, R. G. (1980). Determinants of attitudes toward city police. *Criminology, 17,* 485–494.

Secret, P. E., & Johnson, J. B. (1989). Racial differences in attitudes toward crime control. *Journal of Criminal Justice, 17,* 361–375.

Sherman, L. W. (1980). Execution without trial: Police homicide and the constitution. *Vanderbilt Law Review, 33,* 71–100.

Skogan, W. G. (1990). *Disorder and decline: Crime and the spiral of decay in American neighborhoods.* Berkeley: University of California Press.

Skogan, W. G., & Maxfield, M. G. (1981). *Coping with crime: Individual and neighborhood reactions.* Beverly Hills, CA: Sage.

Skolnick, J. H., & Fyfe, J. J. (1993). *Above the law: Police and the excessive use of force.* New York: Free Press.

Smith, P. E., & Hawkins, R. O. (1973). Victimization, types of citizen-police contacts and attitudes toward the police. *Law and Society Review, 8,* 135–152.

Tennessee v. Garner, 471 U.S. 1 (1985).

Tonry, M. (1995). *Malign neglect: Race, crime, and punishment in America.* New York: Oxford University Press.

Warr, M. (1995). Public perceptions of crime and punishment. In J. F. Sheley (Ed.), *Criminology: A contemporary handbook* (2nd ed., pp. 15–31). Belmont, CA: Wadsworth.

Wilbanks, W. (1987). *The myth of a racist criminal justice system.* Monterey, CA: Brooks/Cole.

 **Article Review Form at end of book.**

Why do many African Americans argue that the criminal justice system is inherently biased against them?

Is Justice Color Blind?

John Diconsiglio

"Suspicion." That was the official reason given by the Middletown, Connecticut, police for handcuffing four Wesleyan College students on the night of November 2.

Suspicion of what?

"Suspicion of being black," says Janel Davis, 18, a Wesleyan sophomore. "If you're out on the street after dark and you're black, that's suspicion enough."

For many African-Americans, the story was eerily familiar. Four black Wesleyan students were walking to their dorm rooms that night when a white police officer stopped them and demanded to see identification. When they refused, the officer arrested them. Later, they were released with an apology, but not before the incident provoked a 200-student demonstration on campus.

"This happens every day to African-Americans," says Francisco Tezen, 20, a Wesleyan junior, "and we need to wake up."

While Middletown officials are calling the incident an honest mistake, many African-American observers say that the four Wesleyan students were given their first taste of how the criminal-justice system routinely treats blacks. Too many blacks, they say, have experienced the same kind of "mistakes" as the students in Wesleyan.

"There is a certain lack of trust of law enforcement [among many African-Americans] because of their personal experiences with the criminal-justice system," says Georgetown University law professor Mark Covering. Some blacks see that system as "designed to keep whites safe and keep them off the streets or in prison."

Even before the Simpson trial, the 1992 videotaped beating of motorist Rodney King at the hands of the Los Angeles police and the subsequent acquittal of those officers polarized black and white views of justice. For some blacks, the criminal-justice system has long meant police brutality, unfair treatment by white juries, and high conviction rates for blacks.

Whom to Blame?

Others, while acknowledging that racial bias may exist in individual cases, insist that the system is largely color blind. Some experts warn against blaming racial disparities in arrest statistics on bias by police, judges, or juries. With crime and drug-use rising in inner cities with high minority populations, "greater proportions of blacks than whites are going to be arrested, prosecuted, and convicted," claims University of Minnesota law professor Michael Tonry.

But many African-Americans say that the criminal-justice system is inherently biased against them. Statistics show that African-American men, who make up only 6 percent of the population, make up 48 percent of all prison inmates. A new study by the Sentencing Project revealed that one in three black men between the ages of 20 and 29 are either in jail, on probation, or on parole. "If these numbers were for young white men, the nation would declare a national emergency," says Marc Mauer, the study's author.

Some argue that those figures accurately reflect the number of African-Americans who commit crimes. William Wabanks, author of *The Myth of the Racist*

Criminal Justice System, says that "the reason so many blacks are in prison is not because the system discriminates. It's because blacks commit a higher percentage of crime."

But others note that many laws seem to punish blacks more than whites. A federal law that calls for mandatory prison sentences for drug possession, for example, distinguishes between crack cocaine, which is used predominantly in the inner city, and powder cocaine, which is popular among wealthy whites. The law calls for a five-year prison term for possessing 5 grams of crack or 500 grams of powder cocaine. "A dealer with less than $1,000 worth of crack receives the same sentences as someone with $50,000 worth of powder," says Mark Moore, professor of criminal justice at Harvard University. "And . . . the one with crack is black and the one with powder is white."

For years, experts agree, blacks have shaken their heads in disbelief as white juries handed down unduly harsh sentences to black defendants. By the time the Simpson verdict came around, the gulf between black and white views of the justice system was enormous.

Those who object to the verdict, says Roger Wilkins, sociology professor at George Mason University, "have no sense of how profoundly antiblack the justice system has been and, in many instances, still is."

Some experts say that so many blacks have been stopped on "suspicion" that their jubilant reactions to the Simpson verdict were not surprising. The real shock, they say, is that after all this time many whites can't see what they are celebrating.

"I don't want to say it's payback time," says Georgetown's Covering, "but many [blacks] viewed [the verdict] as the system finally working in their favor."

 Article Review Form at end of book.

Why are African American jury members reluctant to convict African American defendants?

The Color of the Law

John Leo

In 1991, a visiting Jewish scholar, Yankel Rosenbaum, was fatally stabbed in Brooklyn by a black mob outraged that a black youngster had been run over and killed by a religious Jewish motorcade. Rosenbaum lived long enough to identify Lemrick Nelson Jr. as the stabber, but a largely black jury did not convict Nelson. Later, some jury members went partying with Nelson to celebrate the acquittal. Nelson subsequently moved to Georgia, where he was convicted of slashing a schoolmate.

At the time, it appeared to be an act of race-based jury nullification, and, though the word didn't pop up, it was clear that something very unusual had occurred and that many of the city's Jews had suddenly withdrawn their faith in the local criminal justice system.

Blacks, of course, have their own historic reasons for doubting the fairness of cops and courts. Enormous injustices were inflicted on blacks over the years, and not just in the South, where blacks accused of attacking whites were almost automatically convicted. But as the system has changed, with more black jurors showing up, a different kind of racial surprise appeared.

In New York, a few-high-profile black defendants unexpectedly got off, including a drug dealer who shot several cops and a 19-year-old who shot and killed a white priest, then confessed and claimed that the priest had approached him for sex.

Now, in the wake of Johnnie Cochran's over-the-top, send-them-a-message summation in the O.J. Simpson case, the *Wall Street Journal* reports that what appears to be a racial nullification movement is humming right along. The *Journal* found that some black jurors "are choosing to disregard the evidence, however powerful, because they seek to protest racial injustice and to refrain from adding to the already large numbers of blacks behind bars."

If so, that's a very ominous development indeed. An explicit attempt to politicize jury verdicts along racial lines would clearly put the whole, faltering criminal justice system at risk, with many unforeseen consequences.

The *Journal* lists a string of jury decisions that may reflect the impulse toward nullification, including the acquittal of Washington Mayor Marion Barry, on 13 of 14 counts in a sting operation conducted by the FBI, and the acquittal of some of the defendants charged with beating trucker Reginald Denny during the 1992 Los Angeles rioting.

Racial acquittals. The *Journal* also points out, for what it's worth, that conviction rates are unusually low in heavily minority areas—28.7 percent of felony trials in Washington, D.C., and 30 percent in Detroit ended in acquittals, both significantly high rates. In the South Bronx, more than 47 percent of African-American defendants are acquitted, about three times the national average.

Some racial division on juries is simply the result of different people bringing different life experiences into court and viewing evidence through different lenses. And some is based on the fact that many blacks are less likely than whites to believe the unsupported testimony of a police officer, even if the officer is not Mark Fuhrman. That's well within the normal functioning of juries.

But now we are starting to hear various racial pleas to ignore evidence and free black defendants either as a political protest against a system perceived as oppressive and racist, or as a way of reducing the high number of black males in the prison system. Paul Butler, a black criminal-law professor at George Washington University, takes a cool cost-benefit approach: In cases that don't involve violence, he thinks, black jurors should "presume in favor of nullification" because the community needs the help of accused offenders, even guilty ones, to rebuild itself.

Law professors who advocate freeing guilty people of their own race, but not others, are an excellent indicator of identity politics at work. As columnist George Will wrote last week, the "diversity" people have to accept some responsibility for "the politics of thinking that you are but a fragment of the racial or ethnic group to which you belong and you have few if any obligations beyond it." Obligations beyond the tribe indicate a concern with justice, which used to be of some interest to professors of law.

Because of the anguish of losing so many young men to the prison system, some blacks now seem willing to look past crimes and talk about a system that "criminalizes" its young. The argument buried in "criminalized" —if the defendant shot somebody, it's society's fault—is often made even sharper. A *Boston Globe* columnist wrote recently that "we are rounding up the people our economy does not need and consigning them to concentration camps."

At the law schools, something called "critical race theory" spreads the notion that law is nothing more than a politicized expression of white power and that blacks can never hope for justice from whites. Writing in the *Manhattan Institute's City Journal*, Heather MacDonald says many law students now assume as a matter of course that the law has a color. She says the president of the Harvard Law Review told her: "You can't study criminal law and not have race come up a lot. The mere fact that so many defendants are black means that the law treats blacks differently."

Tribal politics and woolly thinking may be setting the stage for a nullification movement that could inflict some very serious damage, including the isolation of blacks from their natural allies. Don't we all want to rethink this?

 Article Review Form at end of book.

What is the opinion of African Americans regarding government intervention to help reduce the crime problem and improve race relations? How does this relate to the opinion of whites?

Races Worry about Crime and Values, Disagree on Government

What emerges from a *Wall Street Journal*/NBC News poll on black and white America is a picture of an America in which blacks and whites agree, at least superficially, on much: the importance of the crime problem, a sense that some but not nearly enough progress has been made in race relations in recent years and a feeling that integration as a goal isn't as important as it once was.

The survey suggests that blacks may be more inclined than whites to agree with the likes of Republicans William Bennett and Dan Quayle on the severity of some social problems. More blacks than whites say that the quality of public schools and the phenomenon of children being raised in single-parent households are very serious problems. The two races are about even— 74% of blacks and 70% of whites—in citing welfare dependency as a particularly serious problem, according to the survey, conducted by Democratic pollster Peter Hart and Republican Robert Teeter.

But there is a big gap on the approach society should take toward solving such problems. By significant margins, blacks feel that government should play a substantial role in attacking the economic distress they view as the root of society's problems. Whites are more likely to see the nation's problems as based in moral decline, and to see a far lesser role for government in solving most of those problems.

A majority of blacks, 53%, say the country's social and economic problems are mainly the result of financial pressures on families. By contrast, a majority of whites, 58%, say those problems are mainly the result of a decline in moral values. (The lowest-income whites are somewhat more inclined to cite financial pressures rather than moral values as the cause of social problems, but still cite that reason less often than blacks do.) And whereas 30 years ago black activism was focused intensely on integrating society, blacks today seem less convinced than whites

that their basic problems will be solved simply through more integration.

And to the extent that whites make presumptions about what blacks want government to do, they may have it wrong. Blacks don't seem to want the government to create programs; asked to pick among several possible causes for continuing poverty in America's cities, just 7% cited a lack of government funding and programs. Instead, blacks tend to say the government is responsible for creating jobs and other economic opportunities.

In the survey, 65% of whites and 70% of blacks agreed that there has been some or a lot of progress in easing racial tensions in the past 10 years.

The one area in which there seems to be a striking convergence is in what politicians call social values.

Blacks and whites were in virtual agreement on the severity of problems of drugs and violent crime, with 97% of blacks calling violent crime a very serious or most serious problem, while 92% of whites did so. And while 37% of whites rated the phenomenon of children being raised in single-parent households as a very serious or most serious problem, 55% of blacks said it was.

But the convergence of views breaks down on questions about economics, and there are hints of new thinking all around on the fundamental questions of integration.

In the *Journal*/NBC News survey, blacks clearly showed their belief that government has to play a role in creating jobs. Asked which institution—government, business, community groups or individuals—has the greatest responsibility for creating jobs and strengthening the economy, a solid 67% of blacks cited the government. That sentiment was more pronounced among lower-income blacks but only slightly so. Among blacks making under $30,000 a year, 71% cited government, while 60% of those making more than $30,000 did so.

Across the board, whites were less inclined to cite government's responsibility. Just 41% cited government as the institution with the greatest responsibility for creating jobs and economic strength, while 37% named the business community. Even among the poorest whites, only about half cited the government's responsibility.

In dealing with inner-city problems in particular, blacks are more likely to see the need for government intervention, while whites think private initiatives are more useful. Among blacks, 68% called for a greater emphasis on government spending on education and training programs for the inner cities, while just 36% of whites thought those were the right areas for emphasis. A majority of whites said the better option would be to emphasize "private initiative and personal responsibility by people living in the inner cities."

Rethinking Integration

As blacks and whites ponder the persistence of America's social problems, they seem to agree that broader integration of American society is an important goal. But there also seems to be some rethinking among blacks that perhaps integration shouldn't be as high a priority as building up black economic and social institutions.

Among whites, 70% say that racial integration has been good for society, while a similar share of blacks, 65%, also say that integration has been good. But a slightly larger minority of blacks than whites, 23% to 17%, say racial integration has been bad for society.

Whatever the areas of agreement between blacks and whites on hot-button social issues, the survey suggests one area where perceptions are different. Asked whether blacks or whites are more likely to receive welfare benefits, 47% of whites say blacks are more likely, while 30% of blacks say African-Americans are more likely to receive them.

In reality, both groups are partly right. The number of whites on welfare exceeds the number of blacks. Whites comprise 38.9% of Aid to Families with Dependent Children recipients, slightly above the 37.2% of recipients who are black, according to the Department of Health and Human Services. But because blacks make up just 12.1% of the overall American population, the share of the black population on welfare easily outstrips the white share.

In any event, blacks and whites alike seem to have grasped one reality of life in America today: blacks are more likely to be the victims of crime. Crime statistics collected by the Federal Bureau of Investigation indicate that 49.6% of the nations' murder victims in 1992 were black, while 47.2% of the victims were white.

And when asked in the survey who is more likely to be a victim of crime, 53% of blacks said they were; 46% of whites agreed.

 Article Review Form at end of book.

What are the causes of violent crime in the United States?

Disintegration of the Family Is the Real Root Cause of Violent Crime

". . . The popular assumption that there is an association between race and crime is false. Illegitimacy, not race, is the key factor. It is the absence of marriage and the failure to maintain intact families that explain the incidence of crime among whites as well as blacks."

Patrick F. Fagan

Mr. Fagan is William H. G. Fitzgerald Fellow for Family and Cultural Studies, Heritage Foundation, Washington, D.C.

Social scientists, criminologists, and many other observers at long last are coming to recognize the connection between the breakdown of families and various social problems that have plagued American society. In the debate over welfare reform, for instance, it now is a widely accepted premise that children born into single-parent families are much more likely than those in intact families to fall into poverty and welfare dependency.

While the link between the family and chronic welfare dependency is understood much better these days, there is another link—between the family and

crime—that deserves more attention. Entire communities, particularly in urban areas, are being torn apart by crime. We desperately need to uncover the real root cause of criminal behavior and learn how criminals are formed in order to be able to fight this situation.

There is a wealth of evidence in the professional literature of criminology and sociology to suggest that the breakdown of family is the real root cause of crime in the U.S. Yet, the orthodox thinking in official Washington assumes that it is caused by material conditions, such as poor employment opportunities and a shortage of adequately funded state and Federal social programs.

The Violent Crime Control and Law Enforcement Act of 1994, supported by the Clinton

Administration, perfectly embodies Washington's view of crime. It provides for billions of dollars in new spending, adding 15 social programs on top of a welfare system that has cost taxpayers five trillion dollars since the War on Poverty was declared in 1965. There is no reason to suppose that increased spending and new programs will have any significant positive impact. Since 1965, welfare spending has grown 800% in real terms, while the number of major felonies per capita today is roughly three times the rate prior to 1960. As Sen. Phil Gramm (R.-Tex.) rightly observes, "If social spending stopped crime, America would be the safest country in the world."

Still, Federal bureaucrats and lawmakers persist in arguing that poverty is the primary cause

Reprinted by permission from *USA Today* Magazine, May 1996, Vol. 124, No. 2612, pp. 36–38.

of crime. In its simplest form, this contention is absurd; if it were true, there would have been more crime in the past, when more people were poorer. Moreover, in less-developed nations, the crime rates would be higher than in the U.S. History defies the assumption that deteriorating economic circumstances breed crime and improving conditions reduce it. America's crime rate actually rose during the long period of economic growth in the early 20th century. As the Great Depression set in and incomes dropped, the crime rate also fell. It went up again between 1965 and 1974, when incomes rose. Most recently, during the recession of 1982, there was a slight dip in crime, not an increase.

Washington also believes that race is the second most important cause of crime. The large disparity in crime rates between whites and blacks often is cited as proof. However, a closer look at the data shows that the real variable is not race, but family structure and all that it implies in terms of commitment and love between adults and children.

A 1988 study of 11,000 individuals found that "the percentage of single-parent households with children between the ages of 12 and 20 is significantly associated with rates of violent crime and burglary." The same study makes it clear that the popular assumption that there is an association between race and crime is false. Illegitimacy, not race, is the key factor. It is the absence of marriage and the failure to form and maintain intact families that explains the incidence of crime among whites as well as blacks.

There is a strong, well-documented pattern of circumstances and social evolution in the life of a future violent criminal. The pattern may be summarized in five basic stages:

Stage one: Parental neglect and abandonment of the child in early home life. When the future violent criminal is born, his father already has abandoned the mother. If his parents are married, they are likely to divorce by the third year of his life. He is raised in a neighborhood with a high concentration of single-parent families. He does not become securely attached to his mother during the critical early years. His child care frequently changes.

The adults in his life often quarrel and vent their frustrations physically. He, or a member of his family, may suffer one or more forms of abuse, including sexual. There is much harshness in his home, and he is deprived of affection.

He becomes hostile, anxious, and hyperactive. He is difficult to manage at age three and is labeled a "behavior problem." Lacking his father's presence and attention, he becomes increasingly aggressive.

Stage two: The embryonic gang becomes a place for him to belong. His behavior continues to deteriorate at a rapid rate. He satisfies his needs by exploiting others. At age five or six, he hits his mother. In first grade, his aggressive behavior causes problems for other children. He is difficult for school officials to handle.

He is rejected socially at school by "normal" children. He searches for and finds acceptance among similarly aggressive and hostile youngsters. He and his friends are slower at school. They fail at verbal tasks that demand abstract thinking and at learning social and moral concepts. His reading scores trail behind the rest of his class. He has lessening interest in school, teachers, and learning.

By now, he and his friends have low educational and life expectations for themselves. These are reinforced by teachers and family members. Poor supervision at home continues. His father, or father substitute, still is absent. His life primarily is characterized by aggressive behavior by himself and his peers and a hostile home life.

Stage three: He joins a delinquent gang. At age 11, his bad habits and attitudes are well-established. By age 15, he engages in criminal behavior. The earlier he commits his first delinquent act, the longer he will be likely to lead a life of crime.

His companions are the main source of his personal identity and his sense of belonging. Life with his delinquent friends is hidden from adults. The number of delinquent acts increases in the year before he and his friends drop out of school.

His delinquent girlfriends have poor relationships with their mothers, as well as with "normal" girls in school. A number of his peers use drugs. Many, especially the girls, run away from home or just drift away.

Stage four: He commits violent crime and the full-fledged criminal gang emerges. High violence grows in his community with the increase in the number of single-parent families. He purchases a gun, at first mainly for self-defense. He and his peers begin to use violence for exploitation. The violent young men in his delinquent peer group are arrested more than the non-violent criminals, but most of them do not get caught at all.

Gradually, different friends specialize in different types of crime—violence or theft. Some are more versatile than others. The girls are involved in prostitution, while he and the other boys are members of criminal gangs.

Stage five: A new child —and a new generation of criminals—is born. His 16-year-old girlfriend is pregnant. He has no thought of marrying her; among his peers this simply isn't done. They stay together for awhile until the shouting and hitting start. He leaves her and does not see the baby anymore.

One or two of his criminal friends are experts in their field. Only a few members of the group to which he now belongs—career criminals—are caught. They commit hundreds of crimes per year. Most of those he and his friends commit are in their own neighborhood.

For the future violent criminal, each of these five stages is characterized by the absence of the love, affection, and dedication of his parents. The ordinary tasks of growing up are a series of perverse exercises, frustrating his needs, stunting his capacity for empathy as well as his ability to belong, and increasing the risk of his becoming a twisted young adult. This experience is in stark contrast to the investment of love and dedication by two parents normally needed to make compassionate, competent adults out of their offspring.

The Impact of Violent Crime

When one considers some of the alarming statistics that make headlines today, the future of our society appears bleak. In the mid 1980s, the chancellor of the New York City school system warned: "We are in a situation now where 12,000 of our 60,000 kindergartners have mothers who are still in their teenage years and where 40% of our students come from single-parent households."

Today, this crisis is not confined to New York; it afflicts even small, rural communities. Worse yet, the national illegitimacy rate is predicted to reach 50% within the next 12–20 years. As a result, violence in school is becoming worse. The Centers for Disease Control recently reported that more than four percent of high school students surveyed had brought a firearm at least once to school. Many of them, in fact, were regular gun carriers.

The old injunction clearly is true—violence begets violence. Violent families are producing violent youths, and violent youths are producing violent communities. The future violent criminal is likely to have witnessed numerous conflicts between his parents. He may have been physically or sexually abused. His parents, brothers, and sisters also may be criminals, and thus his family may have a disproportionate negative impact on the community. Moreover, British and American studies show that fewer than five percent of all criminals account for 50% of all criminal convictions. Over all, there has been an extraordinary increase in community violence in most major American cities.

Government agencies are powerless to make men and women marry or stay wed. They are powerless to guarantee that parents will love and care for their children. They are powerless to persuade anyone to make and keep promises. In fact, government agencies often do more harm than good by enforcing policies that undermine stable families and by misdiagnosing the real root cause of such social problems as violent crime.

Nevertheless, ordinary Americans are not powerless. They know full well how to fight crime effectively. They do not need to survey the current social science literature to know that a family life of affection, cohesion, and parental involvement prevents delinquency. They instinctively realize that paternal and maternal affection and the father's presence in the home are among the critical elements in raising well-balanced children. They acknowledge that parents should encourage the moral development of their offspring—an act that best is accomplished within the context of religious belief and practice.

None of this is to say that fighting crime or rebuilding stable families and communities will be easy. What *is* easy is deciding what we must do at the outset. Begin by affirming four simple principles: First, marriage is vital. Second, parents must love and nurture their children in spiritual as well as physical ways. Third, children must be taught how to relate to and empathize with others. Finally, the backbone of strong neighborhoods and communities is friendship and cooperation among families.

These principles constitute the real root solution to the problem of violent crime. We should do everything in our power to apply them in our own lives and the life of the nation, not just for our sake, but for that of our children.

 **Article Review Form at end of book.**

Describe the similarities that exist between Irish and Hispanics in relation to their role in the criminal justice system.

Hispanics

The new Irish in the American criminal justice system?

Alejandro del Carmen
Kathleen Korgen
Denise del Carmen
Armando Espinosa

Introduction

The rapid ascension of Hispanics into all sectors of the American criminal justice system today parallels the entrance of Irish immigrants into the system over one hundred years ago. Just as the Irish once used positions in police departments as a means of upward mobility, Hispanics now join the criminal justice workforce as part of an overall effort to improve their standing in U.S. society. The rate of Hispanic entrance into areas of crime control (e.g. police departments, criminology/criminal justice degree programs) indicates that they may soon be the "new Irish" in the American criminal justice system.

Irish

The great Irish potato famine between 1845 and 1848 sent streams of Irish to the United States. In just the years between 1846 and 1850 more than 870,000 Irish men, women, and children arrived in America. By 1860, over 1,600,000 Irish had come to the United States (Duff, 1971). In 1890, the number of Irish descent in America exceeded the inhabitants of Ireland (Hraba, 1994). Today, persons who claim Irish as their ethnicity accounts for approximately 15 percent of the United States population.

While Irish Americans today maintain a higher class standing than the average American, the vast majority of the nineteenth century Irish immigrants were poor and unskilled laborers (Hraba, 1994). Those who managed to find employment toiled in the lowest rungs of the working class. For the first half century after the great migration sparked by the potato famine, between two-thirds and three-fourths of all Irish immigrants were either common laborers or domestics, depending upon their sex (Fallows, 1979).

Upon arriving in the United States, Irish immigrants faced a hostile atmosphere. As early as the 1840's, Boston newspapers carried anti-Irish advertisements with the phrase "None need apply but Americans." The fact that almost all Irish were Catholic added to the abuse they faced in a predominantly anti-Papist America.

Often, anti-Irish Catholic hysteria turned violent. In the year 1844 alone, homes, churches and convents were torched in cities from New Orleans to Louisville to Boston. (Hraba, 1994). Anglo-Protestant Americans also feared potential and purely imaginary Irish attacks. "In 1855, Boston's older families . . . dismissed their Irish servants after hearing a rumor that the women were Vatican agents in a plot to poison the Protestant leadership of Massachusetts (McCaffrey, 1976). Overall, "the stereotype of Irish immigrants centered on not only their Catholicism, but also on the attributions of their being violent, common laborers, drunks, and a drain on the American welfare system" (Hraba, 1994).

Poor and largely unschooled, many Irish immigrants did become criminals or wards of the state. In 1850, almost two-thirds of all persons housed in "charitable and penal institutions" were Irish (Duff, 1971).

Anti-immigrant newspapers in every major city with substantial Irish populations highlighted the large numbers of criminals among the Irish. A December 23, 1853 *Chicago Tribune* editorial asked the following query: "Why do our police reports always average two representatives from 'Erin, the soft, green isle of the ocean,' to one from almost any other inhabitable land of the earth? . . . Why are the instigators and ringleaders of our riots and tumults, in nine cases out of ten, Irishmen?" (Quote found in Wittke, 1970). The following decade, *Harper's Magazine* observed that the Irish 'have so behaved themselves that nearly 75% of our criminals are Irish, that fully 75% of the crimes of violence committed among us are the work of Irishmen.' " (Steinberg, 1989, Quoted in Greeley, 1972).

Discriminated against and demonized, the Irish turned to politics as a way to achieve power in nativist-dominated U.S. society. Alienated by what they saw as an anti-immigrant bent of the Republican party, the Irish flocked to register as Democrats. They had both numbers and location on their side. By 1890, there were almost 5 million persons of Irish descent in the United States (Brown, 1966). The vast majority settled in cities in the Northeast and Midwest. For instance, in 1890, persons of Irish descent comprised one-third of the population of New York City (Glazer and Moynihan, 1970). Within these cities, Irish formed ethnic enclaves centered around parishes, parochial schools, saloons, political clubs, volunteer fire companies, Irish newspapers, and charitable organizations. Entrance into and ultimate con-

trol of local politics was a natural step. As historian John Duff (1971) points out, "how long could Boston, for example, remain a Brahmin bastion when the Irish population increased about 200 percent between 1840 and 1855, while the number of native-born grew only by 15 percent?"

The prevailing view among Anglo-Protestants towards government was to keep it out of business affairs as much as possible. The Irish, on the other hand, saw politics as a means to control business and fight discrimination against them. As their numbers and political organizations grew, they quickly flexed their political muscles.

The Irish first put their budding political clout towards topping such everyday slights as the mandatory use of the King James Bible in the public schools and "the assignment of Protestant chaplains to Catholic inmates of hospitals, jails, and charitable institutions. Next, they fought for the appointment of Irish as schoolteachers and as policemen and firemen. Finally, they sought to take all political power into their own hands" (Shannon, 1964). Their successes were partially evident in the criminal justice system. By 1890 Irish Americans comprised twenty percent of the police force in St. Paul, Pittsburgh, and Cleveland; twenty-five percent in Chicago, St. Louis and San Francisco; and thirty-three percent in New York City (Fogelson, 1977).

Police and political records during the last decades of the nineteenth century illuminate both the struggles and the achievements of Irish Americans. During this period in U.S. history, Irish Americans comprised a disproportionate percentage of those

in political office, on the police force, and in prison. In 1886, while only 16 percent of New York City's population consisted of Irish born, 27 percent of the Board of Alderman, 28 percent of the police force, and 36 percent of those housed in jails and places of charity had been born in Ireland (Shannon, 1964).

The Irish had developed a base in mainstream America by the beginning of the twentieth century that increased in power during the following decades. During the period of the first World War, the Irish entered the professional workforces as Irish . . . men . . . (rose) through the ranks of politics and civil service" (Hraba, 1994). By the 1960s, Irish Americans "enjoyed a virtual stranglehold on the police force" (Fogelson, 1977). Largely due to their history of local political control and domination of the civil service sector, Irish Americans today exceed the national average in education, income, and occupation (Fallows, 1979).

Hispanics

The Hispanic experience with the American criminal justice system today parallels in many ways that of the Irish a century ago. Hispanic is an umbrella term that encompasses Spanish speaking persons from Mexico, Puerto Rico, Cuba, and Central and South America. Nine percent of the population now and projected to be the largest minority in the United States by the year 2007 (AP, 1997), Hispanics are increasingly overrepresented in both the criminal and the crime enforcing sides of the American criminal justice system.

Like the Irish once did, Hispanics deal with both discrimination and negative stereotypes. Portrayed as lazy, inferior, uncultured, and violent, Hispanics are viewed by many Euro-Americans as a drain on the U.S. welfare system and real and potential criminals (Castro et al. in Mann and Zatz, 1998). The recent ads in support of Proposition 187 in California highlight this prejudice against Hispanics. In one ad an announcer ominously states "they keep coming" as if Hispanics are a menace threatening to overrun U.S. society. This prejudice has often turned to violence as Hispanics are increasingly seen as "a threat by some" Euro-Americans (see Garret, 1997).

Again paralleling the Irish immigrant experience, Hispanics today make up a disproportionate number of the poor and those in prison. While the rate varies widely between different Hispanic subgroups, almost a third of all Hispanics live in poverty (Parrillo, 1999). Moreover, while Hispanics comprise 9 percent of the population, 17% of state prisoners and 28% of federal prisoners are Hispanic (Bureau of Justice Statistics, 1998).

On the other hand, Hispanics are also working their way up the class hierarchy in ways similar to the Irish. They have become a population too large and now, too organized, to ignore. While there were 14 million Hispanics in the U.S. in 1980, today there are 30 million. Political players across the nation now realize that they must reckon with the increasingly powerful Hispanic voice. The burgeoning Hispanic political power is evident in the rapidly increasing numbers of Hispanics elected to political office. While there were 3,128 Hispanics in elected office

throughout the United States in 1984, by 1998 there were 5,191. In important electoral states such as Texas and California, candidates for office make a point to try to speak Spanish and actively court the large and rapidly growing Hispanic vote (Kasindorf, 1998). The recent defeat of a city-wide bill to overturn affirmative action programs in the city of Houston provides a good example of Hispanics, in concert with African Americans, making a strong and successful stand for the interests of minorities.

In part through aggressively using affirmative action programs in cities across the nation, Hispanics have increased their numbers in law enforcement agencies. The days when the Irish could use political patronage to secure their slots on the police force no longer exist. Police departments now actively publicize openings and often recruit with affirmative action goals in mind. While Hispanic Americans were only 5.2% of officers in city police departments in 1990, their percentage increased to 6.2% in just the next three years (Walker, Spoh, and DeLone, 1996). This trend continues as civil rights leaders and police reformers strive to create police forces that truly reflect the communities they serve. This need is particularly acute in cities with large Spanish speaking population. Safety as well as equity insists that there be a proportionate number of Spanish speaking police officers.

Today, Hispanics enter all aspects of the field of criminal justice in increasing numbers. More Hispanics are seeking criminology and criminal justice degrees than ever before. This trend was already evident in the 1980s as the numbers of Hispanics earn-

ing a B.A. degree in the social sciences (which includes criminology and criminal justice) rose from 99,752 in 1981 to 103,173 in 1989 (Reddy, 1993). From parole officers to police chiefs to scholars in criminology, Hispanics now establish careers across the spectrum of criminal justice.

Conclusion

As the Irish once did, Hispanics climb the ladder of economic success as they enter the work force of the American criminal justice system. Just as the Irish were once disproportionately poor and without work, Hispanic poverty and unemployment rates far exceed the national average. The criminal justice field has provided a realm of employment for both groups. A century ago, the Irish used their political connections to establish a foothold in employment in crime prevention. Hispanics now utilize their own increasing political power in combination with affirmative action programs to create their own base in the crime fighting field. The parallels between the two groups indicate that Hispanics may soon be the "new Irish" in the American criminal justice system.

Works Cited

American Nationalism, 1870–1890. Philadelphia: J. B. Lippincott Company, 1966.

Bureau of Justice Statistics, (1998). *Criminal Offenders Statistics.*

Brown, T. N. (1996). *Irish-American Nationalism, 1870–1890.* Philadelphia, PA. J. B. Lippincott Company.

Duff, John B. *The Irish in the United States.* Belmont, CA: Wadsworth Publishing Co., 1971.

Fallows, M. R. (1979). *Irish Americans: Identity and Assimilation.* Englewood Cliffs, NJ. Prentice-Hall, Inc.

Fogelson, Robert M. *Big-City Police.* (1977). Cambridge, MA. Harvard University Press.

Garrett, Amanda. (September 6, 1997). *More Crimes Against Hispanics Are Being Reported.* Raleigh, North Carolina. The News and Observer Publishing Company.

Glazer, N., and D. P. Moynihan (1963/19970) *Beyond the Melting Pot: The Negroes, Puerto Ricans, Jews, Italian, and Irish of New York City.* Cambridge, MA: The M.I.T. Press.

Greeley, Andrew. (1972). *The Most Distressful Nation.* Chicago, IL. Quadrangle Books.

Hraba, Joseph. *American Ethnicity.* (1994). Itasca, Illinois: F. E. Peacock Publishers, Inc.

Kasindorf, Martin, (March 18, 1998). *Latinos Tap into Expanding Political Power.* USA TODAY, P. 8A.

Mann, Richey, Coramae and Katz, Marjorie, S. (1998). *Images of Color/Images of Crime.* Los Angeles, California. Roxbury Publishing Company.

McCaffrey, L. J. (1976). *The Irish Diaspora in America.* Bloomington: Indiana University Press.

Parrillo, Vincent., John Stimson., Ardyth Stimson. (1999). *Contemporary Social Problems.* Needham Heights, MA: Allyn & Bacon.

Reddy, Marlita, A. (1993). *Statistical Record of Hispanic Americans.* Detroit, MI. Gale Research.

Shannon, William V. (1964). *The American Irish.* New York: The Macmillan Company.

Steinberg, Stephen. (1989). *The Ethnic Myth.* Boston, MA. Beacon Press.

The Associated Press. July 22, 1997. "Hispanics Discuss Struggle."

Walker, Samuel., Spohn, Cassia., and DeLone, Miriam. (1996). *The Color of Justice: Race, Ethnicity, and Crime in America.* Belmont: California. Wadsworth Publishing Company.

Wittke, C. (1970). *The Irish in America.* New York: Russell and Russell.

 Article Review Form at end of book.

WiseGuide Wrap-Up

- Discrimination takes place throughout the various stages of the criminal justice system.

- The U.S. Supreme Court has decided to review a case based on the claim that federal officials unfairly select minorities to prosecute.

- There are racial differences regarding support for police use of deadly force on fleeing felons.

- African American juries have a tendency not to convict African American defendants.

R.E.A.L. Sites

This list provides a print preview of typical **coursewise** R.E.A.L. sites. (There are over 100 such sites at the **courselinks**™ site.) The danger in printing URLs is that Web sites can change overnight. As we went to press, these sites were functional using the URLs provided. If you come across one that isn't, please let us know via email to: webmaster@coursewise.com. Use your Passport to access the most current list of R.E.A.L. sites at the **courselinks**™ site.

Site name: Criminal Justice Center

URL: http://www.mnplan.state.mn.us/cj/

Why is it R.E.A.L.? This site provides criminal and juvenile justice data. Specifically, in this site you can find Minnesota crime and arrest data showing among other variables the race of the offender.

Try this: What is the difference between an apprehension and an arrest? What are Part 1 offenses?

Key topics: crime rates, firearms forfeitures, arrests and apprehensions by race for state, county, and judicial district

---

Site name: National Archive of Criminal Justice Data

URL: http://www.icpsr.umich.edu/NACJD/

Why is it R.E.A.L.? This site offers the opportunity to retrieve data on-line. In addition, it offers a list of links to related sites. Among the publications available in this site, you will find some that discuss various issues pertaining to crime and race.

Try this: Discuss the issues affecting the race of prisoners admitted to state and federal institutions in the United States.

Key topics: attitude surveys, community studies, court case processing, criminal justice system, crime and delinquency, drugs, alcohol, and crime

---

Site name: Sourcebook of Criminal Justice Statistics

URL: http://www.albany.edu/sourcebook/

Why is it R.E.A.L.? This site brings together data about all aspects of criminal justice in the United States. In this site, you will find over 600 tables and 4 figures from more than 100 sources. Specifically, you will be able to retrieve information regarding the race of victims and offenders (by type of crime).

Try this: Discuss the possible reason why some minority groups are overrepresented in various aspects of the criminal justice system.

Key topics: characteristics of the criminal justice system, public attitudes toward crime, nature and distribution of known offenses, characteristics and distributions of persons arrested, judicial processing of defendants

---

section 5

Victimology

 **WiseGuide Intro**

Traditionally, criminology and criminal justice books have devoted a great deal of attention to topics such as the study of criminological theories and the operation of the criminal justice social control agencies. These topics have also been the center of discussion in criminology classrooms across the country. A trend has also been established that adheres to the notion that we should build on the already existing knowledge regarding theories of crime. Scholars in the field of criminology have actively engaged in research projects, attempting to advance knowledge on particular criminological theories. It is not hard to find academicians in the field of criminology who dispute each other's theories. Moreover, the public has also mirrored the academic interest on the "causes" of criminal behavior. The media, acknowledging the public's interest in the subject, have created television programs that focus on the offender's mind in an attempt to explain the manner in which offenders think. Although we can argue that this attention has been productive insofar as the discovery of new approaches to the study of crime and criminal behavior, it also has created a negative impact. One of the predicaments this has created is the fact that other important topics, such as the study of crime victims, have been largely ignored.

Historically, the criminal justice system has treated victims as witnesses who should tell their side of the story for the sake of contributing to the prosecutor's case. Historians argue that, in the not so distant past, the system of justice was not sensitive to the needs of victims, as they disregarded the trauma created by the criminal incident. However, a few decades ago, several private organizations began to demand publicly that the criminal justice system treat victims in a more humane way. Fortunately, the efforts of these private agencies and citizens to develop a more sensitive approach toward victims found a receptive audience among lawmakers. Ultimately, this resulted in the enactment of laws that not only created support mechanisms for victims but also expanded victims' rights.

Today, victims of crime not only enjoy the benefit of support agencies, which aim at providing counseling and emotional support, but also find that the system of justice is making a conscious effort to be more sensitive to the trauma they have endured. Currently, the statements victims make in court are gaining importance to such a degree that, in some cases, victims can augment or reduce the severity of the punishment given to a defendant. I believe you will find the articles selected for this section to be representative of some of the most complex issues surrounding crime victims today. As you will notice, despite the fact that victim support mechanisms vary from jurisdiction to jurisdiction, most states are making a conscious effort to be more sensitive to crime victims and their needs.

Questions

Reading 32. Why do law professors and attorneys oppose the idea of a constitutional amendment aimed at protecting the rights of crime victims?

Reading 33. How can crime victims benefit from civil litigation?

Reading 34. Does the news media give more attention to white crime victims than it does to black crime victims? Explain your answer.

Reading 35. How have the recent developments in information technology affected crime victims?

Reading 36. How is the overlap between criminals and victims affecting the federal crime victims compensation program?

Reading 37. Describe the dangers associated with a closer relationship between the police and emergency medical departments.

Reading 38. Are disabled men and children abused more frequently than their non-disabled counterparts? If so, what actions must be taken by this group in order to reduce victimization?

Reading 39. Discuss the forces that have led to the emergence of the concept of restorative justice in recent years.

Reading 40. Why do some critics argue that a trial revolves around excuses?

Why do law professors and attorneys oppose the idea of a constitutional amendment aimed at protecting the rights of crime victims?

Victims' Rights Movement Rises to Power

Kelly McMurry

Make no mistake about it, these are heady times for victims' rights advocates.

In the past year, their ultimate goal—to win passage and enactment of a proposed victims' rights amendment to the U.S. Constitution—has received the endorsement of President Clinton and won significant bipartisan support in Congress. Activists believe an amendment would bring into balance a criminal justice system in which the scales are tipped in favor of the accused. An amendment would also ensure that crime victims' rights are enumerated in much the same way the Bill of Rights outlines protections for criminal defendants.

David Beatty, acting executive director of the National Victim Center, said that since 29 states have already approved similar amendments to their constitutions, a federal amendments is likely forthcoming. Beatty's group, based in Arlington, Virginia is an advocacy and resource center that tracks victims' rights laws and related court cases and lobbies at the state and national levels.

States that have passed victims' rights legislation have done so by overwhelming margins. Beatty views the sweeping victories as nothing less than "the kinds of super-majorities our founding fathers intended when considering a constitutional amendment."

But opponents believe that according victims enhanced legal status would undermine existing constitutional protections for those accused of crimes. They believe that a constitutional amendment is unnecessary and that it flouts a system of justice firmly entrenched in federalism.

Advocates and detractors alike punctuate their arguments on the proposed amendment using two words: Oklahoma City. The trial of Timothy McVeigh, who was convicted on June 2 of all 11 counts against him in the bombing of the Alfred P. Murrah Federal Building, showcased the legal struggle to balance the rights of the victim with those of the accused.

A proposal to amend the Constitution was first introduced in Congress in 1996. The Senate Judiciary Committee held hearings on the legislation in April of this year, and more hearings are likely. Senate cosponsors are Sens. Dianne Feinstein (D-Cal.) and Jon Kyl (R-Ariz). Rep. Henry Hyde (R-Ill.) has introduced similar legislation in the House (H.R. 1322). Votes on both are expected sometime later this year.

The movement traces its roots to the 1982 Final Report of the President's Task Force on Victims of Crime. The report castigated the criminal justice system for neglecting victims and recommended a range of victims' rights proposals. A constitutional amendment was one. In the years since, the states and Congress have enacted a variety of measures adopting many of these recommendations.

For example, in 1990, Congress passed the federal Victims Rights and Restitution Act—better known as the Victims' Bill of Rights. (42 U.S.C. §10606(b)(4).) The act gives victims the right to be notified of and present at court proceedings and to be kept apprised of the offender's conviction, sentencing, imprisonment, and release status. (Paul G. Cassell & Robert F. Hoyt, *The Tale of Victim's Rights,* Legal Times, Dec. 23, 1996, at 32.)

Congress also passed the federal Victims of Crime Act, the Justice Assistance Act, and a package of victims' rights legislation as part of the Violent Crime Control and Law Enforcement Act of 1994. (Richard Carelli, *Even with Bipartisan Support, Future Clouded for Victims' Rights Amendment,* Chi. Daily L. Bull., Oct. 18, 1996, at 2.) In 1996, Congress enacted legislation mandating restitution to crime victims. The law also ensured victims' access to closed circuit television broadcasts of relevant trial proceedings that were relocated as part of a court-ordered change of venue.

While advocates are quick to applaud these federal and state measures, they contend that the legislation varies in scope and, when taken together, does not go far enough to ensure a consistent guarantee of crime victims' rights nationwide.

Roberta Roper, who co-chairs the National Victims' Constitutional Amendment Network, said an amendment is the only way to ensure that "justice, fairness, and equity are extended to all innocent victims of crimes, just as we properly do for those accused of crimes."

Finding the precise wording for the proposed 28th Amendment has been a sticking point. In its current form as Senate Joint Resolution 6, the amendment would give victims of violence the following rights:

- to be notified of and to attend all public proceedings relating to the crime;

- to be heard and to submit impact statements at sentencing and parole hearings;

- to be notified of an offender's release, parole, or escape;

- to a final disposition of the criminal proceedings without unreasonable delay;

- to an order of restitution from the convicted offender;

- to have the safety of the victim considered in determining any offender's release from custody; and

- to be notified of these rights.

Opposing Views

In April, as the Senate Judiciary Committee prepared to hold hearings on the amendment, a large and politically diverse coalition of law professors and practioners sent a letter to Capitol Hill urging Congress not to support the amendment. The coalition argued that it would not satisfy victims' needs and that its passage would be counterproductive.

"Crime victims deserve protection, but this should be accomplished by statutes, not a constitutional amendment," the letter argued. "As law professors and practioners, we urge the rejection of the proposed Victims' Rights Amendment as unnecessary and dangerous."

The coalition was coordinated by three prominent law professors: Erwin Chemerinsky from the University of Southern California Law Center, Lynne Henderson from the Indiana University School of Law at Bloomington, and Robert Mosteller from Duke University School of Law.

Noting that the Constitution has been amended only 27 times in the nation's history and only

when there has been a pressing need, the coalition maintained that virtually every right contained in the amendment can be safeguarded by federal and state statutes.

"The constitutional amendment is a practical, administrative, and financial burden on institutions trying to dispense justice," Chemerinsky said. "It would siphon resources away from essential law enforcement efforts and open our entire criminal justice system to a floodgate of claims and differing interests."

The coalition believes the amendment is likely to be counterproductive because it places "enormous new burdens" on law enforcement agencies that could hamstring their prosecution efforts and cripple criminal proceedings. For example, the coalition believes that the proposed right of crime victims to insist on faster resolution could force prosecutors to try cases before they are fully prepared. Or that rushing a trial to a final resolution could jeopardize the defendants' discovery time to gather evidence to demonstrate their innocence.

Victims' rights advocates cannot understand what all the fuss is about. Beatty said that the amendment "would simply elevate the rights of the victims to the same level of protection as those of the accused."

Paul Cassell, a law professor at the University of Utah and a leader in the victims' rights movement, believes that a constitutional amendment is an appropriate response to the imbalance that exists between victims' rights and defendants' rights. According to Cassell, that imbalance was exacerbated in the 1960s, when the Warren Supreme Court expanded the rights of criminal defendants and constitutionalized most aspects of criminal procedure.

Cassell said trial judges who had previously accommodated victims' concerns informally "were suddenly forced to follow prescribed formulas. Without a constitutional basis for considering victims' interests, a defendant's claim of a procedural right always prevailed. The court's one-sided expansion of defendants' rights slid victims out of the picture." (Paul G. Cassell & Steven J. Twist, *A Bill of Rights for Crime Victims*, Wall St. J., April 24, 1996, at A15.)

Oklahoma City

The legal struggle to balance the rights of the victim with those of the accused was played out on a near-daily basis in Denver during convicted killer Timothy McVeigh's trial for his role in the Oklahoma City bombing.

"Oklahoma City has certainly become a test case for victims' rights," said Cassell. "There are still many uncertainties swirling around regarding their rights in this case, and state statues haven't resolved the problem because the defense has raised constitutional objections."

Victims injured in the Oklahoma City bombing and survivors of people who died in the April 1995 blast became angered last summer when Judge Richard Matsch, who presided in the case, barred victims and family members planning to testify in any penalty phase of the case from sitting in the courtroom during trial. He also forbade victims from providing impact statements. His concern? That what they heard and saw in the courtroom could prejudice their testimony. Federal evidence rules allow judges to exclude material witnesses from trial proceedings to prevent them from changing their testimony.

Victims' rights advocates appealed. They argued that Matsch's ruling went too far—and forced them to choose between attending the trial and testifying at sentencing. They lost in the courts in February, when a three-judge panel of the Tenth Circuit upheld Matsch's ruling. (*United States v. McVeigh*, 106 F.3d 325 (10th Cir. 1997).) In March, the full circuit affirmed, turning down a request by federal prosecutors and victims' advocates for an en banc rehearing.

The decision to exclude victims and their families from the courtroom—believed to be the first federal appeals court ruling on the 1990 Victims' Rights and Restitution Act—incensed victims' rights advocates, who say it eviscerated both the spirit and the letter of the act.

Undaunted, the victims' advocates took their campaign to Capitol Hill. There, they were not disappointed. By the end of March, Congress had pushed through a bill that effectively overturned Matsch's ruling. The bill passed by unanimous consent in the Senate. The House voted 418–9 in favor. President Clinton signed the bill into law on March 20. (Robert Schmidt, *Law Passed to Let Witnesses Hear Trial*, Legal Times, Mar. 24, 1997, at 11.)

Matsch chose not to hold hearings on the constitutionality of the new law, saying that to do so would delay McVeigh's trail. On March 25, Matsch reversed himself. But in a five-page order, he noted that victims could be questioned before they testified during the sentencing phase outside the presence of the jury to ascertain whether testimony heard during the guilt phase affected the testimony they intended to offer—and could therefore be barred as tainted.

In effect, Matsch left open the door to reassert his judicial authority by blocking victims' testimony at a later date. Victims who testified at trail were still subject to questioning by the judge during the penalty phase, a prospect that some of them weren't happy about. (Ryan Ross, *Judge Asserts Right to Bar Okla. Victims,* Nat'l L.J., Apr. 7, 1997, at A10.)

In spite of the tragedy and the obstacles they have faced, Cassell said the victims of the bombing hope that Oklahoma City will serve as a wake-up call to expedite passage of a constitutional amendment. "If that happens," he said, "the victims will feel that at least one good thing will have come out of Oklahoma City—fully enforceable rights for all crime victims."

 Article Review Form at end of book.

How can crime victims benefit from civil litigation?

Crime Victims and Psychological Injuries

Beth G. Baldinger and D. Thomas Nelson

Beth G. Baldinger is a senior litigation associate specializing in representing crime victims in civil cases at the law firm of Stark & Stark in Princeton, New Jersey.

D. Thomas Nelson directs the Carrington Victims' Litigation Project and the Coalition of Victim Attorneys and Consultants at the National Victim Center, Arlington, Virginia.

In 1992, a jury awarded "Jane Doe" $2.46 million in civil damages against her father for incestuous abuse and against her mother for failing to protect her from it.[1]

In 1993, a jury awarded $12.6 million dollars in damages to a woman suffering from post-traumatic stress disorder after witnessing her son's death. He was shot by a tenant in their apartment complex.[2]

In 1994, a jury awarded $900,000 to a 33-year-old woman who suffers from post-traumatic stress disorder and multiple personality disorder caused by a former Sunday school teacher who sexually molested her between the ages of 8 and 16.[3]

These awards exemplify a new class of civil cases being brought on behalf of crime victims. Traditional legal principles are being reinterpreted to help people who have been victimized by crime.

Victims are not recognized parties in the prosecution of criminal offenders, and restitution in the criminal forum often falls far short of just compensation for expenses related to medical procedures, rehabilitation, counseling, and lost wages. Therefore, civil litigation can be used to obtain justice for crime victims.

Representing crime victims presents formidable challenges, not the least of which is proving the psychological trauma caused by criminal acts. This is necessary to recover damages other than for physical injuries.

The civil suit expresses the victim's fear, agony, emotional distress, and psychological injuries as legitimate compensable claims. Victims of incest, rape, domestic violence, elder abuse, and child abuse—as well as their spouses and relatives—are suing for intentional and negligent infliction of emotional distress and outrage to recover damages for psychological trauma.[4] To be successful in these claims, lawyers must understand psychological trauma and have a sound strategy for presenting it to the jury.

Psychological Trauma

According to Dr. Judith Lewis Herman, author of *Trauma and Recovery*,

Psychological trauma is an affliction of the powerless. At the moment of trauma, the victim is rendered helpless by overwhelming force. When the force is that of nature, we speak of disasters. When the force is that of other human beings, we speak of atrocities . . . Traumatic events are extraordinary, not because they occur rarely, but rather because they overwhelm the ordinary human adaptations to life. Unlike commonplace misfortunes, traumatic events generally involve threats to life or bodily integrity, or a close personal encounter with violence and death. They confront human beings with the extremities of helplessness and terror, and envoke the responses of catastrophe.[5]

The most prevalent classification of psychological injury in crime victim cases is post-traumatic stress disorder (PTSD). Related psychological traumas include Rape Trauma Syndrome,[6] Battered Woman Syndrome,[7] and dissociative disorders.[8] Many courts now allow evidence of posttraumatic stress disorder as substantive proof that an individual suffered a traumatic event.[9]

Post-Traumatic Stress Disorder

PTSD can result when a person experiences a markedly distressing event that includes actual injury or threat of harm to oneself or someone close.[10]

There are three major groups of measurable symptoms of PTSD. One group involves persistent intrusive and distressing recollections of the traumatic event in dreams or flashbacks.

Another group involves persistent avoidance of stimuli associated with the trauma. For example, a victim may avoid thoughts of the crime, withdraw from activities or situations that arouse recollections of it, experience a feeling of detachment or estrangement from others, and be unable to have loving feelings.

A third group involves persistent symptoms of increased arousal. For example, a victim may experience sleep disorders, irritability or outbursts of anger, difficulties in concentrating, hypervigilance, or exaggerated startle response.[11]

Rape Trauma Syndrome (RTS)

Testimony about this condition is generally admissible in civil cases to help a jury evaluate the rape survivor's actions after the crime. The diagnosis can also prove that the victim experienced trauma.

For example, RTS testimony might be admitted to explain the victim's delay in reporting the crime. Otherwise, the jury could misconstrue delay and conclude either that the rape did not occur or that the victim was not traumatized.

Battered Woman Syndrome (BWS)

A distinctive characteristic of this condition is that victims with BWS usually have experienced a pattern of traumatic abuse rather than a single violent event.

Previously used as a "self-defense" argument for women accused of murdering their abusers, BWS has taken on a new dimension in the civil context. This syndrome has recently been recognized as a cognizable civil cause of action, the elements of which are

- involvement in a marital or marital-like intimate relationship;

- physical or psychological abuse over a significant period of time;

- injury caused by the abuse; and

- past or present inability to change or improve the situation.

Moreover, as BWS is the result of a continuing pattern of abuse, it should be treated as a "continuing tort" for statutes-of-limitation purposes. It may be asserted that BWS constitutes a "mental disability" sufficient to toll the statute of limitations or that the duress inflicted by the defendant is such that the defendant should be equitably estopped from asserting the statute of limitations as a defense.[12]

Other Psychological Disorders

Commonly seen diagnoses of crime victims including survivors of childhood abuse, are somatiza-tion disorder, borderline personality disorder,and multiple personality disorder. They share many common characteristics: depression, agoraphobia or panic, psychosomatic complaints, difficulties with close relationships, and varying levels of dissociative capabilities. These disorders are recognized as complex or chronic forms of PTSD.[13]

Psychological Syndromes

At the other end of the spectrum from recognized disorders is a wave of newly defined psychological syndromes. Some of these are the Parental Alienation Syndrome, Lying Child Syndrome, Confusional Arousal Syndrome, and Child Sexual Abuse Accommodation Syndrome.

- The Parental Alienation Syndrome can manifest itself as one of four types of parent/child behavior: a parent's manipulation of a child's feelings for the other parent, a parent unconsciously rewarding a child for "turning away" affection for the other parent, a child alienating herself or himself for fear of a loss of a parent's love, and a child alienating herself or himself because of situational factors.[14]

- The Lying Child Syndrome might be proffered to explain the propensity of a child to give untruthful statements about an authority figure in order to manipulate events.[15]

- The Confusional Arousal Syndrome has been considered physiological rather than psychological. It is associated with those who suffer from sleep apnea, a defect in breathing patterns. People with Confusional Arousal Syndrome may awaken during a period of depressed mental functioning and may become violent.[16]

- Child Sexual Abuse Accommodation Syndrome describes commonly seen characteristics in sexually abused children: secrecy, helplessness, delayed and unconvincing disclosure, and retraction or recantation.[17]

When evidence of a novel psychological syndrome is proffered, it is necessary to determine whether it is diagnostic or nondiagnostic. Testimony about diagnostic disorders may be admissible to prove causation. Evidence on nondiagnostic syndromes, though not permissible as proof of causation, may be potentially admissible to explain reactions to known causes. The central issue is whether the presence of symptomatic behavior reasonably shows that the existence of a certain cause is more probable.[18]

Pre-trial judicial screening will disallow psychological syndromes that are not sufficiently reliable as evidence. If found reliable, determination as to whether the syndrome is diagnostic or nondiagnostic will ensure that this evidence is introduced for the appropriate purpose.

Assessing Psychological Harm

The degree of psychological harm the victim experiences is most strongly related to the character of the traumatic event.[19] The harm is also influenced by the interplay of personal and situational factors.[20]

Four primary factors can describe the victim's emotional injury to a jury: the nature and extent of physical violence, the victim's pre-incident relationship with the assailant, the location of the crime, and the victim's emotional condition before the crime occurred.

Nature and Extent of Physical Violence

The degree of bodily violation or disfigurement and/or the victim's perception of it are often leading factors in communicating the emotional impact of the crime. Some acts of violence leave visible scars that are easily shown. Others leave no physical evidence.

Physical brutality can be extremely destructive to a victim's sense of competence, self-image, personal safety, and physical integrity. To understand the effect of physical intrusion on a victim, consider how someone standing within one's "personal" space (usually 1 1/2 to 2 feet) or an unexpected physical gesture within this space can evoke feelings of encroachment and uneasiness. Now imagine the sense of violation a woman feels when she is trapped, pinned, and raped.

Victim's Pre-Incident Relationship with Assailant(s)

Violence perpetrated by someone who the victim knows can be experienced more intensely than violence committed by a stranger. When victims are violated by people they trust, respect, or love, the betrayal has impact in addition to the violation itself.

This can be devastating to the victim's sense of self-esteem and identity. Violations of personal trust are paramount in civil cases of incest, domestic violence, and sexual abuse committed by professionals or the clergy.

Location of the Crime

Where the act of violence took place is often a highly influential factor in a crime victim's psychological injury. For example, victims suddenly awakened in bed to face a gun may be more traumatized than people who are attacked on a street. People usually assume they will be safe inside their homes and at their places of work. When the sanctity of these places is violated, the experience can be shattering, resulting in phobic reactions.

Victims injured at their workplace may not be able to return to the same workstation, if they are able to return to the same employer at all. People violated in their own homes may eventually move, but their psychological injuries often go with them, bringing fears of intrusion to their new surroundings.

Victim's Prior Emotional Condition and Susceptibility to Harm

Children and people who are elderly, infirm, or generally dependent on others before victimization may be more likely to suffer psychological injuries from a violent crime. A significant factor in a victim's ability to cope with the aftermath of a crime is a sense of control over events. Those who had little control over their daily activities before the crime are likely to be more susceptible to psychological injury.[21]

People with rigid personalities or those who were emotionally fragile before the crime may

Details of the crime allow the jury to appreciate the victim's emotional trauma.

also suffer greater psychological impact.[22] "Traumatic life events, like other misfortunes, are especially merciless to those who are already troubled."[23]

Psychological Trauma Claims

Significant damage awards for psychological trauma are based on several key elements: aggravating conditions of the defendant's actions, insensitivity of defense counsel, clear testimony on causation from the plaintiff's expert, and lay witnesses who credibly establish the victim's deteriorated condition.

Working with crime victims suffering from psychological trauma requires extraordinary patience, understanding, and sensitivity. Victims are often apprehensive and overwhelmed by the demands of a civil suit.

Obtaining the necessary information often requires several meetings. Every effort should be made to accommodate special needs for safety and comfort. For example, it is often helpful to give these people a sense of control by asking simple questions about where they want to sit, what name they prefer to be called, and who they want present during the consultation.

To help assuage the client's fears of the unknown, the attorney should explain what to expect during a civil lawsuit, particularly during depositions and expert examinations. The attorney must be forthright about the impact of broad civil discovery rules—what can be protected against disclosure/admissibility and what cannot.

During the last 10 years, a wealth of technical and anecdotal information has been published about crime victim psychological trauma. The attorney should be familiar with this literature and speak to victim service professionals. If possible, the attorney should arrange to attend a support group meeting. True believers make the best convincers.

The attorney should compile detailed pre-incident, incident, and post-incident histories of the victim. The pre-incident history should include information about family, school, occupation, social and recreational activities, medical and psychological treatment, and accidents or other traumas. The attorney must obtain all relevant records.

An exhaustive incident report of the crime is crucial. This information goes much further than merely establishing liability; it forms the basis for the expert's testimony on trauma causation. The horrific details develop compelling evidence that allows a jury to appreciate the victim's emotional trauma.

For the post-incident history, an on-going dialogue with the client, therapist, and others in the client's support network provides the means to monitor the nature and extent of the trauma. It is common to learn that the victim has engaged in self-destructive or anesthetizing behavior (alcohol or drug abuse, suicide attempts, self-infliction of injuries, eating disorders). For purposes of civil litigation, these negatives can be turned into positives. "Abnormal" behavior is normal when it arises from "abnormal" circumstances. Juries should judge a victim from the victim's perspective.

The attorney must find common ground with psychologists on the best way to present the victim's emotional trauma in court. Legal and mental health professionals must operate as a team.

What will be expected of the therapist? To treat the client? Testify as an expert? Both? The attorney and experts must find a way to effectively communicate mental health findings in the courtroom. They must communicate with each other and with the client to avoid surprises.

It may be to the client's advantage to have the attending psychologist focus on treatment and to retain an appropriate expert to testify about the cause of the psychological injury. If this option is chosen, the expert should be retained early and should examine the client as soon as possible to establish an accurate post-incident, baseline assessment of the client's condition. Periodic reevaluations by the causation expert strengthen the expert's testimony, especially in comparison with the defendant's expert, who will usually see the client only once.

The expert will need all prior and on-going medical and psychological counseling records and reports. The attorney must be aware of the interrelationship between the victim's physical and psychological injuries. Oftentimes, severe psychological trauma will manifest itself into physical conditions such as nervous disorders, rashes, or unexplained fevers. These should be put into context for the jury by expert testimony.

Presenting Damages at Trial

The attorney may consider using a three-step approach for presenting psychological injuries to the jury: develop a theme, present proofs in a "building-block" style, and submit specific jury instructions on psychological injury.

Theme

The character of the traumatic event and the victim's pre-incident and post-incident histories can serve as a framework for the theme. For example, a single working mother who had lived a full and active life, once raped, developed agoraphobia and became a prisoner in her own home. The theme here might be one of being trapped or wrongfully imprisoned.

If possible, before trial the client could write a letter to the attorney describing how the traumatic event has affected her or his life. The letter can be a useful tool for counsel in determining a case theme.

Despite expert testimony, there is rarely anything more powerful than the voice of the victim. The theme of the case can be intensified and the jury's awareness heightened by creating images. For example, when a rape victim describes how she had her lover move out of the bedroom because she couldn't bear to look into his eyes at night and tell him, "Not yet, I can't," *that* is powerful.

Building Blocks

Expert testimony should begin with the treating physicians, because they usually refer victims to psychologists or counselors. A treating physician can testify to the onset of the client's physical and emotional symptoms.

Next, the treating psychologist will be able to provide a detailed account of the victim's subjective complaints and furnish a psychological diagnosis. The psychologist can describe areas where the client has difficulty, where improvements have been observed, and where the client continues to decline.

An expert psychologist on causation can then explain the victim's psychological trauma. The testimony must be communicated clearly in a step-by-step manner, with minimum scientific terminology for the maximum effect.

The victim should testify only briefly. The attorney may want to consider having the plaintiff outside the courtroom while psychological proofs are presented, because it is difficult for victims to listen to this testimony. The attorney should discuss this option with the client, the treating psychologist, and the physician.

If the plaintiff is not going to be present during this part of the trial, the jury should be informed that this is due to doctor's orders and with the court's permission. Members of the victim's family in the courtroom will usually compensate for the victim's absence by "standing in" for the victim. This helps to illustrate the seriousness of the case to the jury.

The presentation of testimony should conclude with several credible lay witnesses. Spouses, friends, relatives, co-workers, and others with personal knowledge can testify about the plaintiff's fears and attest to altered behavior.

Jury Instructions

The attorney should draft jury charges before trial and keep them in mind while presenting the case. It is helpful to be especially well prepared on issues of aggravation of preexisting conditions and the client's predisposition to emotional trauma. The attorney should take a full offensive position on these issues. Tailoring the proofs to the jury charges will help focus the jury's attention on the preferred evidence.

Forum for Justice

For crime victims with psychological injuries, civil litigation can be a healing process. It can furnish a restorative sense of empowerment.

Civil actions grant victims a forum to receive justice, regardless of the outcome of a criminal prosecution. The significance of this cannot be understated.

Civil judgments or settlements give victims and the public a confirmation that others were responsible for the violence perpetrated against them. Victims often blame themselves for being in the wrong place at the wrong time. They may be overcome by "if only I . . . ." misgivings. Particularly for victims suffering from psychological injuries, a judgment can go a long way toward healing their irrational feelings of guilt.

Finally, jury verdicts are respected for their power to send strong messages about safety, crime, and societal change. Verdicts for crime victims can foster the hope that defendants have learned a lesson and will change their behavior—so that others might not have to endure the same kind of violence.

Notes

1 Doe v. Doe, No. 91–03635 (Minn., Scott County Dist. Ct. Oct. 2, 1992), 36 L. REP. (ATLA) 55 (1993).
2 Arnett v. Linda Manor Ltd. Partnership, No. A–300222 (Nev., Clark County Dist. Ct. Mar. 10, 1993), 37 L. REP. (ATLA) 23 (1994)
3 Doe v. Komarek, No. 91–5870 (Mass., Middlesex Super. Ct. Feb. 22, 1994), 37 L. REP. (ATLA) 312 (1994).
4 *See generally* Annotation, *Modern Statues of International Infliction of*

Mental Distress at Independent Tort: Outrage, 38, A.L.R. 4th 998 (1985); Cheryl M. Bailey, Annotation, *Sexual Child Abuser's Civil Liability to Child's Parent*, 54 A.L.R. 4th 93 (1987).

5 JUDITH L. HERMAN, TRAUMA AND RECOVERY 33 (1992).

6 Ann W. Brugess & Lynda L. Holmstrom, *Rape Trauma Syndrome*, 131 AM. J. PSYCHIATRY 981 (1974); *see also* Cohn v. State, 849 S.W. 2d 817 (Tex. Crim. App. 1993). Illinois law states: "In a prosecution for an illegal sexual act . . . testimony by an expert . . . relating to any recognized and accepted form of post-traumatic stress disorder shall be admissible as evidence." ILL. ANN. STAT., Ch. 725, para. 5/115–7.2 (Smith-Hurd 1992).

7 LENORE E. WALKER, THE BATTERED WOMAN'S SYNDROME (1984).

8 HERMAN, *supra* note 5, at 115–29.

9 Gregory G. Sarno, *Admissibility at Criminal Prosecution of Expert Testimony on Rape Trauma Syndrome,* 42 A.L.R. 4th 879 (1985).

10 AMERICAN PSYCHIATRIC ASS'N. DIAGNOSTIC AND STATISTICAL MANUAL OF MENTAL DISORDERS (DSM-IV) 209 (1994).

11 *Id.* at 209, 210.

12 Cusseau v. Pickett, No. L–6086–92 (N.J., Bergen County Super. Ct. Aug 4, 1994); leave to appeal denied.

13 HERMAN, *supra* note 5, at 122–29; *see also* INCEST RELATED SYNDROMES OF ADULT PSYCHOPATHOLOGY (Richard P. Kluft ed., 1990).

14 RICHARD A. GARDNER, THE PARENTAL ALIENATION SYNDROME AND THE DIFFERENTIATION BETWEEN FABRICATED AND GENUINE CHILD SEX ABUSE (1987). *See* Weiderholt v. Fischer, 485 N.W. 2d 442 (Wis. Ct. App. 1992).

15 Jennette v. State, 398 S. E. 2nd 734, 737 (Ga. Ct. App. 1990).

16 People v. Cegers, 9 Cal. Rptr. 2d 297 (Ct. App. 1992).

17 Roland C. Summit, *The Child Sexual Abuse Accommodation Syndrome,* 7 CHILD ABUSE & NEGLECT 177 (1983); *see also* State v. J.Q., 617 A. 2d 1196 (N.J. 1993).

18 FED. R.EVID. 401; JOHN E. B. MYERS, EVIDENCE IN CHILD ABUSE AND NEGLECT §4.32 C (2d ed. Supp. 1994).

19 HERMAN, *supra* note 5, AT 57.

20 *See* Diana S. Everstein, *Psychological Trauma in Personal Injury Cases, in* PSYCHOTHERAPY AND THE LAW 27 *(Louis Everstein & Diana S. Everstein eds., 1986).*

21 *HERMAN, supra* note 5, at 60.

22 Everstein, *supra* note 20, at 33.

23 HERMAN, *supra* note 5, at 60, *citing* Margaret S. Gibbs *Factors in the Victim That Mediate Between Disaster and Psychopathology: A Review,* 2J. TRAUMATIC STRESS 489–514 (1989).

 Article Review Form at end of book.

Does the news media give more attention to white crime victims than it does to black crime victims? Explain your answer.

Paying More Attention to White Crime Victims

Peter Downs

Downs is a freelance writer based in St. Louis.

Eddie Burton faced the cameras to send out a plea for information on the abduction and murder of young LaChrisha "C.J." Jones. To his right, C.J.'s mother placed a black and yellow ribbon on the site where the body of the 17-year-old African American was found 10 months before. Once the cameras stopped rolling, Burton, a spokesman for Families Advocating Safe Streets (FASS), an organization of clergy, concerned citizens and African American support groups, gave the assembled press corps a piece of his mind. He angrily contrasted the lack of attention from the St. Louis media at the time of Jones' murder with the week of headlines that followed the abduction and murder of a 22-year-old white woman eight months later.

"Black victims don't get the attention," Burton vented, so their families "feel the press and the police don't care." The press conference's organizer, Jeanette Culpepper, who founded FASS after her own son was murdered, agreed. "When a black kills a white, all hell breaks loose," she said. "But when it's black on black, it's all right."

The St. Louis Post-Dispatch's index bears out Burton's and Culpepper's claims. In the three weeks following the disappearance of 9-year-old Kimbre Young in 1993, for example, the newspaper ran only two stories on the African American girl's case. Five months later Cassidy Senter, a 10-year-old Caucasian girl, was the second to disappear from a suburban neighborhood. In the four weeks following her disappearance the newspaper ran more than 23 stories about her.

It appears there has been little research on the issue of racial imbalances in reporting on crime victims. But the data that are available indicate a real disparity that is pervasive in many American cities.

A 1994 Chicago study on violence in television news and "reality" programming (shows such as "COPS" and "Rescue 911") by Robert Entman, then an associate professor of communications at Northwestern University, found that, on average, stories about white victims of violent crimes lasted 74 percent longer than stories about black victims. The total time given to white victims was 2.8 times more than the total time devoted to both black and Hispanic victims.

"In comparable cases, you will find a greater number of column inches or seconds on TV for white victims than for black victims anywhere in the Midwest," says Sonia R. Jarvis, professor of communications at Washington, D.C.'s George Washington University.

Dr. Alvin Poussaint, a Harvard University psychiatrist, says anti-black bias in reporting on murder victims "isn't arguable." No newspaper he's seen "isn't guilty of giving more attention and sympathy to white murder victims than to black murder victims," he says, "giving even more sympathy to the white victim if the perpetrator is black."

Tim Larson, news director at KSDK-TV in St. Louis, admits that the critics are right. But he says the media are caught in a double bind. If a news organization emphasizes reports on black victims, he says, "we get criticized for only covering crimes in the black community."

Not so, counters Jarvis. "We're not suggesting that the media report more crime or that whites get less coverage," she says. "We're suggesting that black deaths also get treated [with a] sense of loss."

Many argue that prejudice and stereotyping inevitably play a role in the media's coverage of black crime. Marsha Houston, professor of communications at Tulane University, says the "killing of a white person is always treated as a significant loss," while the killing of a black person is usually dismissed with an "assumption that that person was involved in the drug scene" and is not worth reporting.

Jarvis adds that this assumption holds true across the country. The only exception she's seen was in the East Coast media, she says, when it reported the death of Len Bias, who had just been drafted by the Boston Celtics. In general, she says, the news media depict African Americans as "throwaway people who can be ignored."

Jim Amoss, editor of the New Orleans Times-Picayune, argues that any such bias is probably inadvertent. "Most metropolitan dailies are essentially white-run organizations," he says, "and still, in 1995, white readers and editors gravitate to whites as their own kind. Their hearts go out more to white crime victims than to black victims."

Arthur Silverblatt, professor of communications at St. Louis' Webster University, says that economics, not prejudice, are at the heart of decisions to play up homicide stories with white victims. He says that such decisions derive from competition for viewers with money. "As the white community is the community with more income," he says, "they are the people whose viewership matters more."

Mike Ward, news director at WMAQ Channel 5 in Chicago, says that with newsrooms becoming increasingly diversified, there is a good chance that coverage of crimes against blacks is improving, even though the sheer number of black homicide victims in urban areas complicates efforts to provide in-depth analysis. "There is no way," he says, "that we or anyone else can cover the totality of crime in the city and suburbs of Chicago, where there are over 900 murders a year."

Ward says that in his newsroom, staffers try to concentrate on the objective facts of the story. "Whether reporting on a drive-by shooting or whatever," he says, "we look at what is the crime rate, is it going up or down, and are people forming [neighborhood crime watch] units or do they already have them?"

But Jarvis says that providing context for the news involves more than simply reporting whether or not the crime rate is up or down. The problem, she says, is that "we're not seeing the issue framed in a way that would encourage a positive public policy response. . . . If the kinds of killings we see going on daily in urban centers were instead being committed by foreign terrorists, would the American people stand for it?"

 Article Review Form at end of book.

How have the recent developments in information technology affected crime victims?

Enhancing Victim Information in the Information Age

Anne Seymour and David Beatty

Anne Seymour is project manager of "Promising Strategies and Practices in Using Technology to Benefit Crime Victims," and chairs ACA's Restorative Justice Committee. David Beatty, who directed this project, is director of public policy for the National Victim Center in Arlington, Va.

Technology Greatly Enhances Transfer of Information about Offenders and Victim Services

If the very core of the victim services movement were boiled down to one concept, it quite possibly would be information. In corrections, access to information literally can mean the difference between life and death; if victims are not notified about the release of their assailants, or if they do not receive information about measures of protection, the effects can be devastating. At the very least, information can provide victims with peace of mind as they rebuild their lives.

When corrections professionals consider the possibilities of-fered by the Information Age, they also should consider the benefits of technology in the delivery of corrections-based victim services. Technology plays a significant role in providing victims with information related to their cases, as well as serving as a link to corrections-based victim services.

In February 1998, the National Victim Center sponsored the first national symposium on "Promising Strategies and Practices in Using Technology to Benefit Crime Victims," with support from the U.S. Department of Justice's Office for Victims of Crime. A number of innovative technologies were presented at the symposium that offer opportunities for collaboration between victim services, corrections and allied justice agencies; link victims more efficiently to programs and services offered by correctional agencies; and provide vital information to victims in six key areas.

Variety of Applications

Nobody chooses to be the victim of a crime. Therefore, the ability to choose becomes an important factor in the victim's recovery process. The choices victims must consider often are related directly to statutory rights in their states. "Do I want to provide a victim impact statement at the time of sentencing?" "Do I want to be notified about the status of my offender and/or any release hearings?" "Do I want to seek protective measures so my family and I will be safe?" "Do I want restitution?" Today, technology offers impressive solutions to better enforce victims' rights.

In San Diego County, Calif., victim impact statements provided at the time of sentencing are videotaped and captured on CD-ROM, creating a "permanent record" for future review during parole hearings. In addition, paroling authorities in states with electronic case management systems have the capability to include victim impact information in secure electronic files that promote victim confidentiality.

Victim notification—one of the core rights victims seek from correctional agencies—is now automated in many states. When an offender is due to be released from jail or prison, voice-automated telephone calls are made to the victim from a central call center that operates 24 hours a day, seven days a week. The victim enters a

Personal Identification Number (PIN) on the telephone dial pad to indicate that notification has been made and to stop the calls. With this system, victims also can dial a toll-free number at any time to access information about the status of an offender, or to receive information and referrals from a human operator. Voice automation also can be integrated with victim case management systems to generate notification letters.

Recent innovations in technology offer greater opportunities for victim and community protection than ever before. Programs to monitor and track the location of offenders under community supervision use Global Positioning Systems (GPS) with wireless communications and a centralized database. Community corrections agencies determine locations which are "off-limits to offenders (such as the victim's home, or locations where children are present in cases of offenders who prey on children), or which will keep the offender within certain geographic boundaries. These locations are loaded into a portable tracking device worn by the offender (that cannot be removed), which then notifies both the offender and the central surveillance operations about violations. Notification interfaces also can be provided to victims using a telephone or pager.

Financial restitution has been simplified in numerous jurisdictions and correctional agencies through the use of technology. The Court Ordered Payment System (COPS), developed by the Florida Department of Corrections in 1991, is designed to receive payments of fines and fees from offenders, apply the money to the vic-

tims'/payees' accounts, and quickly disburse checks within 72 hours of the offenders' payments.

Once a month, the Washington Department of Corrections (DOC) bills offenders under its authority for their outstanding court-ordered legal financial obligations (LFOs), which include victim restitution. Felony offenders are required to make payments toward their LFOs to one of 39 court clerks. These clerks record any payments they receive on the mainframe Judicial Accounting Sub System (JASS). Once a month, identified data is downloaded to a file, which the DOC matches against its database, updating offender records and creating a billing file of all matched offenders who have outstanding balances. That billing file is then transmitted to a vendor, who produces the actual monthly billing statements and mails them to offenders.

The Offender Obligation System, developed by the Utah Department of Corrections in 1994, uses an Informix database and a Unix/PC Windows-based client-server network to automate the collection and disbursement of an offender's financial obligations. These include restitution, fines, fees and other charges, including the cost of electronic monitoring for those on home detention.

Access to Information

The Electronic Age has revolutionized the accessibility of information to victims of crime. No longer do geographical location, physical ability, culture or language create a barrier to information. Innovative applications of technology have changed the ways victims can identify and re-

trieve information and services. These innovations range from the simple to the complex.

- The Web site of the Florida Department of Corrections provides status information about incarcerated offenders, including a current photograph, as well as data on location and dates of release hearings.

- More widespread use of TDD equipment has expanded information and services for hearing-impaired and deaf victims from corrections-based victim service programs.

- Applications of telemedicine—similar to those used by prisons—electronically link medical and mental health experts in cities with remote rural regions and jurisdictions in need of such expertise, to provide consultation and review victims' medical histories and cases.

- The proliferation of toll-free telephone numbers helps break barriers for victims who cannot afford a long-distance telephone call to access information and services from correctional agencies.

Information-Sharing

When integrated management information systems within and among justice agencies incorporate victim information, both the quality of and access to information are significantly improved. Lost paper files and misplaced case information become obsolete when victim-related case information is electronically attached—with appropriate security restrictions—to the electronic case file of the offender as it makes its way "virtually" through the justice process.

In addition, the need to interview and re-interview victims to obtain the same information for different victim services and justice agencies can be significantly decreased. Case information captured at one source, such as a police station or prosecutor's office, can be entered and shared between agencies, eliminating the need for redundant data entry, as well as multiple, traumatic contacts with victims.

At the National Victim Center's symposium, two issues relevant to systems integration were raised:

- As corrections and justice agencies plan and design shared management information systems, victim representatives need to "be at the table." Too often, victims and the information they need are an afterthought, resulting in the elimination of victim-related databases, or limited victim data incorporated only as a low priority.

- Corrections officials must consider the security of victim data when planning management information systems. Victim confidentiality is vital to enforcing victims' privacy rights as mandated by law, and can be enhanced by security screens, limited access with private PINs, and encryption.

Information Management

The benefits of technology when applied to information and case management are substantial. Databases can be designed to capture not only vital information about individual victims, but also helpful data about case histories, relationships with offenders, and prior receipt of services.

In addition, basic organizational management is enhanced by information systems that expand an agency's ability to design programs, secure funding and strategically plan for the future. For example:

- Statistics that provide valuable information about the scope and level of services provided to victims offer valuable trending data that can be used for program planning.

- Information about the status of victim compensation claims is being managed electronically in some states, eliminating the need to rely on paper-based files that are not always easily accessible.

- Basic statistical information about victim demographics is more easily managed and accessed by justice professionals today which, in turn, augments the ability of the U.S. Department of Justice to track important trends in crime and victimization.

Information about Advocacy

Many victims today seek opportunities to get involved in victim advocacy efforts and to make a positive difference in others' lives through victim assistance, crime prevention and public education activities. Visits to the Web sites of local, state and national victim assistance organizations provide extensive information about opportunities for victim advocacy.

Electronic newsletters contain timely resources related to current legislative and public outreach efforts. And the increased use of "listservs" on the internet can provide timely information to multiple parties at the press of a key.

Public awareness of, and community involvement in, victims' rights and services comprise a key goal of victim services and allied justice agencies. Many innovative applications—from computerized graphic design software packages, to CD-ROM training, to the widespread use of the World Wide Web—have both complemented and simplified the presentation and transfer of information to parties interested in victims' rights and services. Technology has enhanced collaboration efforts between correctional agencies and victim services. For example, the Web site of the Ohio Department of Rehabilitation and Correction offers electronic links to key national victim services organizations.

The speed of information processing has resulted in community awareness and timely public education activities, matching the need for such response and support in the victim community. However, it is important to remember that technology, though it simplifies the transfer of information, should remain only a tool to help augment the "human touch" essential to helping victims reconstruct their lives in the aftermath of a crime.

 Article Review Form at end of book.

How is the overlap between criminals and victims affecting the federal crime victims compensation program?

Guilty Victims

How states' failure to separate the innocent from the guilty is costing the victims compensation program millions

Joseph Hallinan

More than a decade ago, when Congress established a fund to provide financial compensation to crime victims, it no doubt intended to aid society's least powerful members, especially abused women and children. It probably did not intend to help the likes of Hussein Barmil, a New York fugitive on the lam from the FBI. Or Dean Rossey, who gunned down a Milwaukee teenager. Or Tony Rigor, a twice-convicted California dope dealer with 17-inch biceps.

But it did. What's more, Barmil, Rossey, and Rigor are just a few of the hundreds, perhaps thousands, of convicts who receive money each year from the victims compensation program, set up in 1984 for the purpose of reimbursing victims with no in-surance or savings. But there is nothing illegal here. No tricks, no fraud. Just an unpleasant truism: Victim and criminal are often one and the same person.

Victim advocates seldom mention this fact. Thugs, after all, don't make good poster children. Instead, in their testimony on Capitol Hill and in statehouses around the country, victim advocates almost universally portray their clients as innocents. Which is fine, except that all too often, a surprisingly small share of victims comp money goes to women and children, while significant amounts are shelled out to adolescent and adult males, many of whom have been injured in bar-room brawls or street violence, some of whom have serious criminal records. Moreover, unless we tighten the current requirements under which compensation is granted, these not-so-innocent victims will continue collecting hundreds of thousands of dollars in government handouts—often at the expense of the very people the program was designed to assist.

Crime Does Pay

Meet victims compensation recipient Dean Rossey, a 19-year-old inmate at the Wisconsin state prison in Green Bay. Back in 1995, Rossey recalls, "I was smoking weed and drinking just about every day." He had dropped out of school, dropped out of Narcotics Anonymous, and his mom had kicked him out of their Milwaukee home. On the night of December 13, Rossey, two friends, and a fourth teenager, John Giese, were on a road trip to Illinois to buy some dope. Instead, they turned down a dead-end street and ordered Giese out of the car. They took his coat, the $1,850 they were going to use to buy the dope, a gold bracelet, his pager, and his stocking cap. "And after that," says Giese, "they just told me to turn around."

Rossey, according to court records, pointed the gun at the back of Giese's head. Giese remembers him saying, "This ain't nothing personal, it's just business." Then Rossey fired. Amazingly, Giese lived. But Rossey was the one who collected victim's comp. Five months earlier, Rossey and some friends had gotten into a brawl with a carload of gang members."[One of them] just—POW—hit me right in my jaw," says Rossey. "That's when my jaw broke. And I went like that and I spit out my tooth in my hand." Wisconsin's victim comp program paid more than $14,000 to wire Rossey's jaw shut. It also paid for the two weeks of work he missed at Builder's Square.

Not a particularly sympathetic beneficiary of his state's victims comp program, Rossey is also not untypical. Milwaukee resident Jon Walecki lost a few teeth (but gained nearly $3,500) after he supposedly called another gay "a fag." Down the road in Madison, I found Toby Vale, a convict injured in a bar fight when he was so drunk he couldn't even remember who, or what, had hit him. He wound up with a broken leg—and $16,723 in victims comp money. When I pointed out these cases to the head of the state's compensation program, she said, "I can't believe they paid this."

But people who work with victims day to day know this goes on all the time. "Unfortunately, there are career victims just as there are career criminals, and they cross back and forth across the line," says Bobbie DeLarRoi, coordinator of the Office of Victim Witness Advocacy in Burlington County, N.J. "One day they might be a victim and the next day the offender."

Criminologists have recognized this pattern since at least 1987, when a research team led by University of Pennsylvania Professor Marvin Wolfgang found young offenders "being predator one day, prey the next" Wolfgang's studies also showed that, in adult years, the chance of being a victim of aggravated assault was more than three times as great if the respondents were also offenders. For robbery, the odds were between six and eight times as great.

Just how significant is the overlap between criminal and victim? No one knows. The Office for Victims of Crime at the Justice Department, which administers the federal dollars involved in the program, has never studied the issue. The agency's statistics are so paltry it cannot even tell how many of the compensated victims are men and how many are women; how many are black and how many white—nor does the program as established by Congress require states to keep records of or even to ask questions about an applicant's criminal past.

By my admittedly unscientific sampling (achieved by comparing state prison records with victims comp records in four states), I estimate about 8 percent of compensated victims have a recent criminal record. And this number in no way takes into account the barroom brawlers and street scrappers who have managed to keep their police records clean, if not their noses.

Criminal Negligence

About 40 percent of each state's victims comp money comes from the federal government (save for Nevada, which pays its own way) with essentially no strings attached—i.e., almost no restrictions on eligibility. Each state, in turn, covers the remaining costs of its program, then pays victims as much as it likes for nearly any crime it likes. (And considering where much of the money winds up may give you pause for thought about the wisdom of other federal programs that hand money over to the states without smart standards) West Virginia, for example, compensates injured turkey hunters. "Turkey hunting's horrible here," says Cheryle M. Hall, clerk of the state Court of Claims, which administers the fund. "They wear camouflage and they nail each other." But since West Virginia considers negligent shooting to be a crime, the state treats hunters as victims.

All 50 states have guidelines under which victims are technically ineligible for aid if they contribute to their own victimhood. "If you're dealing drugs and you get shot, you're denied," asserts Dan Eddy, who heads the National Association of Crime Victim Compensation Boards. But often it's not that simple, says Jackie McCann Cleland, director of the compensation and assistance division of the federal program. Deciding whether a victim's conduct played a role in his injury, she explains, "is one of the most difficult challenges facing a comp program." And different states interpret their responsibilities differently. In Massachusetts, says Barbara Boden, the state's deputy program director, "the only thing we can do is deny [payment] for contribution [to the crime], and that's a pretty hard burden for us to prove. It they provoked a crime or something like that, it's difficult for us to track that down."

Ohio, on the other hand, bars victims comp to those with recent criminal histories. "This just seemed so logical to me" says state Rep. Ann Womer Benjamin, who co-sponsored a recent law to further tighten requirements. It deals with a category of people who have committed offenses against society and says that they're not going to be able to get something back from society no matter what happens to them. At present, however, Ohio is one of only five states with such a policy.

Moreover, even with clear eligibility guidelines, separating the deserving from the undeserving can prove difficult. Many victims comp programs have tiny staffs; administrators say this makes it difficult, if not impossible, to do thorough background checks on applicants. Illinois, for instance, has just three fulltime employees to process more than 4,000 cases a year; Georgia has just two.

Such personnel shortages may explain why, for instance, it took Wisconsin years to figure out the truth about Hussein Barmil, alias Nassar Alian, alias Miko Hussein. By the time it did, Barmil had collected more than $21,000 in medical payments—all while he was a fugitive or behind bars. Barmil's trial began in 1989 in New York City, where he jumped bail after being arrested for armed robbery. Four years later, he was arrested in Milwaukee and convicted of carrying a concealed weapon after he pulled a 38-caliber revolver during a street-corner argument.

The following year he was arrested again, this time for a felony, after police found more than 10 pounds of pot in his motel room. In an effort to get the charge reduced to a misdemeanor, Barmil agreed to work undercover for police, who still did not know he was wanted in New York. Five months later, while trying to sell marijuana as an undercover informant, Barmil was shot. Although he was still wanted in New York and had been twice arrested for crimes committed in Wisconsin, Barmil was granted victims compensation. In November of 1995, while still in jail, he received $8,849.93 from the state of Wisconsin. It went on to pay thousands more, too, even though, as the checks were being written, Barmil would: a) escape from jail; b) be hunted down by the FBI in Florida; and c) be reincarcerated in Wisconsin. After reviewing his case, Gillian Nevers, who administers Wisconsin's program, told me, "I can't believe this."

Women and Children Last

Of course, many of the criminal/victims I spoke with (and, in fact, many of the people who handle their compensation payments) see nothing wrong with giving money to people who play both sides of the street. "You could be a felon for something real small—beating your girlfriend or something like that," says Tony Rigor, an ex-con from Los Angeles. "And to not allow you to have benefits, I don't think that's right," he says. "I done my time."

A twice-convicted dope dealer paroled from prison, Rigor once had 17-inch biceps and

could bench-press 320 pounds. Today, he sits in a wheelchair in an apartment in East Los Angeles, a quadriplegic. He moves only with the aid of a pad he manipulates with his chin. Rigor, 30, was crippled by a single shot fired from a car during the Rodney King riots in 1992. He has received more than $40,000 from California's victims comp program, including a $36,000 customized van and a $2,000 mechanical bed.

The question of whether Rigor's criminal past should disqualify him from receiving government aid would not matter so much if the programs serving such victims were flush. But many programs are struggling, and when money goes to compensate gang bangers or drug dealers, this leaves less in the pool for truly innocent victims. "We just ran out of funds," complains Sandra Morrison of Mississippi's program. Last year, she explains, demand simply exceeded supply. Likewise, Dara Smith of the Montana program recalls that in 1996, "We broke the bank. . . . We just couldn't pay any claims out in the month of June."

Although the lack of national statistics makes it hard to generalize, many administrators confirm that much of their money goes to pay men behaving badly. "Baseball bats—that's the weapon of choice in Newark or Camden," said Sharon Koch, an administrator in New Jersey, where assault payments eat up 66 cents of every victim dollar. In Idaho, says case manager Paige Fincher, "We have lots of bar fights. It's mostly, you know, if you're a man you do it with your fist and bite somebody's ear off." Assault payments in Idaho last year outnumbered sexual-crime payments 6-to-1.

The data that do exist suggest that the program is not fulfilling its original intent. In 1995, according to the most recent figures from the Department of Justice, compensation programs paid $247.6 million to 119,000 crime victims, with payments classified according to one of eight crime categories. That year, North Carolina paid not a dime to children who were physically (as opposed to sexually) abused, according to its annual federal report. Neither did Alabama, New York, or Louisiana. All told, 10 states reported no payments in 1995 on behalf of physically abused children. Women fared little better. Three states—Connecticut, Rhode Island, and West Virginia—reported issuing no aid whatsoever to victims of domestic violence, who are almost always women, while Louisiana reported paying just seven victims. Maryland paid 10. Illinois, including the entire Chicago area, paid only 22.

What's more, the average cost of payment runs higher where men are concerned, with the highest average payments going to cases of homicide and non-familial assault, two crimes in which the victims are traditionally overwhelmingly male. In 1995, the average payouts for these two categories were $2,837 and $2,752, respectively. By comparison, the average payment for adult sexual assault, whose victims are almost always women, was only $1,126. For child sexual abuse, it was $1,221. For "domestic assault/spouse abuse," $1,421.

Without a doubt, tens of thousands of innocent victims, many of them women and children, are helped each year by the victims comp programs. Since 1993, for instance, approximately $10,000 in payments have gone toward counseling and medical services for Amy Parker Hodgett and her two young children. "I think the program is very helpful and very essential," says Parker Hodgett, who was reportedly beaten and nearly killed by her ex-husband.

But $14,866.58 in compensation payments went to Dean Rossey, the teenager who shot John Giese in the back of the head. By the time the money arrived, however, Rossey had already begun serving his 15-year sentence. So, he says, his mom cashed the check and deposited some of the money into his prison bank account. "It worked out good," reports Rossey from prison. "It's a nice program. It helps out victims. It really does."

 Article Review Form at end of book.

Describe the dangers associated with a closer relationship between the police and emergency medical departments.

Should Doctors Be More Proactive As Advocates for Victims of Violence?

Jonathan Shepherd

University of Wales College of Medicine, Cardiff UK

Jonathan Shepherd, professor of oral and maxillofacial surgery

Currently the management of adult victims of violence by general practitioners and accident and emergency departments is reactive, concerned almost exclusively with the management of physical injuries. Professor Jonathan Shepherd outlines some ideas for a more proactive approach on the part of doctors to improve the protection and support of vulnerable people; to deal with psychological sequelae; to take the responsibility of making an official complaint to the police away from seriously injured people, who are unable to give or withhold consent to disclosure; and to prevent assailants inflicting further injuries. BMJ asked a sociologist, a psychiatrist, a moral philosopher, and a police surgeon for their comments.

Towards Interagency Procedures to Protect Victims and Prevent Violence

A public health approach to violence has focused so far on risk factors such as alcohol consumption,[1] availability of firearms,[2] and links between deprivation and crime[3] but has yet to include trying to bring violent offenders to justice. Yet there is now strong evidence of a link between the incidence of violence and the rate at which offenders are convicted. Increasing the rate of conviction is therefore likely to be an effective way to prevent injury.

Criminal justice and public health have much in common. Both use deterrence (health warnings), incapacitation (isolation), and rehabilitation. A public health approach, however, focuses on the injured rather than the offenders. It can therefore be concerned with the very large number of violent incidents on both sides of the Atlantic that are neither reported to nor recorded by the police.[6][7] In Britain only about a quarter of the assaults resulting in treatment at accident and emergency departments are recorded by the police.[8]

Although criminal law treats all assaults as offenses against society, the initiation and maintenance of the prosecution process depends on the injured themselves.[9] Many of these people are repeatedly injured by assailants in whose "web of power" they are trapped.[5][9] This applies not just to women who are injured in domestic violence but to many other people.[9] Many victims do not report violence or make complaints that trigger police action because they are incapacitated by their injuries, afraid of reprisals, habituated to violence, or have a continuing relationship with their assailants. Furthermore, because the police judge that many victims who report offenses will drop the prosecution, investigations are often perfunctory or abandoned at an early stage.[9] This results, in part, from the fact that the offender and the state are central in the criminal justice system and means that many of society's most vulnerable people are not being protected as they should be. People who are at the same time victims and patients are, however, central to health care. This means that doctors should be influential advocates for victims as part of a much wider, proactive, interagency approach in which psychological sequelae can also be recognized and dealt with.

When it is in the medical interests of victims (in relation to preventing future physical and psychological harm) health professionals should counsel them to report offenses or to allow the health professionals to do so on their behalf.

There are dangers, however, in a closer relationship between the police and accident and emergency departments—in particular that victims of violence, who may themselves be on the edge of the law, might be dissuaded from seeking medical help. Nevertheless, the General Medical Council's current guidance, that each disclosure be considered individually, implies that the participation of other agencies should be considered when treating anyone injured in an assault. Violent offenses should be reported to the police, without the patient's consent if necessary, if injury is very serious or if failure to disclose appropriate information would expose the patient or someone else

to a risk of serious harm. When injuries are not serious and the victim does not wish to initiate a police investigation, making available anonymous details of violence could still help to prevent future crime. The collection of this information would be straightforward, particularly integrated with the recording of information already necessary for Criminal Injury Compensation Authority reports.

Organisations such as Crime Concern should include data on injury from accident and emergency departments in their assessments of urban violence, and department computers should be networked to facilitate annual reports on violence. Accident and emergency departments need to be more integrated with community policing. A crucially important barometer of civil order is the incidence of injury, but this is being ignored both locally and nationally. Apart from the valuable contribution of the charity Victim Support, few attempts have yet been made to bring together the desperate agencies responsible for the care and protection of injured adults. Many of them are young men.[7] There is a need for a joint forum to develop, monitor, and review policy based on a sound legal and ethical framework. Area child protection committees are a model, though terms of reference for adults would differ.

In relation to violence, the implications of a community approach are clear. Health care should be organized not only to provide treatment for people injured in assaults but to reduce the risks of further injury in the communities and families from which they come.

1. Shepherd JP. Violent crime: the role of alcohol and new approaches to the prevention of injury. *Alcohol Alcohol* 1994;29:5–10.
2. Kellerman AL, Rivara FP, Somes G, Reay DT, Francisco J, Banton JG, et al. Gun ownership as a risk factor for homicide in the home. N Engl J Med 1993;329:1084–91.
3. Shepherd JP. Violent crime in Bristol: an accident and emergency department perspective. *British Journal of Criminology* 1990;30:289–305.
4. Farrington DP, Langan PA, Wikstrom P-OH. Changes in crime and punishment in America, England and Sweden, between the 1980s and 1990s. Studies in Crime and Crime Prevention 1994;3:104–31.
5. Farrington DP, Langan PA. Changes in crime and punishment in England and America. *Justice Quarterly* 1992;9:5–46.
6. Bastian LD, DeBerry MM. *Criminal victimization in the United States, 1990.* Washington, DC: Bureau of Justice Statistics, 1992.
7. Mayhew P, Maung NA, Mirrlees-Black C. *The 1992 British crime survey.* London: HMSO, 1993. (Home Office research study No 132.)
8. Shepherd JP, Shapland M, Scully C. Recording by the police of violent offenses: an 8 accident and emergency department perspective. *Med Sci Law* 1989;29:251–7.
9. Clarkson C, Cretney A, Davis G, Shepherd JP. Assaults: the relationship between seriousness, criminalization and punishment. *Criminal Law Review* 1994 Jan: 4-21.

The Sociologist's View: More Convictions Won't Help Victims of Domestic Violence

Rebecca Morley

School of Social Studies, University of Nottingham, Nottingham UK

Rebecca Morely, lecturer in social studies

Women victims of domestic violence constitute an unknown but undoubtedly substantial percentage of admissions to accident and emergency departments for injuries sustained through violence.

Although the authoritative British crime surveys have shown consistently, for all violence, that men are more often victims than women, they have also shown that much domestic violence is not reported to the police. The 1992 survey showed that 80% of domestic violence was directed at women.[1]

Medical records of women attending hospital emergency departments in the United States indicate that up to 25% have a clinical profile consistent with domestic violence, though few are identified as such as by medical staff.[2,3] An adequate approach to handling such admissions must accommodate the circumstances and needs of victims of domestic violence.

The underlying premise of Professor Shepherd's argument—that increasing rates of conviction is an effective way to prevent injury—is flawed in the case of domestic violence. North American research echoes more circumstantial evidence from Britain that criminal justice responses alone do not effectively deter offenders or protect victims, except sometimes in the very short term; indeed, without community supports to enable victims to protect themselves, arrest and prosecution may result in more severe violence from an angry assailant on release.[4] [5] Many women do not wish to take police action, not because they are habituated to violence[6] but often because they fear reprisals or a coercive criminal justice response, or both. In some North America jurisdictions the number of calls to the police for help fell after mandatory arrest and prosecution policies were introduced.[4] Integrating accident and emergency departments with community police in the way pro-posed by Professor Shepherd would almost certainly dissuade some women from seeking medical help and would make others even less able to disclose the cause of injury.

Rather than concentrating on procedures for reporting to the police, whose role is limited, staff in accident and emergency departments would be more useful advocates for victims by adopting a believing and non-judgmental attitude towards them, ensuring that they are interviewed in confidence and away from their partner, and providing them with information about the range of community supports available and how to access them. Though these supports include the police, women's refuges provide the key protective and supportive role by helping women escape repeated violent attacks and providing empowering advocacy and support.[7] [9]

The British Association for Accident and Emergency Medicine produced guidelines for handling domestic violence in 1993 that are a good starting point for an effective response by accident and emergency departments.[3] They need to be fully implemented and integrated with the responses of other agencies in ways that are geared to protecting and empowering victims rather than to policing them. It is not true that, apart from Victim Support, few attempts have yet been made to bring together the disparate agencies responsible for the care and protection of injured adults. More than 150 multiagency forums on domestic violence exist throughout the United Kingdom and bring together a wide range of statutory and voluntary sector agencies.[10] Though accidental and emergency departments are active in a few, they are much less likely to be involved than many other agencies, including the police.[10]

Accident and emergency departments clearly have an important role in protecting victims of violence from further injury. To the extent that other victims share the circumstances and needs of victims of domestic violence, models of interagency work now being developed to deal with domestic violence may also be more appropriate for them than that advocated by Professor Shepherd.

1. Mayhew P, Maung NA, Mirrless-Black C. *The 1992 British crime survey.* London: HMSO, 1993. (Home Office research study No 132.)
2. Kurtz D. Emergency department responses to battered women. *Social Problems* 1987;34:69–81.
3. British Association for Accident and Emergency Medicine. *Domestic violence: recognition and management in accident and emergency.* London:BAAEM, 1993.
4. Morley R, Mullender A. Hype or hope? The importance of pro-arrest policies and batterers' programs from North America to Britain as key measures for preventing violence against women in the home. *International Journal of Law and the Family* 1992;6:265–88.
5. Morley R, Mullender A. *Preventing domestic violence to women.* London: Home Office Police Department, 1994. (Police Research Group, Crime Prevention Unit, series paper No 48.)
6. Smith LJF. *Domestic violence: an overview of the literature.* London: HMSO, 1989. (Home Office research study No 107.)
7. Women's National Commission. *Violence against women: report of an ad hoc working group.* London: Cabinet office, 1985.
8. Victim Support. *Domestic violence: report of a national inter-agency working party on domestic violence.* London: Victim Support, 1992.
9. Home Affairs Committee. *Domestic violence.* Vol I. *Report together with the proceedings of the committee.* London: HMSO, 1993.
10. Hague G, Malos E, Dear W. *Against domestic violence: inter-agency*

initiatives. Bristol: SAUS Publications, 1995. (Working paper 127.)

The Psychiatrist's View: Preventing Violent Crime Is Not a Medical Role

Gwen Adshead

Department of Forensic Psychiatry, Institute of Psychiatry, London UK

Gwen Adshead, lecturer in forensic psychiatry

The maintenance of civil order is a political issue, which may not be improved by becoming "medicalised." Not only does this let central government off the hook it may also marginalise the problem. It is already too easy for the Home Office and the Department of Health to bounce the needs of crime victims between them. Doctors do not necessarily have any training or expertise in social policy matters, and, more importantly, no public mandate to take them over.

Being involved in crime prevention can backfire on health carers. If health carers have some role in crime prevention, should they not be held partly responsible if crime occurs? By comparison, the police (whose principal role is actually crime detection) are offered specialist training in crime prevention and are offered legal immunity from prosecution if crime occurs. Will health carers be so fortunate?

I would argue that crime prevention is a dangerous (and impossible) extension of the medical professional role. Reporting violence to the police with or without the victims' consent will not necessarily help with either crime prosecution or crime prevention. However, victim protection and support is an essential part of the medical (and nursing) role. A change of attitude towards interpersonal violence is needed, and all doctors (not just those in accident and emergency medicine) can and should play their part. Doctors may need to be reminded that all interpersonal violence is a crime; even when it takes place within the family and especially when it is sexual.

This has extensive educational and training implications. Many health carers are still ignorant about how to assess and treat all aspects of violence. More doctors need to know about the assessment and treatment of trauma, and how to refer patients for specialist help. Some specialist clinics provide psychological treatment for victims of crime, but more are needed. There is also a need to advise and educate the judiciary about victims of violence. The adversarial nature of the criminal justice system is biased towards "stranger danger," when, in fact, most physical violence occurs between people who have some sort of relationship. The degree of danger from strangers has been exaggerated, and criminal justice procedures, from the police station through to the crown court, may have to alter appropriately.

The health service is now led by demand. Research into costs and needs assessment for victims of crime is therefore vital. Other strategies for protecting and supporting crime victims could include better cooperation between the Department of Health and the Home Office, between voluntary groups and health care providers, and different medical disciplines.

Finally, Professor Shepherd has rightly argued that services for adult victims of crime should mirror those provided for children. Research into the effects of trauma suggest that a small proportion of both child and adult victims of interpersonal violence may become violent themselves. The physical and psychological effects of violent crime may turn out to be the most expensive drain on scarce health care resources, present and future. No sensible manager could afford to ignore this.

The Moral Philosopher's View: The Victim Should Decide

Grant Gillett

Bioethics Research Centre, Medical School, University of Otago, Dunedin, New Zealand

Grant Gillett, professor of medical ethics

Professor Shepherd recommends a cooperative arrangement between accident and emergency and criminal justice services such as the police in an attempt to prevent injury. The justification for this arrangement is that increasing rates of conviction is an effective public health measure to prevent injury. The problem is then to reconcile this goal with victims' reluctance to pursue their complaint. This is not easy. It requires consideration of the ethics of disclosure of patient information beyond the therapeutic relationship, the conflict between respect for autonomy and protection from harm, and the ethics of intervention in the face of uncertainty.

A patient's willingness to have the results of medical communications shared is, in general, the determining factor in deciding what a doctor or health care team can share.[1] There are, however, a number of exceptions to this rule of clinical conduct. One exception is created when, in the doctor's opinion, the safety of the community is at stake or the community needs to be protected. We have made special provision for this in, for instance, legislation covering communicable diseases, but the same ethical arguments could be made when someone threatens society in other ways. The argument for unauthorized disclosure to prevent harm is obvious: if a person does not tell then someone who is hurt as a result has been preventably harmed. This is used in relation to the at risk partners of people positive for HIV and was evident in the famous Tarasoff case.[2][3] The argument against unauthorized disclosure takes two forms. The first is a direct appeal to the doctor's duty of confidentiality. The second invokes a consequentialist reason not to disclose based on the likelihood that such a practice will prevent others from seeking help and advice and therefore will have worse consequences for a larger group of people than the non-disclosure would have affected. Whether this is so in either AIDS or in relation to violence is debatable.[4] The problem in cases of violence is that it is unclear whether the victims wish to be prevented from harm. One would, however, credit any person with a wish to avoid suffering violence if the other things they value are safeguarded. This suggests that the most that could be done is to have a process of skilled negotiation based either in health care or in some collaborative venture, as proposed by Professor Shepherd, to secure crime prevention without compromising the patient's interests.

The next issue concerns the extent to which someone needs protection from their own bad choices. In suicide, for instance, doctors are entitled to intervene to counteract the potentially damaging consequences of a patient's act. Thus, if we were able to say that a person's wish not to report serious danger was similar to the misguided reasoning that might lead to a suicide attempt, we could invoke a similar justification to intervene to prevent mortal or grievous harm to the victim. At what point, however, does a person's resolve to run risks to maintain a lifestyle cross the line from being a reasonable choice to being an unreasonable one that may result in personal harm and impose a burden of care on others? One could argue that the potential victim is better placed than anyone else to decide on acceptable levels of personal risk.

Finally, we should consider the efficacy of the measures we intend to take. If there is no proof that a particular procedure prevents injury we cannot justify sacrificing any of the patient's considered choices. In the face of genuine uncertainty we cannot advise a person at risk that proceeding in a particular way will protect him or her.

1. Black D. Absolute confidentiality. In: Gillon R., ed. *Principles of health care ethics.* Chichester: Wiley, 1994: 479–88.
2. Gillett G. AIDS and confidentiality: the doctor's dilemma. In: Almond B., ed. AIDS: a moral issue. London: Macmillan, 1990:56–67.
3. California Supreme Court. Tarasoff v Regents of the University of California. 17 Cal. 3d 425, 551 P.2d 334, 331 California Reporter, 1976.
4. Crisp R. Autonomy, welfare, and the treatment of AIDS. In Almond B, ed. *AIDS: a moral issue.* London: MACMILLAN, 1990: 68–81.

The Police Surgeon's View: Medical Paternalism Is Unacceptable

M. A. Knight

Association of Police Surgeons, Clarke House, Harrogate, North Yorkshire UK

M. A. Knight, honorary secretary

Police surgeons (otherwise known as forensic medical examiners in metropolitan London and forensic medical officers in Northern Ireland) are mostly general practitioners, and they may see both the victims and the perpetrators of violent and sexual assaults. They may be asked to attend accident and emergency departments and sometimes paediatric wards in order to assist with the documentation of injuries, the compilation of police statements, and to conduct joint examinations with paediatricians in cases of alleged physical and sexual child abuse.

Police surgeons may also see those accused of such assaults, who may themselves be injured, with a view to establishing their fitness or otherwise for continued detention in a police station and their fitness for interview.

Professor Shepherd states that violent offenses should be reported to the police, without the patient's consent if necessary, if injury is very serious or if failure to disclose appropriate information would expose the patient or someone else to a risk of serious harm. Although any attempt to reduce the often tragic consequences of violent crime is laudable, the steps he proposes strike at the very heart of the right of the individual patient to self determination.

It is also stated that victims of violence might be dissuaded from seeking medical help. Whether the victims are "on the edge of the law" or not his proposals might well result in them being reluctant to seek medical help—with the inevitable consequences of undiagnosed fractures, poor healing of unsutured wounds, and the even more serious results of untreated trauma—once it became known that attending an accident and emergency department was likely to lead to police involvement.

Most people would agree that the police should be involved in the case of stranger danger, particularly if others are at risk, and consent from the patient is much more likely to be forthcoming in such circumstances. In the case of domestic violence, when others are rarely at risk, the right of the patient to confidentiality is paramount. In this case the patient may wish to have a continuing relationship with the assailant despite the risk of further violence—and that is the patient's right.

Professor Shepherd draws a similarity between a possible legal and ethical framework for the reporting of assaults on adults and the work of area child projection committees. There is, however, no similarity since the work of these committees is to protect those who are unable to protect themselves rather than those who are competent to determine their own destiny.

The challenge to confidentiality is further compounded by the suggestion of networking computers in accident and emergency departments. Anderson has pointed very strongly to the dangers of networking in health care without adequate safeguards.[1] Concerns about declining levels of confidentiality were expressed in several motions put to the annual representative meeting of the BMA at Harrogate in July.

It must be right to encourage patients to report injury, but many would take the view that to extend this principle to a point where doctors should be influential advocates for victims implies a degree of medical paternalism which would be unacceptable to most doctors.

1. Anderson, R. NHS-wide networking and patient confidentiality. *BMJ* 1995; 311:5–6.

 Article Review Form at end of book.

Are disabled men and children abused more frequently than their non-disabled counterparts? If so, what actions must be taken by this group in order to reduce victimization?

Violence

Are the disabled more abused?

Robert Mauro

There has been a lot in the news recently about domestic violence and spousal abuse. (Ninety-five percent of the victims of domestic violence are women.) There are six million reported cases of battered women each year. According to the FBI, only one in ten cases are actually reported, so that means there are possibly sixty million women being battered every twelve months.

In the U.S., 21% of married women report psychical abuse by their husband, says Angela Browne in her book When Battered Women Kill.

One British woman in seven is raped by her husband reports Ruth E. Hall in her book *Ask Any Woman: A London Inquiry into Rape and Assault.*

The figure for battered disabled men is slightly higher than the 5% figure for non-disabled men, according to the director of the Buffalo, NY, S.A.F.E. House for the Developmentally Disabled. In most of these cases, it is a wife battering her husband who has Alzheimer's. (Also, we have heard of the abuse that goes on in nursing homes.) Men must

report abuse when it does happen. Never be ashamed.

According to the Health and Human Services Department, children with disabilities are maltreated at 1.7 times the rate of other children. In nearly half of those cases of abuse or neglect, the child's disability was at the root of the violence. (I could not find the rate for disabled adults.)

A shelter director for the developmentally and learning disabled estimates about 50% of the incidence of domestic violence among marginally developmentally disabled persons is caused by the mental illness or some type of substance abuse by either the abuser, abused or both.

Family violence includes harassment, reckless endangerment, assault or attempted assault, menacing or kidnapping. According to the Domestic Abuse Intervention Project of Duluth, domestic violence is also about power and control. The batterer uses economic abuse, coercion, threats, intimidation, isolation, and emotional abuse. At the same time, the batterer can be denying or minimizing the fact that he/she is committing this abuse

—claiming instead that he/she is the victim.

Occasionally a couple might begin fighting verbally. Name calling. Yelling. Screaming. As mom always said, "Sticks and stones can break your bones, but names can never hurt you." Nevertheless, verbal or emotional abuse can indeed hurt. In fact, verbal and emotional abuse can quickly escalate to pushing, slapping, punching. And this is the beginning of a very vicious cycle.

Besides the physical, psychological, and emotional toll to the victim, according to Domestic Violence for Health Care Providers, 3rd Edition, Colorado Domestic Violence Coalition, 1991, the medical expenses from domestic violence total as high as $5 billion a year.

What can you do to avoid being battered? Never give a batterer a second chance. If someone pushes you, slaps you or hits you, end the relationship. If you have been cut, bruised, or in any other way hurt, get photographic evidence of the injuries. Get a doctor to look at them. Report them to the police. Hopefully, the batterer will leave you alone after a police warning or an arrest.

Reprinted from *Accent on Living*, Fall 1994, Vol. 39, No. 2, pp. 50–52. Reprinted by permission of Cheever Publishing, Inc.

If not, where can you get protection? Get an Order of Protection. At least it will create a paper trail of evidence if nothing else. The National Women's Law Center says an Order of Protection works in 40% of the cases by successfully keeping the batterer away. In some states there are mandatory arrest laws for the batterer. New York state is working to pass such a law.

Change your phone number or even move from the area. Leaving is often impossible for a disabled person, though. There is little funding to support the disabled victim of domestic violence or to help him/her find a safe haven, a shelter, a new apartment. Most shelters are already full. According to the Senate Judiciary Committee Hearings of 1990, there are three times as many animal shelters in the U.S. as there are shelters for battered women. As a result, up to 50% of all homeless women and children in our country are fleeing from domestic violence, says Elizabeth Schneider in Legal Reform Efforts for Battered Women, 1990.

If you need help, call a domestic violence hotline, rape hotline, the police, 911, or the National Coalition Against Domestic Violence at 303-939-1852.

According to "From Access to Equity," a report written by Jane Thierfeld Brown and Grace Gibbons Brown of the Office for Disabled Students, Barnard College, "Agencies serving abused women have usually included provisions for women with disabilities as an afterthought, if at all." (All facilities providing medical, psychological, or crisis counseling for victims of abuse or domestic violence must be wheelchair accessible and have a TDD. A sign language interpreter should be available if needed.)

 Article Review Form at end of book.

Discuss the forces that have led to the emergence of the concept of restorative justice in recent years.

Training Enhances Victim Services

Donald G. Evans

Donald G. Evans is president of Donald G. Evans and Associates in Toronto.

Victims have been an invisible and forgotten part of the criminal justice system for too long. Today, they are emerging from the wilderness and claiming their rightful place. In an October 1996 article in State Government News, Anne Seymour notes that "today in America, more than 30,000 statutes at the state and federal levels provide victims with basic rights and practices" in the form of victims' bills of rights or statutes requiring victim notification. This change in attitude and approach currently is bolstered by a growing interest in restorative justice.

At the core of restorative justice is the issue of reparation. Punishing or rehabilitating inmates is not enough; in the wake of a crime, victims need to feel that their needs have been addressed by both offenders and the justice system. It is inconceivable that programs designed to meet this end should be executed without the victim's input. Probation agencies are taking this into account and are designing victim

services and training service workers to address these needs.

Since its inception, the American Probation and Parole Association (APPA) has taken a strong role in advocating the rights of victims. Joining with the Office for Victims of Crime (OVC), APPA initiated "Victim Assistance in Community Corrections," a train-the-trainer seminar geared toward enhancing services provided to crime victims by community corrections.

Two seminars were conducted this past fall. The first, held in Nashville, Tenn., Sept 24-26, 1997, attracted 28 trainers representing 14 states and Canada. The second, held in San Diego, Oct. 15–17,1997, included 27 trainers representing 14 states. The purpose of the seminars was to enable the participants to develop and deliver victim service training within their organizations and to be a resource for community correctional agencies and practitioners within their jurisdictions. Each three-day seminar was an interactive, skill-building program that covered the following topics:

- the impact of crime on victims
- victim notification

- restitution programs
- restorative justice concepts
- workplace violence
- community relations and outreach
- program evaluation

Instructors taught participants leading-edge training techniques that will aid in the dissemination of information and the implementation of programs.

One of the highlights of the seminar was the victim impact panel. Comprised of crime victims, the panel conveyed the need for balance between the rights of the offender and the needs of the victim. A common result of victimization is the feeling of powerlessness; including victims in the justice process empowers them. Understanding this need will help probation agencies see the importance of victim impact statements and the role of victim notification systems which advise them on the status and disposition of a particular case. Joy McLeod, a trainer with the Canadian Training Institute, suggests that all probation and parole agencies encourage victim input and keep victims informed of case status.

Reprinted with permission of the American Correctional Association, Lanham, MD.

Seminar Coordinator Tracy Godwin says many of the seminar participants had responses similar to McLeod's and indicated that they plan to use the information and techniques derived from the sessions to improve services to crime victims in their areas. She also notes many of the participants now wish to educate agency staff on the needs of victims and to promote victim services in probation and parole agencies.

As part of this project, APPA has developed a compendium of Promising Victim-Related Practices in Probation, which Godwin says is in the publication stage and will be available in the near future. The major lesson learned in the seminar is awareness of the stake that victims have in any community/restorative justice initiative.

In her article, Seymour suggests that "without victims' support, understanding and involvement, this effective approach is doomed to failure." In other words, restorative justice restores nothing if the victim isn't involved.

 Article Review Form at end of book.

Why do some critics argue that a trial revolves around excuses?

Watching 'As the Jury Turns'

John Leo

Prediction: If Tonya Harding is put on trial for the attack on Nancy Kerrigan, she will use the domestic abuse defense, just like everyone else. She can position herself as the victim of some sort of unsuspected awfulness inflicted by her accuser, ex-husband Jeff Gillooly.

Another prediction: If the Menendez brothers are tried again for killing their parents, the prosecution will try them first for the murder of the mother. Since the father was the prime villain in the brothers' story, it will be hard to employ the abuse excuse to justify killing her. Unless, of course, they can come up with some new and very graphic memories of maternal horrors.

We are deep into the era of the abuse excuse. The doctrine of victimology—claiming victim status means you are not responsible for your actions—is beginning to warp the legal system. "Get ready for a huge burst of criminal defenses based on abuse," says Allan Campo, a litigation analyst in Lafayette, La., whose firm helps prepare lawyers for trial. "In about 10 years, the public will

be bored with it, but that will be after a lot of murderers get off."

This is a profound change. Juries have traditionally been very openminded about whether a defendant committed an alleged crime, but very tough on excuses. Now the trial revolves around excuses. Traditionally, defense lawyers tried to create doubts. Now they just put the actual victim on trial. The irony of this seems to escape victimologists. A movement that began with the slogan, "Don't blame the victim," now strives to blame murder victims for their own deaths. Virginia Postrel, the editor of *Reason* magazine, writes, "We have created a culture of excuse, and it has conquered our courtrooms."

It isn't just victimology. Part of the problem is that one of the central teachings of American pop psychology—feeling is more important than thinking—has also penetrated the culture. Critic Michiko Kakutani wrote last month that "I feel is replacing I think" in Washington talk-show discourse. Bobby Ray Inman signed on with feelings of comfort and signed off with expressions of discomfort. On campus, this is an old story. Many profes-

sors complain that their students are free with feelings and attitudes but very reluctant to analyze or argue about ideas.

In the jury box, the culture of feelings is a threat to the whole enterprise. Jurors are supposed to put aside their biases and feelings and analyze evidence. On "Dateline NBC," one of the Menendez jurors said she felt that Lyle was uncertain about whether he had reloaded his shotgun to blast away at his wounded mother. Correspondent Stone Phillips reminded her that Menendez had clearly testified that he did reload. No matter. The juror had an unshakable feeling that he might not have. No one knows what went on in the jury room. But it's my guess that this juror, at least, worked backward from a feeling of sympathy, erasing inconvenient evidence that pointed to a cold-blooded, methodical killing.

Television, too, is part of the problem. The daily parade of bizarre creatures on "Oprah" and "Geraldo" has a long-term effect. It erases judgment and induces a generic tolerance for any kind of dysfunctional behavior. Weirdness goes mainstream every afternoon.

In highly publicized trials now, the defense attorney has the same function as "Oprah"—to create and enlarge pools of sympathy for the beleaguered and allegedly victimized underdog.

In the second Menendez trial, Court TV's coverage provided the defense with daily feedback on what was working to increase sympathy. "What we're seeing now," said Mark Crispin Miller, the writer and social critic, "is the defense attorney as chief propagandist in and out of the court, drawing attention away from evidence and the law, making it more likely that people will make their minds up on the basis of images they see."

Much of the commentary on the Bobbitt and Menendez trials revolved around images, chiefly the powerful effect of the defendants' crying during testimony, but also Lyle Menendez's smile at the end of his trial and the courtroom smirks by both brothers earlier in the case. TV deals in images and emotions, so many televised trials will depend more heavily on performances by defendants than on actual evidence.

Juries are often sequestered in high-profile cases, but because Court TV is a hit, there is bound to be some feedback between the public and juries. More and more, abstract issues of true-false and guilty-innocent will be upstaged by questions of how it looks and feels on television and how much weight should be given to the heartache expressed by the accused. Are we only a few steps away from drama coaches being as important as a good defense lawyer?

This is just the dawn of nationally televised trials. But already the mix of victimology and sympathy-inducing TV theatrics is imposing big changes. "Jurors are beginning to behave like social workers," says Alan Dershowitz, who has worked with a great many juries himself. What comes next?

 Article Review Form at end of book.

- Civil litigation by crime victims against their offenders can be an empowering experience and can serve as a message to the public regarding safety and social change.

- The news media give more attention to white crime victims than to African American crime victims.

- Recent developments in information technology are improving information services to crime victims.

- Men and children who have disabilities are abused more frequently than their nondisabled counterparts.

R.E.A.L. Sites

This list provides a print preview of typical **coursewise** R.E.A.L. sites. (There are over 100 such sites at the **courselinks**™ site.) The danger in printing URLs is that web sites can change overnight. As we went to press, these sites were functional using the URLs provided. If you come across one that isn't, please let us know via email to: webmaster@coursewise.com. Use your Passport to access the most current list of R.E.A.L. sites at the **courselinks**™ site.

Site name: National Criminal Justice Reference Service

URL: http://www.ncjrs.org/victhome.htm

Why is it R.E.A.L.? This is a very informative site containing on-line documents and links regarding numerous topics including, but not limited to, child abuse, domestic violence, fraud, juvenile victims, missing children, rape/sexual abuse, restorative justice, stalking, victim assistance, victim impact, and victim's rights.

Try this: Describe some of the age patterns of victims of serious violent crimes. What are some of the costs associated with crime victims in the Untied States?

Key topics: Child abuse, civil remedies, crime victims fund, domestic violence, fraud, juvenile victims, grants

Site name: National Center for Victims of Crimes

URL: http://www.ncvc.org/

Why is it R.E.A.L.? It is held that this is the "most comprehensive" site for crime victim information on the internet. It contains information regarding crime victimization statistics, law and public policy affecting victims of crime, a virtual library and links to other crime victims-related web sites.

Try this: Describe some of the recent crime victimization rates.

Key topics: news, legal issues, law and public policy, safety strategies, job bank

Site name: Office for Victims of Crime

URL: http://www.ojp.usdoj.gov/ovc/

Why is it R.E.A.L.? This site is supported by the Office for Victims of Crime (OVC) which was established in 1984 for the purpose of overseeing diverse programs that benefit victims of crime. The site contains a comprehensive list of links and addresses to various types of crime victims organizations as well as a number of publications on crime victims. Some of the organizations listed are responsible for victims of child abuse, elder abuse, hate crimes, drunk driving, and stalking.

Try this: Describe some of the characteristics associated with female victims of violent crimes. Discuss some of the initiatives in place to fight child abuse.

Key topics: resources for international victims, assistance for victims, resource center, training and technical assistance, state compensation and assistance division, National Crime Victims' Rights Week

Index

Note: Names and page numbers in **bold** type indicate authors and their articles; page numbers in *italics* indicate illustrations; page numbers followed by *t* indicate tables; page numbers followed by *n* indicate notes.

Court TV, 177
crack cocaine, racial bias in crimes involving, 118–19, 121*t*, 123–24, 133
crime control
  growing federal role in, 84–85
  by health professionals, 166–71
  Hispanics in, 141, 143
  plea bargaining for, 36
  and police reform, 18–20, 23–28
  and restorative justice, 103–4
  and three-strikes rules, 84–90
crime reporters, stresses on, 12–17
crimes of opportunity, 25
crime victims. *See* victims
criminal courts. *See* courts
criminal gangs
  influence on juveniles, 139
  police as, 18–19
criminal intent, by children, 48
Criminal Justice Center web site, 145
criminology, traditional focus of, 146
critical race theory, 135
cruel and unusual punishment, death penalty as, 94
Cullen, Francis T., 125

D

Daily Tar Heel, 58–60
data, on World Wide Web, 145
Davis, Len, 19
Davis, Richard Allen, 85
D.C. Code cases, 82
deadly force, attitudes about, 125–30
death penalty
  public attitudes about, 94–101
  racial discrimination in, 119, 122
del Carmen, Alejandro, 141
del Carmen, Denise, 141
delinquency, preventing, 49, 50, 139–40
Denny, Reginald, 54
Department of Justice, 65
deportation, 68, 78
deterrence
  methods of increasing, 28
  and police pursuit, 4, 5, 11
  See also crime control
Diconsiglio, John, 132
disabled people, victimization of, 172–73
disciplinary systems
  for police department employees, 21–23
  in schools and universities, 24–25, 58–60
Discretion to Disobey, 45
discrimination, 116–17
  in arrests, 18–19, 119, 120, 132–33
  in crime victim news coverage, 157–58
  in incarceration, 88, 118–22, 132–33
  in juvenile justice system, 112
  and police use of deadly force, 125–30
  in sentencing, 119, 123–24, 132–33, 134–35
dispositional reviews, 73
dissents, 51

doctors, victim protection by, 167–71
domestic violence
  as commonplace defense tactic, 176–77
  protecting victims of, 166–71, 172–73
  psychological trauma from, 152, 153
  victim compensation for, 165
Dowd, Michael, 19
Downs, Peter, 157
drug crimes
  federal penalties for, 71
  jury responses to, 55
  racial bias in treatment of, 118–19, 121*t*, 123–24, 133
  roots of, 113
  support for use of force against, 128*t*
drunken driving
  pursuit for, 7–8, 9*t*
  use of force against, 128*t*
due process, plea bargaining for, 36
Dukakis, Michael, 85

E

economics, role of race in views of, 136–37
education
  law-related, 105–7
  state and federal interference in, 24–25
elderly people
  abuse of, 172
  psychological effects of crime on, 153–54
electronic monitoring, 81, 82, 160
emergency departments, victim protection by, 167–71
entrepreneurial skills, 33
error. *See* constitutional error
escapes, police use of force in, 126–30
Espinosa, Armando, 141
ethnic stereotypes, 142, 143
Evans, Donald G., 108, **174**
Executive Order 8641, 70
expert testimony, 154, 155

F

Fagan, Patrick F., 138
fairness, in discipline, 22
Falcone, D., 4
families, importance to crime control, 50, 138–40
federal agents, 1
Federal Bureau of Prisons web site, 115
federal courts, jurisdiction of, 52–53
Federal Death Penalty Act of 1994, 95
federal government
  growing role in crime control, 84–85
  interference in local policing, 24–25, 28
  victims compensation by, 163
Federal Juvenile Delinquency Act, 68
Federal Parole Decision Making, 79
Federal Parole Decision-Making Project, 75–76
federal parole system, history of, 64–74, 75–83

Federal Probation Act of 1925, 67
federal questions, 51, 52
felonies, and support for police pursuit, 7–9
Fifth Amendment rights, 30
finality, 53
Find Law web site, 61
firearms, possession by juveniles, 139, 140
Florida Department of Corrections web site, 160
force, use by police officers, 125–30
Frank, Antoinette, 19
Frank, James, 125
Franklin, Richard H., 92
Fuhrman, Mark, 18

G

gangs, 18–19, 139
Garcetti, Gil, 87
get-tough legislation, 84–90, 92–93
Giese, John, 162–63
Gillett, Grant, 169
global positioning systems (GPS), 160
Goldwater, Barry, 84–85
good-time provisions, 65–66
Gregg v. Georgia, 94
grief, reporters' encounters with, 14–15
Groves, Kim, 19
gun accidents, impact on reporters, 13–14

H

Hallinan, Joseph, 162
harmless error, 41
Harvey, Chris, 12
hate, among police officers, 18–20
hearing examiners, 76–77
high-speed chases, 3–11, 23
Hispanics, parallels with Irish immigrants, 141–43
Hoffman, Peter B., 64, **75**
Honor Court, 58–60
Horne, Malaika, 118
Horton, Willie, 85
hunters, victim compensation for, 163

I

incarceration
  racial discrimination in, 88, 118–22, 132–33
  total rate of, 119
  trends in, 62, 88–89, 92–93, 118
  web sites about, 115
  See also prisons
information technology. *See* technology
injury, legal, 53
inmate lawsuits, 56–57
integration, 136, 137
Intensive Supervision Project, 82
intentional errors, 22–23
internal affairs, 33
Irish, parallels with Hispanics, 141–43

Putting it in *Perspectives*
-Review Form-

Your name:_____   Date: _____

Reading title: _____

Summarize: Provide a one-sentence summary of this reading. _____

_____

_____

_____

Follow the Thinking: How does the author back the main premise of the reading? Are the facts/opinions appropriately supported by research or available data? Is the author's thinking logical?

_____

_____

_____

_____

_____

Develop a Context (answer one or both questions): How does this reading contrast or compliment your professor's lecture treatment of the subject matter? How does this reading compare to your textbook's coverage?

_____

_____

_____

_____

_____

Question Authority: Explain why you agree/disagree with the author's main premise.

_____

_____

_____

_____

_____

_____

COPY ME! Copy this form as needed. This form is also available at http://www.coursewise.com
Click on: *Perspectives*.